# Two Amazing Introductions

**I live a very quiet life.**

I haven't always. I have had dumb jobs and passionate boyfriends, heartache and noise; I've had plenty of watching bands play in bars, puking on commuter trains, and sobbing into the phone (and sometimes all three on the same night).

But for a couple of years now I have lived and worked very quietly on the second floor of a two-story brick apartment building with my cat, the illustrious and exalted Trixie. Trixie has plush black fur and an expressive tail, and she sleeps curled up on the round papasan chair in my bedroom like she's an eagle perched in a giant nest. She is a perfect animal and I am too. I am perfectly animal. Every day I eat and breathe, look at Fortrees, smell the air, and pull the laces on my sneakers tight. Some days I have a zine day, which means I sit on the hardwood floor of my living room and slice through paper with my delicious paper cutter. Then I do things like carefully arrange rubber stamp letters and stroke paint onto paper with a little-kid paintbrush.

But I am also perfectly spirit. I feel and think all the time. I'm not saying I think well or figure much out, but like all of you, my mind and heart are almost always busy. I composed this essay in my mind last night while I lay in my bed in the dark. I'd had a migraine all day long and although it had already broken and the pain had leaked away, I was feeling a little crazy. That kind of pain often makes me feel like that - wild when I have it, drifty and almost bereft when it's gone. To comfort myself I pulled my *Stevie Smith* book off the bedside table and into the bed with me. Other books in my bed include: *Notebooks of a Naked Youth* by Billy Childish (another comfort book because it's probably my favorite novel of all time), *These Demented Lands* (I haven't started that one yet but other things I've read by Alan Warner were really good), and *The Opposite of Fate* by Amy Tan, a book about writing that I acquired in a zine trade. Trixie was asleep in her eagle's nest at the foot of the bed, and as I lay there with my books I thought about what I wanted to tell the readers of the *Zine Yearbook* about my life, and about what zines mean to me. That means I went to sleep last night thinking of you.

Through doing zines I have made some wonderful friends, real friends, and we write emails and letters to each other.

One thing I've noticed ........................ folks, especially people who are a fair ........................ o are 20 years old or so ........................ he things that we like— ........................ d touching, and althou ........................ lf, I love zines. Dreaming ........................ m, and bringing them to the post office all snug in their packages makes me feel whole in a way not much else does. It's hard for me to explain exactly why. I think I love zines for the same reason I loved writing in the beginning, before it got hard. The medium of zines reminds me of the point of the work: the deep and sincere need to be heard, the yearning for communion. I sign most of my zines "love, Katie" as though they're letters because they feel a lot like letters. I mean, I wouldn't bother saying something if I didn't think there was someone to say it to. Some of you have heard what I've said in my zines and I've heard what some of you have said in your zines and that honestly amazes me. The connection people make with each other through writing and reading is as human as we get, and zinesters know this, they live it. I'm writing this now and you're reading it in another now, which means we're here together in a way; wherever we are, we're both crackling with the same kind of life. Can you think of anything more incredible than that?

—- Katie Haegele, **www.thelalatheory.com**

I've been thinking about Gertrude Stein and letters of introduction. Like, say it was 1912 and I was a misfit something; someone who wanted something and couldn't find where. And I was about to leave my little home town of confinement and travel up to Paris.

Paris.
Maybe I had a friend of a friend who had once met Gertrude Stein. She would say, "Oh, you should go to 27. Here, let me write you a letter of introduction." and she would write with ink on fine letter paper, seal it with her wax stamp seal, and I'd carry it safe in my breast pocket as I rode the steam trains across the countries.
Gertrude and Alice had people over every Saturday. Lots of people. Their house was a centering point, a sanctuary. They had art from floor to ceiling, tons of food. They would introduce a topic and the conversation would go from there to all directions.
But how do you get invited in the first place if you are just a no one coming in from nowhere? I have a letter of introduction in my pocket. Shy. Too shy to actually knock, I slip the letter of introduction under the door. I would have scratched the address of the boarding house I was staying at on the back , and in the morning there is an invitation from Alice and Gertrude waiting for me at the front desk..
I've been thinking of letters of introduction. I've been thinking about looking for the punks or freaks in new towns I

was passing through, and
*"here, here's my zine."*
and they'd page through it. *"There's a basement show tonight, do you want to go?"*
I've been thinking about the way we stood around outside shows trying to sell zines to get a couple dollars to get in, and the quiet way we became part of something we couldn't otherwise find a way into. We didn't play music. We were not sure about dancing. But we had this. shy glance up. *"do you want to buy my zine?"* *"oh, here, you can have it for free."* That was part of it. It wasn't that we were trying to introduce ourselves exactly, but there was something of that, something about changing the normal dialog of our lives. something about opening up subjects that weren't in the public realm. something about creating a different path for us to go down. We don't have to be professionals and recognized by the system in order to be real. We can create our own standards. we can teach each other and make a world worth living in.
I liked the non-anonymity about it. The bravery of handing out something, secrets or not. music reviews or history. stories or essays.
*here, have this.*
There was writing and there was a face to it. It was secret code. It said, I think we might have something to talk about. I think we might be able to make friends. I think I might have something you could learn from. I think you might have something I could learn from you.
In a world of alienation and anonymity, where you could go whole days and months and years without any real connection to anyone and no way of figuring out how to find one; where the art of conversation had been lost to triviality and gossip, it was a way of reclaiming these things we felt missing. and laughter. and pushing ourselves to do something interesting so we'd have something to write about, stupid as that reason may be.
Zines were what you did with your friends when everything else was screwed. When the hearts were broken and there wasn't enough money to pay for heat and you all sat crammed into one room with the space heater and took turns venturing into the kitchen to bring back coffee and nourishment; to flip the record over. Delirious from lack of sleep and asphyxiated from propane heat, Melissa would tell a story.
*"you should write that down."*
There were doodles turning into drawings, stories turning into secrets, our screwed up lives coming into perspective as not so screwed and actually kind of hysterical.
*"We should write a zine. Everyone, two pages by midnight."*
*"but I don't have any stories."*
*"but I don't know how to write."*
*"what could I possibly have to say?"*
Zines were how we learned to exist outside ourselves when the world told us to disappear. They were focus. A way to sort though our lives and look for what was most important. Because paper. Copies. We had to make them small. Cram it all into tiny pages, bike to the Kinkos at 2 am which when our friend started their shift and the manager was in the back room doing the paperwork. We took turns working at photocopy stores. We broke into our shitty office jobs at night and scammed copies. We found ways around every system designed to keep us out. And when that failed, we got jobs at the copy stores again.

20 copies of an issue was kind of a lot. This is the thing I liked; that it wasn't about getting a ton of readership or getting it out everywhere or taking over the world or getting recognition. It was the making of it. the sound of the typewriter, the going over the words, the asking your friend *"do you think this sentence makes sense? Do you think I should write about when the moose almost stepped on my head?"* the trying to peal off some text laid down with glue stick and the paper ripping instead of pealing and then having to type it all over again. It was the late night bike rides the *"yes, we made our self-imposed deadline!"* It was bad donuts and bent staples and paper cuts. It was about being out in the world when everyone else was sleeping. And running into someone new at the donut shop up all night.
*"What are you working on?"*
*"A documentary about my week in prison."*
*"Here do you want mine? I just finished it. It's the story of my grandma's immigration."*
It was urgency and the feeling of a mission and a way to create meaning. It was what you did when you felt awkward somewhere. Leave the show. Go down to the railroad tracks and write. People wrote. It was as accepted as getting drunk.
*"Do you want a 40?"*
*"No, I'm going to go to the loading dock and write."*
And there were different zines for different reasons. It was about public life, making private public. It was the hand touching hand as the zine was passed between you. It was confronting the fear of rejection over and over until it didn't matter so much any more.
It was creating a culture. It was about culture. It was about creating real physical connection in the face of nothingness. It was folded well loved pages falling apart and holding you together, kept safe in your pocket as you rode the train under the bay from Oakland to San Francisco, and knowing that there was someone else out there, someone you met in passing for a second who had given you this gift who had secrets like your own. and that you weren't alone. you could live safe. you could tell the truth too, despite the blank suffocating stares.
We can make ethical decisions about our technologies, and what works and what is falling through the cracks. we remember the feeling of paper and touch, and think about how connection and community is foraged in a million different ways. and sometimes the wires make the most sense, and sometimes we need this: face and voice, realness and a way in; to confront fear and learn support. humility, honesty. a shy glance. *"here, have this."*

—- Cindy Crabb
**po box 29**
**Athens, OH 45701**

# ZINE YEARBOOK #9

edited by Joe Biel, Steven Stothard, Sparky Taylor, Dillon Vrana, and Brittney Willis

This is Microcosm #76067
ISBN 978-1-934620-07-6

All content owned by original authors and artists.

Designed by Sparky Taylor
Cover designed by Richard Springer

Originally published by Become the Media
First edition of 3,000 copies - Jan 1, 2009

Distributed in the booktrade by AK PRESS
sales@akpress.org
(510)208-1700

Microcosm Publishing
222 S Rogers St.
Bloomington, IN 47404
(812)323-7395
www.microcosmpublishing.com

Printed in Canada

**(a letter we recieved in reponse to our yearbook flyer. we thought this might be a good jumping-off point for our staff introductions.)

dear
microcosm
dear
zine yearbook

you asked for anote regarding
our intentions ; i wasn't sure
t hat meant. ther's a bit of a
manifesto on the inside front
cover of our zine, if that's
what you're looking for.

Nothing is Real stems
from our (jesse & dan-
iel's) love of creating
nonsense. this began
to take shape when i
first got a type-
writer a few years ago.

We've often had the idea of
making a magazine (for a while
jesse wanted to make something
called laughter.)this past year
i began to better understand
the whole zine thing and making
our own publication seemed
more feasible. it was probably
a year from conception to
copying, in july. initially
10 copies were made, then 20 more
we might do another run soon.

we're working on a couple new
editions right now, one with
a travel theme another with
maybe a gender theme -- trying
to correct the gender imbalance..
hopefully one of em' 'll be done
before your december deadline

## Check Your Attitude

actually a note explaining your

intentions would be welcome...
what is the zine yearbook? does it
reprint excerpts of the zine?
oor does it just list 'em off?
is the whole concept really even
in keeping with what a zine is?

i was thinking about the fact that
our zine is gonna look pretty
dinky alongside all the other
well-established contributions
and it occurred to me t'at a zine
is about something very personal
it's about each human that makes
it your fiends see it and some
strangers see i the strang ers
(ideally) feel touched

violence is also something very
powerful but our culture is very
desensitized to it

zines in a book sounds to me ii
a little like violence on television. desensitizing.

you know?

zines collected in books always
confuse me. if you can get a book
why are you still making zines?
zines are to me all about the
alternative to books.

but who am i to tell you this--
i am new to zinedom. you are microcosm. you live and breathe zines.
you will do a good job.

whatever form it takes, i am looking
forward to seeing the zine yearbook.
peace out,

daniel brandt.
(204)452-0594
sorry, no Electro-mail

P.S. IT'S PRINTED
ON PAPER RESCUED FROM
BEING THROWN OUT

4

# AN INTRODUCTION OF SORTS

For those unfamiliar, the Zine Yearbook was published from 1996-2004 by Jen Angel and friends. It was mostly self-published with some previous efforts at publishing by Tree of Knowledge and Soft Skull Press.

For those whose lives have yet to be touched by the medium, zines are generally self-published periodicals, like magazines. Their exact definition is hard to grasp. They exist in a medium where creators mostly create and exchange with each other, with money and profits as an afterthought.

When Jen offered us at Microcosm the opportunity to publish the Yearbook, I got the impression that we were not the first party that she had asked and we initially also said no. A year and a number of staff changes later, the group perspective was totally different and we decided that it sounded like a really fun project.

Microcosm had never edited anything that it published before; let alone group edited. Normally we just receive finished books from the author and then do the nuts-and-bolts work to see it to the printer and through its distribution. This book was edited collectively, through a system of individual endorsements, long meetings, and endless discussion over the merits of various zines and pieces. The selections that made it into the final product were agreed upon as a group and then the actual production work of scanning, contacting the authors, sequencing, and placement was shared and divided as well.

This collection represents a shining moment where it all comes together--the hard work, the long hours, the years of endlessly reading mountains of zines, even the fear that our community may not always be going to new places or trying new things—It all felt worthwhile for me in working on this project.

That said we had a lot of financial hesitations about working on this project. Unlike many of the similarly expensive, book-length projects that we work on, this one was unlikely to break even--let alone turn a profit.

For maximum transparency, we have decided to publish our projected finances for this project. We thought it would be neat to show folks how the money gets divided around here. While we think capitalism is seriously flawed, we also think it's best that people have an idea of where our capital goes.

Expenses:
We print 3,000 copies for $6,704.90
(with possible 10% overrun)
approx $770 to ship the books to us and distributors
$1,871 for wages of Yearbook meetings
(does not include time spent editing the Yearbook or working on it, or reading submissions for it - actual figure would be higher)
$70 for poster paper
$25 for ISBN
$45 for mailing out posters and flyers for Yearbook
$43.68 on photocopies
$12 for Snakepit book in trade for poster printing

$9,541.58-$10,141.58

Revenue to be expected:
The most probable situation is:
A retail price of $12
150 free copies to contributors
250 review copies
We send 1,000 copies to AK Press on consignment at $4.80 each.
They sell 2-20 copies per month = $1,296
We sell 200 copies to Counter Culture at $4.80 each = $960
We send 50 copies to Last Gasp at $4.80 each = $240
We sell approximately 500 copies retail for $10 direct = $4,000
We sell approximately 400 wholesale for $7.20 = $2,160

$8,656 (-9,541.58) = a loss of $-885.58
and we are left with about 380 copies

You might be wondering why we're printing 3000 copies, since we're going to have 380 copies left over. It's just not practical to print fewer copies because of the pricing structure most book printers use. Printers give price quotes in increments of 1,000, and the cost per book increases at 2,000 copies. But 2,000 copies wouldn't be enough to fully distribute the book to all of the places that we normally would. 3,000 insures that we get a cheaper price per book and a cheaper cover price, while still allowing the book to be distributed as widely as we'd like.

It's hard not to acknowledge that zines are best for their immediate, ephemeral qualities. That feeling that you've found something truly unique and special, from a seemingly unlikely source. For these reasons, putting zines in a mass-produced book is seemingly contradictory.

But like many of our projects, our mission in publishing this book is to promote the existence of zines. To make them accessible to people who might otherwise not know what zines are. After much debate we decided that the benefits of releasing this book far outweighed the perceived negatives. We're not attempting to co-opt zine culture, but to help it thrive in an age of blogs and websites. We hope that zines will be around for a long time to come, and that this book is a step in that direction.

We want you to be so inspired by reading this collection of zine reprints that you are motivated to make your own. Maybe it will be such a simple and logical conclusion that you won't even think about it. Maybe inspiration will simply strike you for a project that you hadn't thought of previously. Maybe it'll be a new avenue for producing your art.

This collection showcases what we thought were some of the best and most unique zines published in 2007. Every day we are told that print is dying, but as our co-worker Chris says, "If print is dead, it's another reason to like zombies."

Best,
Joe Biel

The Zine Yearbook is done! After endless meetings, tons of reading, and one very corrupted file, we've finally finished it! We had seriously laid out the entire book when the file refused to open. The Yearbook so nice, we had to lay it out twice!

First of all, thank you so very much to all the people who shared your zines with us!!!

Even though we spend a whole heckuva lot of time around zines, we're no experts. A zine's value is totally subjective, and there are so many more zines than this out there!! Just because we didn't excerpt from a zine doesn't mean it's not awesome, and we highly encourage you to keep an eye out for the honorable mentions located in the back!  Also we tried to select some things that we don't distribute in the hopes that people would be encouraged to support other distros, or look elsewhere for new zines.

Please forgive us in advance for whatever mistakes we made. We're human beings, not zine-bots, (although that would be kinda cool) and we've really done our best to make this book awesome! There will undoubtedly be typos, cut-offs, and layout choices that were made due to space constraints. We did try to keep the formatting the same whenever possible,

but obviously we couldn't always, and we mean no disrespect to the authors or to you the reader.

This project was a huge undertaking, much harder I'm ashamed to say, than we initially anticipated. This is a shout-out to all those who've worked previously to make one of these things!  Jen, Jason, Tree of Knowledge, and anyone and everyone else who put together previous editions, you are badasses!

My greatest hope is that the Yearbook inspires people to write and draw zines of their own. That people will read through this book and realize how diverse the zine world is and continues to be. That it will be the spark a first-time zinester needs to get started. That an aging zinester who's proclaimed print is dead will dust off their typewriter and crank out a new issue.

A girl can dream.

We hope you like it!!!
-Sparky

# TABLE OF CONTENTS

# Shotgun Seamstress #2

Osa
5225 N Concord Ave
Portland, OR 97217
shotgunseamstress@gmail.com

## black punk zine that never happened

SEVERAL YEARS AGO WHEN I LIVED IN WASHINGTON, DC, I GOT THE IDEA TO MAKE A ZINE ABOUT BLACK PUNKS, BUT I NEVER FINISHED IT. I HAD THIS BOOK CALLED BANNED IN DC ABOUT DC'S EARLY-TO-MID 80s PUNK/HARDCORE SCENE, AND IT HAS MORE BLACK PEOPLE IN IT — BOTH IN BANDS AND IN THE AUDIENCE — THAN ANY OTHER PUNK BOOK I'VE EVER SEEN. IN A WAY IT MAKES SENSE BECAUSE OF DC'S HUGE BLACK POPULATION. BUT WHILE I WAS LIVING THERE, THE CITY WAS STILL MAJORITY BLACK, BUT I WAS PRETTY MUCH THE ONLY ONE AROUND AT SHOWS. I THINK MORE BLACK PEOPLE WENT TO SHOWS BECAUSE OF BAD BRAINS. (HR) →

JUST THAT ONE BAND PROBABLY MADE ALL OF THE DIFFERENCE IN THE WORLD.

There's this one photo from Banned In DC that shows these two black dudes standing outside the Wilson Center (punk show space), and one of the guys is holding a sign that says "All Ages: PUNK THROWDOWN with Trouble Funk, Government Issue and Grand Mal." I've probably looked at that photo a hundred times imagining what that show must've been like. Government Issue is a white hardcore band and I don't know who Grand Mal is, but Trouble Funk is a black go-go band from Washington, DC (more on go-go later). They played several shows with hardcore bands during the time, including Minor Threat.

Before seeing that picture, I'd never really imagined a punk show looking like that. I started fantasizing about what it must've been like to be a Black Punk in DC in the 80s instead of now. I wanted to make a zine of interviews with all races of people, but especially including black kids that went to shows at the time. I wanted to know the approximate ratio of black people to white people, what it felt like to go see a black band and to hear reggae and/or go-go at a punk show, what the feel of the shows were... In my imagination, it just seemed like so much richer of an experience.

I got intouch with a couple people, but I never did set up any interviews or get anywhere with the project. At that point in my life, I didn't know any other black kids in punk, so it made it so much harder to think about how to frame the things i wanted to communicate. My interest in DC's punk scene in the 80s grew out of a deep feeling of longing for something I wanted but couldn't have. Thinking about communicating that to a white audience felt awkward and uncomfortable to me. So I never finished the zine, but Iwas still left with a million questions that needed answers. For one, how and why did the punk scene in DC turn so white again? It's always interesting when you learn that things haven't always been the way they are now, and that communities/movements of people aren't always making progress.

I mean, who knows, maybe it wasn't all that different back then. Black kids probably still only made up a tiny minority of band & audience members. I know I'm romanticizing a past that I don't know very much about. But that fantasy is just me imagining the possibilities. That's what this is about, is black people expressing, representing and documenting the fullest range of our beings collectively and individually.

Exploring ALL of our possibilities.  Instead of allowing the dominant culture to tell us what it means to be
black, we can create and recreate what that means all
the way to infinity.  And we can do it with music and
with art.

# okay, now back to GO-GO...

When I went to DC as a kid, I remember seeing bucket
drummers by METRO escalators or on the Washington Mall
by the Smithsonian museums.  Mostly it was guys beating
those white, 5 gallon industrial buckets with drum sticks.
I imagine them beating dozens of different buckets till
they found the ones that sounded JUST RIGHT.  and they
always sounded tight.  If i remember correctly, it was
kind of modeled after a drum set with one bucket as a
snare, the others as toms with different pitches and a
bass bucket.  genius!  I don't even wanna try to explain
what a go-go beat is, so if you can go online, go here:
http://www.youtube.com/watch?v=3nPKkj8COGg and you'll see
a video of a guy playing go-go beats on bucket drums!
His bass bucket is an upside down garbage can.

One day in 9th grade algebra class, me and my friends
Brandis, Atia and Monique all hatched this plan to go
to a go-go show in the city.  The next day we all returned
with the same results. Each of our parents had vetoed
that shit before the full request could even leave our
lips.  It seemed like every night on the news, there
was something about another shooting at a go-go show
and the police having to break it up.  Understandably,
my parents didn't want my 14-year-old black ass getting
shot by accident.

They'd show footage on the news of black kids at go-gos
getting buckwild, cussing and fist fighting.  Like I said,
I wasn't there, but from the outside it seems to me
like another case of the media and the cops uniting to
criminalize public gatherings of black people.  They
hate it when we're out in public having any kind of fun.
When we do it, it's loitering.  When white people do it,
it's the Alberta Street Art Walk or whatever.

Anyway, the 80s were a rough time for black communities
considering poverty, crack, homelessness and most social
programs and public resources being cut or underfunded

Members of this group were 8-11 years old when they started out. Here they are outside of **junkyard band** the Berry Farms Housing project in Anacostia, SE Washington, DC in July 1986.

thanks to Ronald Reagan. This was post-black power. All of our leaders were dead. There were several major reasons at the time for black communities across the country to be experiencing despair, defeat and a sense of hopelessness. Combined with a lack of resources or opportunity to do anything about the situation, lots of people turned to violence. It is also out of these same circumstances that hip-hop in NYC and go-go in DC began to blow up. We all know the trajectory of hip-hop, but what happened to go-go?

My best friend since elementary school, Koren, moved down to Georgia to live with her dad when we were in 9th or 10th grade. I remember her telling me that when she told her new friends in Georgia about go-go, they told her she was making it up. They'd never heard of it. And we hadn't been thinking about go-go as a local phenomenon. We thought everyone (at least black people) knew about it, but in reality, go-go barely made it out of DC. Even within DC, because of the violence associated with it, go-go music started to be banned at different clubs and events. At least E.U. enjoyed brief national success with "Da Butt" (yep, that's a go-go beat!)

The go-go bands that still play are pretty much funk bands with keyboards, horn sections and heavy go-go percussion. That stuff is cool, but the stuff I'm truly inspired by are the groups of raggely little kids that some of those bands evolved from, banging buckets, pots and pans, and playing toy instruments until they could acquire real ones. That's more DIY than anything I've ever seen in punk. I've heard people say that hip-hop is our punk rock, and maybe it used to be, but I really think

# it's GO-GO.

John Porcellino
PO Box 18888
Denver, CO 80218
www.king-cat.net

## DIOGENES OF SINOPE

DIOGENES was born in Sinope, an Ionian settlement on the Black Sea (at present-day Sinop, Turkey), circa 412 B.C. At some point he was exiled from Sinope for "adulterating the coinage" and travelled to Athens, where he became a student of the philosopher Antisthenes.

Antisthenes had studied under Socrates, and had founded a "school" of Philosophy called CYNICISM (from the Greek "kynikos", meaning "Like a dog."). Cynics "held the view that virtue is the only good and that its essence lies in self-control and independence." (Merriam-Webster's Collegiate Dictionary, 10th ed., 1993)

The object of Cynicism was to achieve true personal freedom and self-realization within everyday life, and its adherents used unconventional methods to that end, disregarding social customs, public opinion, and popularity, as well as traditional notions of wealth and honor. Cynics turned superficial values upside-down in their quest for true value.

Diogenes, inspired by watching the adaptability of a mouse, took residence in a tub outside the Temple of Cybele, and taught there through the example of his life.

On a voyage to Aegina, Diogenes was captured by pirates, and offered for sale as a slave on the island of Crete. When asked by the auctioneer what his job skills were, he replied "I can govern men" and asked to be sold to a man who needed a master. He was sold to a Corinthian, Xeniades, who made Diogenes a teacher to his children.

Diogenes lived the rest of his life in Corinth, and died there in 323 B.C.

# DIOGENES and the BOWL

DIOGENES OWNED ONE POSSESSION: A BOWL

SLURP!

ONE DAY, AT THE FOUNTAIN...

A BOY APPROACHED

SCOOP

DRINK DRINK

SMASH!

JP 2007

# DIOGENES IN: "AN HONEST MAN"

ONCE, DIOGENES WAS FOUND WANDERING THROUGH THE AGORA WITH A LANTERN— IN BROAD DAYLIGHT:

?!

WHAT ARE YOU DOING??

I'M JUST LOOKING FOR AN HONEST MAN

JP 2007

# DIOGENES IN: "MEN and SCOUNDRELS"

ONCE, DIOGENES SUDDENLY CRIED OUT:

MEN! HURRY! COME QUICKLY!

WHEN A CROWD HAD GATHERED, HE BEAT THEM OFF WITH HIS STICK—

NO, NO— AWAY, ALL OF YOU!!

!!!

IT WAS MEN I CALLED FOR... NOT SCOUNDRELS!

JP 2007

# Figure 8 #4

**Krissy**
**PO Box 14613**
**Portland, OR 97293**
**ponyboypress@yahoo.com**
**www.ponyboypress.com**

# alli™

## The Poop Your Pants Diet!

By the time you read this will have no doubt heard of the new diet drug Alli. Between the TV campaigns, store displays and radio spots it is hard to miss. The 2007 marketing budget for Alli is $150 million and seven ad agencies have been hired. An intense guerilla marketing campaign was started with the launch of Alli which included creating a "professional" organization that fed the media stories about the effectiveness of Alli and the dangers of weight loss drugs that were not Alli. News programs, magazines and talk show hosts took the bait and reported "news" stories based on this propaganda masquerading as legitimate news. A "documentary" was also sponsored by the company who sells Alli. It was called "Fat: What No One is Telling You" and it ran on PBS stations, falsely appearing as an objective program interested in the real truth of this issue and promoting Alli. At the same time, one million copies of a diet book also went on sale, along with 3.5 million starter kits.

Alli (pronounced Al-EYE) is the first over-the-counter diet drug approved by the FDA. GlaxcoSmithKline paid $100 million for the U.S. rights to Xenical (orliostat) and for its petition to the FDA to market an over-the-counter version of a diet drug that had been previously available by prescription only. They gave it the friendly sounding name of Alli and made it available to any one who chooses to spend the 2 bucks a day. GlaxcoSmithKiline are anticipating sales of 1.5 to 3.9 billion per year. Launching this diet pill has

been the largest investment made in any over-the-counter brand in the past decade, said Steve Burton, a company president.

Over the past five years, prescription sales of Xenical have been steadily declining. In 2000 sales were at 202 million, by 2005 it was down to 86.6 million. GlaxoSmithKline knew all too well that an over-the-counter diet drug would now be available to consumers who would have not been able to get it before, including people with eating disorders, teenagers and people who are already thin. This new consumer market translates to big profits.

According to Prescription Access Litigation (PAL), a consumer advocacy coalition of more than 125 organizations, there actually are prescription diet drugs out there that have better safety records. These could have been used as an over-the-counter drug. Alli, however, is not one of them. It is very dangerous to be used without supervision. It has little effectiveness, it compromises your health and it offers the user a host of disgusting side effects, which PAL lists as "diarrhea, oily spotting, oily stools, flatulence with discharge and fecal urgency".

Because of the heinous lack of responsibility on the part of

## With Allies like this, who needs Enemas?

GlaxoSmithKline for putting out Alli, PAL gave them the first "Bitter Pill" award of 2007, titling it "With Allies like this, who needs Enemas?"

Part of Alli's campaign is to "break through the clutter with straight talk". Advertisements say that losing weight is hard work and that Alli only helps. Good diet on exercise on your part is just as important as taking the pill. The marketing states "It won't be easy, nothing worth it ever is. But greater weight loss is possible, 50% more than with dieting alone…if you have the will, we have the power." However, in clinical trials, people taking Alli along with dieting and exercise for a two-year period only lost an average of 3 pounds more than those who were dieting and exercising alone. Those three pounds will cost an average of $750.00. But, money isn't the worst way you will pay.

Alli claims to help you lose weight by working to block the absorption of fat by the body. If you take in too much fat, your body expels it in an incredibly embarrassing and smelly way. Alli's own advertising states that one of the side effects is gas with oily spotting, "in fact you may recognize it as something that looks like the oil on top of a pizza". This is what they say in the advertising and marketing! This is what they are using to sell it to us! Imagine what it is really like!

On the website the company tells you how to prepare for the side effects. This is a hint at how really bad it is:

…pick a day to begin taking Alli, such as a weekend day so you can stay close to home…You may feel an urgent need to go to the bathroom…it is probably a smart idea to wear dark pants, and bring a change of clothes to work…the bathroom is the best place to go [if you get gassy].

This is the sugar coated version. Here is how one healthcare practitioner put it when responding to a thread about Alli on a healthcare blog:

HOWEVER, and this is VERY important…you will LEAK orange, foul-smelling oil from your tushy if you eat fatty foods! It will not clean with toilet paper, it will stain the toilet bowl until scrubbed with bleach, and it will leak THROUGH your pants uncontrollably, also staining your clothes (it is VERY hard to get out, even with bleach). This will happen only once to convince you to decrease your fat intake..lol. No fast food on this medicine, no greasy foods, no pizza especially. I don't know why they don't warn people about this. I am an ARNP[Advanced Registered Nurse Practitioner] who prescribed it to many patients, but I gave them the warning to be careful. Carry baby wipes, and an extra set of pants!! At least until you know how it will affect you. Sorry, but somebody needs to warn the public. I will be afraid to sit on a cloth seat (think theater) anywhere in public when this comes out! The leaking stain is 99% permanent (smell too!).

GlaxcoSmithKline has taken the reality of these side effects and done some incredible marketing on this product. First off, they don't call them side effects, instead they use the more harmless sounding term "treatment effects" and they make it seem like they are doing you a favor by giving you crippling diarrea, leaving you smelling like death and permanently ruining your outfit.

While no one likes experiencing treatment effects, they might help you think twice about eating questionable fat content. If you think of it like that, Alli can act like a security guard for your late night cravings.

They make it all seem so nice and benign. The truth is that you cannot eat more than 15 grams of fat per meal without getting these side effects. That is a tablespoon of butter/margarine, oil or salad dressing. And you cannot splurge and use your three whole tablespoons of fat on one meal! You have to spread it out evenly through-out the meal or you will be going through a lot of clothes.

The average recommended fat intake for healthy adults is 65-80 grams. The average fat intake needed for growing teenage boys is 100 and for teenage girls it is 73 grams. Young people still growing, the elderly, pregnant women and anyone with gastrointestinal or absorption problems are of special concern.

> ..they tell us it is for our health and when the surgery or drug backfires, killing us or making us sick, it is our fat that is the culprit..

Because this drug is the first of its kind over the counter, there is no way to regulate who takes it.

Susan Norris, M.D., of the Centers for Disease Control and Prevention states that the lack of actual weight loss and the common "gastrointenstinal adverse effects (expolsive diarrhea, fecal incontinence, abdominal cramping anal leakage and oily discharge") are not the issues that worry medical proffesional the most. The most disturbing thing about the release of Alli is that there is no clinical support or long term benefits for actual health outcomes of taking the drug, such as cardiovascular disease or death.

Alli reduces the absorption of fats. Yet the absorption of those fats is necessary for good health. There are certain vitamins that need fat to benefit our body. With use of Alli, the body cannot get the nutrients from vitamin A, D, E and K. Vitamin A is important for growth, healthy bones and teeth, reproduction and vision. Vitmain D is critical for helping to maintain bones and teeth, muscular strength and more. Vitamin E is essential for healthy skin, plays a key role in immune function and promoting healthy red blood cells. Vitamin K is needed for normal blood clotting and bone health. Twelve percent of Xenical users became Vitamin D deficient within 2 years. Vitmain E deficinces were docmented in 6 percent of those taking it. Now that millions of people have access to Xenical in Alli, the numbers of these deficiencies will surely climb!

It makes me so mad thinking about this. Everyday there is a story in the paper about how fat Americans are costing so much in medical bills. Through the complete irresposibility and greed of GlaxoSmithKiline and business like them, millions of Americans who believe that they are to blame for everything including high insurance costs will take this drug. They will get sick from using it and then WILL end up costing more at the doctors office than someone who didn't feel shamed into taking it. And what will go down on the record is that this person, this FAT PERSON needed more medical care than a thin person.

This is what is repeated over and over with each new pill or surgery. They shame us into doing it, they tell us it is for our health and when the surgery or drug backfires, killing us or making us sick, it is our fat that is the culprit, not the greed or short-sightedness or just plain fat bigotry of these so called medical professionals.

Alli says often in its advertising and literature that losing the weight is work that YOU have to do, Alli can only help. It is an easy out that masks itself as honesty.

The real honest truth is that corporations like GlaxoSmithKline will keep producing and marketing dangerous consumer products as long as we keep buying them! They will fund "studies" that are reported as news to scare us and shame us into feeling like we are sick and then they will market a new pill or surgery that will supposedly save us all. In the meantime we get sick and die and they get richer off of our own money and we are partly to blame. Do not participate! Do not accept all news reports or marketing. Question and research for yourself and speak to you friends and family about it. Once we stop buying the products, they will stop making them.

Epilogue:
After I wrote this I discovered the Alli forum on the website. People who are using Alli can post topics and ask for help, support or in some cases just rant. It is suprisingly engrossing. Many people state it isn't working for them, many people say it is and they have lost x amount of weight, some people have gained weight. Almost everyone beats themselves up and wonders what they did wrong. They all still look to Alli to help them understand how to make it work for them. A few people have questioned the whole thing and don't seem to be getting any response from the moderators. But, the most fascinating thing is the people who have strayed from the diet and have had terrible side effects - although few people on the site call them side effects, most have totallly fallen for the marketing and call them TE's, short for Treatment Effects.

The people who strayed from the diet, ate something fatty and then experienced terrible side effects ("my body won't stop leaking," ruining clothes, pooing oil, having terrible smelling gas and pains – sometimes for days) all laugh it off. They all have completely bought into the "plan" and say, oh well, it is my fault. And yet other users still feel the need to chastise them abut staying on the plan. It is a bizaare thing to witness.

Sources:
Prescription Access Litigation -
http://www.prescriptionaccess.org

JunkFood Science - http://junkfoodscience.blogspot.com/

Alli official site- www.myalli.com

# Publick Occurances #9 & 10

Danny Martin
Tucson, AZ
bullmooseallstar@yahoo.com

# Barefoot and in the Kitchen #4

**Ashley Rowe**
**c/o AK Press**
**674 A 23rd St.**
**Oakland, CA 94612**
**socialobscenity@yahoo.com**

### 'KARMA' SPRINKLES

A sort-of substitute for parmesan cheese- as in, you can use it in the same situations, but don't expect it to taste the same. I'm not sure if the name of this recipe refers to the good karma you'll have for not eating real cheese, or the bad karma I'll have for blatantly ripping off a similarly-named, very expensive product that I like to eat but don't like to pay for. Wait a second, I don't think DIY is every bad karma. Nevermind.

- ½ Cup chopped walnuts
- ½ Cup nutritional yeast
- ½ Tsp. salt

Find some way to crush the shit out of the walnuts. You could use a food processor if you have one, or do it old-school style with a mortar and pestle (that would rule), or find some even more crafty DIY way to do it, like using a hammer, or the bottom of a small jar, or some kind of handle of something. Or whatever.
Once the walnuts are sufficiently pulverized, mix in the salt and nutritional yeast.
Store in an airtight container in the fridge.

# Mylxine #17

**Scott Satterwhite**
**110 North F St.**
**Pensacola, FL 32501**

## Langston Hughes' 100th Birthday

I was riding my bike up to the public library downtown when I was greeted by this giant picture of Langston Hughes at the front entrance. It was a younger picture of him so i didn't instantly recognize him, but thought "I wonder if that's Langston." Then I saw a flier that said the library was holding a 100th birthday party for Langston Hughes. I asked the librarian about the party, but he didn't know so I just walked into the meeting room.

"Is this where the Langston Hughes' birthday celebration is going to be?"

"Yeah, it sure is," said this middle aged man named James, who bore a slight resemblence to an older Mr Hughes. James was blowing up balloons when we came in. I asked if they needed any help.

"OH BLESS YOU, CHILD! BLESS YOU, BLESS YOU! Do you want to start by blowing up some balloons?"

So I blew up a few balloons and asked if they minded if I called a friend to come help. Of course they didn't, so I ran to the phone and called Adee up, who besides my neighbor was the only other person I knew that was really into Langston.

"Hey, guess what! Today's Langston Hughes' birthday and the library's throwing a party. Do you want to come help set it up? It sounds really cool. You should come."

Adee was there in 30 seconds and we went to setting up chairs and blowing up red balloons to decorate the room.

James was running around the place like a chicken with his head cut off, straightening seats, evenly distributing balloons, and getting the cake ready. I was really excited. Langston Hughes is my favorite poet and I love things like this. I'm a sucker for tradition and memorials. Not all of them on either, but there aren't enough opportunities to celebrate great lives. I don't give a shit about George Washington's birthday or Abe Lincoln's. When I'm down, I can't curl up with the Gettysburg Address for comfort. Poetry is one of the few solaces in a scary world and to have a celebration for my ace was more than I could dream of. As close to heaven as I believe is possible.

After Adee and I blew up a million balloons and set up a couple dozen chairs, we walked around the library killing time until the ceremony was going to begin. We were really excited. Then promptly at 4pm, on the day Langston Hughes would have turned 100 years old, the party began.
"Today is a very special day. It's Langston Hughes' 100th birthday and the library is going to celebrate this great African-American's life."

James went on to say that we would have a few readers come up and read some of their favorite works by Langston, followed by an audio tape of him discussing a few of his poems, and a short video. Then James announced his surprise to the audience, a special guest.

"Since today is Langston's 100th birthday, I thought it was only appropriate that I invite my auntie to come be with us," he said in a tone that meant he was talking to the handfuls of kids in the front row. "Auntie is 100 years old herself. That means she's a centurion. Does anyone know what that mean?" The kids were as puzzled as the adults. "A centurion is the name for a person who is over 100 years old. You may have read about centurions in books, but my auntie is a real thing," James said, looking around at the audience. "So after the birthday party is over... just come up here and touch her!"

She just sat in her wheel chair, covered in a blanket, straining to hear what James was saying, waving to all the kids in the room.

The presentation started with a brief discussion of Langston Hughes' life, broken up by tapes of him reading his poetry as well as guests from the community reading their favorite poems. It was really sweet.

"It's also nice to see people of the "lighter hue" here today as well," referring to me I assume since I was the only white person there except the head librarian. James and I had talked about Langston Hughes for a long time when we first met. Mostly about his short stories and his poetry, but a little about his life. Since he knew I was familiar with Langston Hughes, and there weren't a lot of readers, he asked if I would care to read a few of my favorite poems. I said that I didn't have a book of his work with me, and then this woman from the audience handed me a collection of his poetry.

What an honor! I couldn't find my favorite poems in the book she handed me, but I did find a few that I liked and I went up to the podium and nervously read them. One of the poems I found was this one on McCarthy and the House Un-American Activities Committee. Before I read the poem I went and did a little rant about McCarthyism and how Langston was a Communist and how he had written a lot of poetry about his politics several years earlier around the time he went to Spain during the civil war. For that, he was later hounded for being a premature anti-fascist. A lot of people had forgotten that part of his life, and just focused on certain parts that went better with what the mainstream liked to think of Langston. They do this a lot, this "whitewashing" of radicals, especially with African-Americans-unless they've just decided to make a villain out of them, like Paul Robeson for instance. I just wanted to bring this up, but was a bit apprehensive because I wasn't sure where the people who put the event on stood politically. But I went ahead and spoke anyway.

"And even though there was tremendous pressure on him to rat out his friends, Langston Hughes stuck to his guns and never gave McCarthy a single name. It was a difficult thing to do back then, and he paid the price for it. He was blacklisted and had trouble reading his poems for a while. It was a hard thing to do back then, to stand up to fascists, and it is today. But no matter how much Langston Hughes was hounded by McCarthy and his unscrupulous cronies, he never gave the scoundrels one single name."

Almost everyone in the room gave a firm "uh huh", nodding their heads in agreement like we were in church. You never know how things like that will go over in unfamiliar crowds, and it relieved me to no end that I could basically tell a whole room of people that the person this birthday party was for was a Communist and I loved him for it, and everyone nodded approvingly and were proud of that, too.

James got back to the podium and thanked me for reminding everyone about that part of Langston's life.

Now it was time for the special guest—the centurion.

"Before we cut the cake, my auntie wanted to say something to all of you. Now go ahead, auntie."

"Well," she said in a labored, crackly voice you'd expect from a 100 year old woman "I'm going to be with Jesus really soon," she said, looking around the room from behind her thick, thick glasses. The people in front of me started looking at each other, a little uncomfortably. "I'm going to be with Jesus really soon, but I lived a very good life. In fact, I worked for this nice white family until I was 80 years old, taking care of them." She said.

"Then when I turned 80, they gave me pension of four hundred dollars a month. And then I get about $450 a month from social security and another two hundred..."

"Hold on, Auntie!" James jumped in, stopping her from giving a full financial disclosure to all of us. "Hold on! I gave you the floor, now YOU give it back to ME!"

Everyone in the room got one of those timid grins.

"Girl, that man is crazy!" The woman in front of me whispered to her friend.

Adee and I just smiled, trying to hold in the laughter. I couldn't believe he said that. It was a little strange that his aunt started going into her weekly paychecks with us, but Auntie didn't seem to care. She just went back to being 100 and smiling at the kids in the room.

Then James played a tape of Langston Hughes reading some poems and we all listened. James read a poem about how Langston's favorite color was red and he gave everyone who wanted one a red balloon, then a rose, and an apple. The apple had a card attached to it that said "Apples are like people, sweet on the outside and rotten to the core." I liked that and laughed. Adee did, too.
James had brought a cake to the ceremony with a symbolic piece missing (for Langston supposedly...or for James when no one was looking). We all had a piece of the cake and, as Langston was reading in the background, I thought to myself that this was the best day of my life. I went up to the centurion and shook her hand (couldn't resist touching her!). She was nice and thanked me for reading. I thanked her for talking, too and making my day.

It was all so beautiful that day. None of it diminished from the fact that there was a war going on, that the next morning we'd be protesting it, or that the world seemed to be crumbling around us. I find solace in poetry and Langston's words were the words that healed my hurt heart. That we celebrated his birthday shouldn't be that big a deal, but it was to me. It was like me being able to say to him "Thank you for keeping me here."

My favorite poet, my great friend, my favorite place...ah, almost makes me religious. Almost.

# Three Minute Girlfriend

**Toronto, ON**
**http://zeesypowers.com**
**3 Minute Girlfriend DVD available**

Everyone loves to be in love, but dating is tedious when the first bloom fades. Drawing out the inevitable is worse than being lonely, that's not true. There is nothing worse than being lonely. I will be your girlfriend for three minutes, Sunday, March 18, 2007, at xpace, 58 Ossington Ave., 1-6 P.M. No risk of rejection, no messy break-up, no hard feelings.

Mar 12, 2007 3:52 PM
subject          RE:3 Minute Girlfriend

Interesting idea. How does it work? Thanks.
*******************************

Mar 12, 2007 5:05 PM
subject          3 Minute Girlfriend - w4m

I'm confused as to what a 3 minute girlfriend consist of...I am intrigued.
I am a 32 year old Hispanic male who's considered quite attractive and I don't have any mental issues.

Please give me a little more insight as to what you have in mind.

Mar 12, 2007 8:02 PM
subject          3 Minute Girlfriend - w4m

Is it ok if I only need 2 minutes? Ok, honestly, how many people have tried that joke on you? I'd like to think I was original there but I have a feeling I wasn't

WOW - what a caption. Hey just a little reminder, you should never place your address on the internet. Anyways, drop me a line, whenever you have some time!
Tony
******************

Mar 13, 2007 8:27 PM
subject          3 Minute Girlfriend

I'm curious, is this going to be performance art?
Or are you just looking to hook up with someone for 3 minutes?
You have piqued my interest.

you are actually pretty freakin cute! would you like to kareoke sometime sugar? my story is I feel people in Toronto dont like intelligent black men like myself. I dont want to be racist but I find it hard to find a cool smart funny stress free person. Just faith that there must be someone out there that could like me is keeping me sane. Any ways sugar...you seem like a hit! I am sure you could never be alone and you will get many responses...respect that must be cool idea...3 minute girlfriend
Chow Bella! keep in touch?
Uric

I have seen your add on here for the past week or so and have a kind of stupid question for you if that is OK?

Why doyou want to have a botfriend for 3 minutes and then breakup? I think you sound like a smart enough girl and you're obviously VERY cute, so why don't you just persue a good guy with morals, confidence and lots of self respect. I think if you land a guy like that, you won't be lonely anymore.

My name is Luke, I'm 27 and I would totally meet up with you and take you out for a night of good conversation and all sorts of fun, but not if I can expect tonever see you again at the end of the night.

I hope you respond to this but I won't be hurt or disappointed if you don't.

I hoep to hear from you soon,

~Luke
*********************

Hey,
Your ad sounds really interesting.
I am 35, IT professional, I like atravelling a lot and have trravelled to almost every part of the world at least northof the equator. I like outgoing and having fun.
I m a fun romantic guy I like to spend romantic time. I would sit with you hours and hours talking while you have your head on my shoulder and i move my hand on your hair. Or in the bed and feel your breath while close to you.
I like to spend time while you are close to me and feel your warmth.
I like to give a long french kiss, if you can get a 15 min long french kiss non stop then you are ok :)
any ways lots of things to be said but can't write all of that.
Let me know if you wish to get together ot not.
Regards,

Mar 16, 2007 4:13 PM
subject          3 Minute Girlfriend

only three minutes...what if you really do like me?
*********************************************

Hi,

Very cool initiative that you re taking tomorrow. I will not be able to make it to xpace but would love to hear about how it goes for you...

Best,
Chris
*************************

The text you have just read was compiled from the responses to the craigslist posting pictured on the front cover. The event took place Sunday, March 18, 2007.

# Rum Lad #2 and 3

Steve Larder
stevejipwit@hotmail.com
www.stevelarder.co.uk

I DON'T TRUST FAIRGROUND RIDES. THEY'RE TAKEN APART AND RE-ASSEMBLED SO MANY TIMES THAT I JUST THINK, EVERY NOW AND THEN, THERE HAS TO BE A COUPLE OF NUTS AND BOLTS THAT GET MISPLACED IN THE PROCESS...

# So Longview

Kyle Frail
136 Tanglewood Dr.
Longview, WA 98632
kjcelement@yahoo.com

 ERIC

**What was the Lance MagHahn benefit that you helped with?**

Lance Hahn, singer of J Church, got kidney failure and he has heart problems. So, to help pay medical bills, this guy named Chad Riley basically got together on MySpace and must've emailed about a kazillion bands and somehow ended up emailing me. He wanted to know about putting a song on the comp, doing either a J Church or a Cringer cover. At first it sounded like a small thing and somehow it ended up getting bigger and bigger and No Idea (Records) got involved and actual good bands got involved.

**Does it sound like it's actually coming out?**

I still get updates all the time from him on MySpace saying the deadline has been reached for all the songs to go to the mastering guy. The last I heard, it's going to be a double cd and it's actually going to be on No Idea Records but there's some other smaller labels that are going to help No Idea fund the pressing of it. Like, Vinehill Records is doing a lot. They've done, like, a J Church 7" in the past.

**Who hasn't done a J Church 7"?**

And it's supposed to come out Spring 2007. He sent me a little banner (laughs) that I can't figure out how to put up on MySpace, on my page. But it says that it's going to be on No Idea. It has The Queers and The Parasites. A bunch of good bands.

Well, it's gotten more business-oriented. It's a ᴋxxᴇxᴋ career move now for kids. Its like, "I could go to college, I could work in a mill, or I could get a band together and make a bunch of money." It's way more bottomline driven than it used to be. Before it was just any excuse to get together and play, 'cause there was nothing else to do. Now everything's so inundated with shit, you know. It makes things a little less special. Jill and I saw on MySpace for Reid's Pit Stop. Their last show a couple weeks ago was a benefit show for Community House, I think. It was $8 or 6 bucks with a can of food to get in and all the bands were just fucking shit-local bands. Like Rico and the Glaciers and shit like that. I don't care what benefit it's for, I'm not going to spend $8 or $6 just to see a bunch of crap. At least make an effort to get some bands people want to see. If you're going to go to the effort to do a benefit, you know, do it right. Don't just "Benefit Show: Half-Ass." Community House is probably sitting there like, "Rico and the fucking who? Couldn't you get Jackmove? Are they busy? Is everybody busy? Can we do this next weekend?"

**You said it's so bottomline-oriented now, but for some people being able to make a living off music is a dream. So, where do you see the line between punk rock as volunteer time (like playing free shows) and busting your ass so you feel like you deserve to get something out of it?**

I think ifyounever go into anything artistically, thinking that, "Well, if I work this hard I should get something out of it." First and foremost, it should be about fun or maybe expression or something. Maybe getting some sort of point of view across or just having a good time. It should never be like, "I want to go on tour for two weeks and sell a bunch of t-shirts. See how many fans we can make." If you want to do that, be a fucking recruiter.

# Hack This Zine #5

**Hackbloc Collecive**
staff@hackbloc.org
www.hackbloc.org

## Free Jeremy Hammond!

### Hacker   ANARCHIST   Programmer

In January 2007, we lost one of our fellow hacktivists and friends to the federal prison system. Jeremy Hammond has been charged and convicted of obtaining credit card information from right wing website protestwarrior.org. Not one of the credit cards was charged with a single cent and the website was not defaced. As a result of this 'crime' he will spend the next two years in Federal Prison. That is two years in a cemented room with a bed and a toilet, that's two years where all he can do is walk to the 'workshops' to make license plates and/or furniture, walk to the yard and walk to the cafeteria. That is two years to avoid getting beaten or worse. That is two years of no freedom, try to imagine living in a big closet and never leaving your parents house (you can go to the backyard), try to imagine that for two years thats all you will see. You will not be able to travel, you can not sit in the forest with trees all around, you can't come any near a computer, or go to the movies, you can't hang out with friends and you sure as hell can not access the net. All for a 'crime' that has cost nothing in damages to protest warrior or its customers (despite having to fix their crappy code).

HackThisSite.org, our hacker training ground, was co-created by Jeremy. When I received the news about Jeremy, I went to the front page of this site to see what actions were going to take place to free Jeremy. There was a 104 comments to the news about Jeremy and these were the common remarks:

He'll definitely be missed... Best of luck to you, Jeremy.. I really have nothing to say except whats next? or better yet WHO is next.Jeremy, make sure you don't drop the soap, and get out alive or something resembling that.

If anyone gave two shits about Jeremy I really didn't see it here, and this was a community he built. The apathy that permeated those comments was something to behold.

"(Apathy) is a common reaction to stress where it manifests as "learned helplessness" and is commonly associated with depression." -wikipedia.

Why are there not more people upset about this? Why does this not set a fire under anyone's seat? Why are there no actions in support of our friends?

The reason there are so few action in support of Jeremy's inpresionment comes down to FEAR. See the last issue of Hackthiszine (summer 2006) about why we fear and how to over come this fear. But plain and simple it's this: The government and the corporations that run it, need you to be scared so they can keep you soft and juicy like the cow meat they feed you. Placated you vote the way they want you and you stay humble and speechless in your cubicle just the way they like you. This way you won't make waves and upset their imbalance of power so they can be at the top of the political and monetary food chain. A hacker != a cow. A hacker is someone who thinks and looks for knowledge. This knowledge can damage the corporate government and it's lackeys because what you see, you won't like. A hacktivist is a hacker that get's upset about this bondage and wants to break the chains by spreading the knowledge to everyone by any means necessary and usually via a computer.

If you are not asleep and you KNOW what I'm typing about then hear this. better than this. We can get the word out there in all the electronic formats we know. By freeing Jeremy, we are letting the corporate government know that we are not taking their shit! He should have been slapped on the hand, given probation. Not the kind of punishment given to killers or rapist! He gathered information. He gleaned it in his own way. That scares those in power. The corporate government is FEARful of us. There punishment is based on FEAR.

For more information on how you can help free Jeremy go to hackbloc.org. Sign on the forums and see what you can do to let everyone know that the government is scared of us!

**You can also write to:**
*Jeremy Hammond #18729-424*
*FCI Greenville*
*PO Box 5000*
*Greenville Il 62246*

# Pound the Pavement #10

Josh MacPhee
Brooklyn, NY
josh@justseeds.org

Make Not War!

VILLAGE IDIOT

VILLAGE IDIOT

STARTS WARS

PUBLIC URINAL

Only one of these men
was popularly elected

The other guy just backed a military coup.

# Funwater Awesome #2

Zach Mandeville
118 4th Ave E
Olympia, WA 98501
zachboyofdestiny@gmail.com

A rundown of my day, the palate of my poetry.

At 8:30 I'd arrive at beauty school and clock in. All my cosmetology friends would go into the classroom for the morning theory class. I'd go to my station on the salon floor, listen to my walkman, and read the barber textbook. It would tell me something like:

*When shaving a man, do not breathe in his face. This is unhygienic and annoying to the customer.*

Or

*A good deal of barbering is the appearance you give. You want to be a trustworthy, respectable professional. This means showering often.*

And I would think, *How interesting!* And I'd write it down in my notes, in preparation of test day.

Some days I would work in my workbook, as a change of pace. With questions like:

*Q. By being honest and conscientious when an injury occurs, what will you protect?*

*A. Your reputation.*

And after a week or two of this I would take a test, where "showering often" and "your reputation" became multiple choice answers.

After an hour of theory all the other students would filter into the salon floor and the school would be open for business. We'd plug in our clippers and fill up our water bottles, the radio would be turned on and the two students working the front desk that day would call up different classmates to tell them they had appointments.

Then we would all wait, wait for someone to come in for a coloring or a haircut, or until it was time to go home.

A requirements sheet was given to us every Tuesday, the duties and services we were expected to do that week. It was always the same, a computer printoff with boxes for haircuts and styles and shampoos. I was given the same requirements as the cosmetology students, except where it said "perms" I crossed out and wrote "shaves".

I had tallied and divided the sheet to figure out I needed to do one style, one shampoo, one haircut, and one shave a day to fulfill my requirements. So in the morning I'd bring Magnum over to the shampoo bowl and wash his long, luxurious hair. Then I'd call over Ms Jo to check my job. She'd look at his hair and then put her signature on the sheet. Then I would dry his hair and braid it and call her over again. I'd put Magnum away and pull out Bridget, my female mannekin. I would practice shaving on her, using the correct hand movements and positions while Ms. Jo would watch and then check off my shaves box. I could get 3/4 of my daily requirements done in about half an hour, and spend the rest of the day waiting for a haircut to come in.

The other students would be completing their worksheet as well, but doing perms and colors along with styles and cuts. So the school would fill up with all the different smells of all the different services being performed. Bleach for the coloring, ammonia and other strange chemicals for the perms. I'd spend a good part of my days trying to come up with the right description for the awful smells wafting and combining around my station.

I also passed the time by reading. This was risky activity as reading was not allowed on the salon floor. I brought War and Peace just to have the longest, heaviest book to work through, and I'd read it sitting in my barber chair, until a teacher came behind me and said, "Should you be reading right now? Get to work." And I'd stash War and Peace away and stare at Magnum, working.

When it was an especially slow day I'd finally attempt to write. I could usually write for long periods of time, but could never think of anything to write about. Perhaps the smells were getting to me, perhaps it was Roxy Radio blaring out the same seven hits each hour, perhaps it was only my own failure, but nothing good could be written. I looked through my notebook after school ended, to see if there was anything I could use for the zine(as I had hoped). Instead, it was filled with pages of statements like:

"My hairdryer broke and then I fixed it, though all I did was bend the nozzle up. I hope halfway through a thermal [style] it doesn't erupt into lightning and flames and burn up Magnum."

Or

"I thought my friends Chris and Jeremy were coming in. But it was another Chris and Jeremy."

And

"I'm sleepy. And that is all I am."

Sheer poetry I'd write! And then a teacher would come up behind me and tell me I needed to stop writing and get to work and I'd put the notebook away and stare at Magnum and his bountiful mane.

I thought that maybe I should just think and meditate, like a monk. I could use these six months of idle time to explore my mind, or to work on my stillness. But again, the smells and radio got to me and as soon as I'd achieve some mental peace the song would change and I'd scream, internally, "Are they playing fucking Gavin Degraw AGAIN?!" And shatter any stillness I had.

I developed new lonely ways to cope with my day, to wile the hours away without doing the monotonous schoolwork. I'd fill up my water bottle often-so my clients(and Magnum) would have fresh water spraying their head- but would take the longest possible route to get to the sink. I'd walk around the entire outside perimeter of the school-leaving out the front door, entering through the bottom back door- to get to the dispensary sink 15 feet away from my desk. A single water bottle fill up, if done right, could last a half hour.

I'd fill up my back pocket with quarter sized zines to read in the bathroom. With so few men in the school, the men's room was almost always empty. It became like a prayer cell for me in there-silent and lemon-scented- and I'd spend an hour in the last stall reading *America? 13* and *Ghost Pine 6* and thinking, *I want to do this.*

Sometimes I'd just sit on the toilet and stare at the graffiti for half an hour.

I'd wash my combs repeatedly, one by one, walking in shuffled steps back and forth between the dispensary and my desk. Anything to get out of staring into Magnum's eyes and knowing I'm not straightening his hair well enough, no matter how many times I washed his hair and tried.

I realized one day, on my seventh comb and umpteenth walk to the dispensary, that this new existence I was subversively living was no better than actually doing the school work. Sure, I found a way to slack off and leave my desk, but it was by washing combs, all day, over and over. And pooping. And so, resigned, I would sit and stare at Magnum or myself in the mirror, and let the hours pass.

On the third or fourth day of this, I developed an eye twitch. I felt it first, a rapid trembling in my left eye, so I stared at myself in the mirror, waiting, and saw it happen again, my eyelid twitched and trembled like a cartoon blind being pulled up too quick.

*Who'll come to a barber with an eye twitch?!*, I worried, *they'll think I'm a serial killer! Who else's eye twitches like this?!*

I'd try to control it, try to calm myself and my eye, then I'd hear my name called over the intercom and feel lefty twitch like crazy. I'd go say hi to the guy who's hair I was going to cut, and lead him over to my station, my face acting normal. Then I'd look at him in the mirror and ask, "What kind of haircut would you like." And my eyelid would flutter and shake and I swear he looked unsettled, thinking of all the legs and arms I had locked up in my freezer. It didn't help that War and Peace started to get really good, and I got swept up in it, so even after my eye would calm down and we'd be starting up small talk, in my head all I could think about was, *Andrew Bolkonski is dead! How can we talk like this when ANDREW BOLKONSKI IS DEAD!* and these thoughts would spill over into real conversation, and I'd tell some stranger, while running clippers over his head, that the Russians burned Moscow down so the French couldn't control it.

# La La Theory #5

**Katie Haegele**
**PO Box 284**
**Jenkintown, PA 19046**
**www.thelalatheory.com**

Blizzards, Blindfolds, Squatters and Cartoonists:
The La-La Theory #5

Nineteenth century philosophers were very interested in figuring out the origins of language, and some of their theories were pretty fanciful. A Dutch linguist named Otto Jespersen certainly thought so; he gave the theories teasing nicknames, such as The Pooh-Pooh Theory, which suggested that human speech came from the instinctive sounds early man made out of frustration and anger. The one he called The La-La Theory put forth that language was borne of the human need to express poetry and love.

May 2007          katie@thelalatheory.com

www.myspace.com/thelalatheory

blizzard — 1859, origin obscure, possibly from "blizz," American dialectal for violent rainstorm. Blizzard came into common usage during the hard winter of 1880 – 1881.

boycott — In 1880 English land agent Charles C. Boycott refused to lower rent to his Irish tenants in County Mayo. Locals organized and refused to do business with him. It became a verb, then a noun, adopted in German (Boykott), Russian (boik st), Spanish (boicoteo), Polish (bojkot), Croatian (bojkotirati) and other languages worldwide.

outlaw — from Old English utlega, "one put outside the law." Recorded as early as 924. Meaning "one living a lawless life" first recorded in 1880.

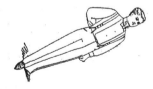

# Coffeebreath #2

**COFFEEBREATH #2**
winter 2006

RADON interview
Hotel Life    Warehouse Life
Life at the Beach
Florida propaganda

Replay Dave
PO Box 13316
Gainesville, FL 32604

## TOM GABEL

New Year's Eve 2005, Tom and I were celebrating at the same bar. We did a shot to help ring in 2006. He mentioned he was staying in a hotel, and looking for a room to rent. I'm constantly looking for ways to make a little extra money here and there, and my brain did some rapid calculating. He's on tour most of the year. I spent most of my nights at Lauren's house anyway. I could charge Tom storage space rent in my room and let him have it when he's in town. I made the offer. It was brilliant, but we're experienced drinkers enough to not commit to drunk talk that seems brilliant at the time.

I called a couple days later to hash out the details. I was expecting a 'No' more than a 'Yes', but his apologetic tone seemed reserved and out of place. He explained that he wanted to try living in hotels for a complete year. Fair Enough. I've also put myself in living environments that minimize or eliminate rent as well as push the limits of my psyche. I can hardly stand hotels on the road for a night, I couldn't imagine a year. My brain started spitting out all kinds of questions. I collected them and Tom was open enough to answer them.

Interview conducted via email from May - October 2006

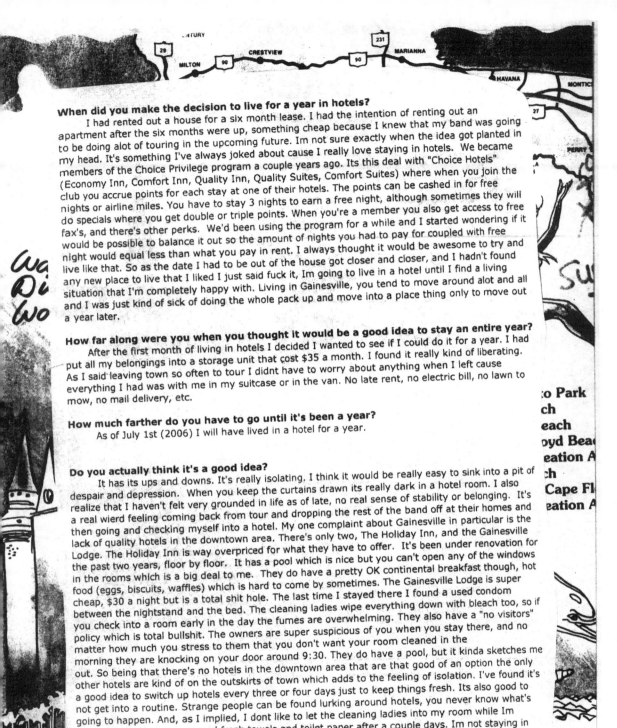

## When did you make the decision to live for a year in hotels?

I had rented out a house for a six month lease. I had the intention of renting out an apartment after the six months were up, something cheap because I knew that my band was going to be doing alot of touring in the upcoming future. Im not sure exactly when the idea got planted in my head. It's something I've always joked about cause I really love staying in hotels. We became members of the Choice Privilege program a couple years ago. Its this deal with "Choice Hotels" (Economy Inn, Comfort Inn, Quality Inn, Quality Suites, Comfort Suites) where when you join the club you accrue points for each stay at one of their hotels. The points can be cashed in for free nights or airline miles. You have to stay 3 nights to earn a free night, although sometimes they will do specials where you get double or triple points. When you're a member you also get access to free fax's, and there's other perks. We'd been using the program for a while and I started wondering if it would be possible to balance it out so the amount of nights you had to pay for coupled with free night would equal less than what you pay in rent. I always thought it would be awesome to try and live like that. So as the date I had to be out of the house got closer and closer, and I hadn't found any new place to live that I liked I just said fuck it, Im going to live in a hotel until I find a living situation that I'm completely happy with. Living in Gainesville, you tend to move around alot and all and I was just kind of sick of doing the whole pack up and move into a place thing only to move out a year later.

## How far along were you when you thought it would be a good idea to stay an entire year?

After the first month of living in hotels I decided I wanted to see if I could do it for a year. I had put all my belongings into a storage unit that cost $35 a month. I found it really kind of liberating. As I said leaving town so often to tour I didnt have to worry about anything when I left cause everything I had was with me in my suitcase or in the van. No late rent, no electric bill, no lawn to mow, no mail delivery, etc.

## How much farther do you have to go until it's been a year?

As of July 1st (2006) I will have lived in a hotel for a year.

## Do you actually think it's a good idea?

It has its ups and downs. It's really isolating. I think it would be really easy to sink into a pit of despair and depression. When you keep the curtains drawn its really dark in a hotel room. I also realize that I haven't felt very grounded in life as of late, no real sense of stability or belonging. It's a real wierd feeling coming back from tour and dropping the rest of the band off at their homes and then going and checking myself into a hotel. My one complaint about Gainesville in particular is the lack of quality hotels in the downtown area. There's only two, The Holiday Inn, and the Gainesville Lodge. The Holiday Inn is way overpriced for what they have to offer. It's been under renovation for the past two years, floor by floor. It has a pool which is nice but you can't open any of the windows in the rooms which is a big deal to me. They do have a pretty OK continental breakfast though, hot food (eggs, biscuits, waffles) which is hard to come by sometimes. The Gainesville Lodge is super cheap, $30 a night but is a total shit hole. The last time I stayed there I found a used condom between the nightstand and the bed. The cleaning ladies wipe everything down with bleach too, so if you check into a room early in the day the fumes are overwhelming. They also have a "no visitors" policy which is total bullshit. The owners are super suspicious of you when you stay there, and no matter how much you stress to them that you don't want your room cleaned in the morning they are knocking on your door around 9:30. They do have a pool, but it kinda sketches me out. So being that there's no hotels in the downtown area that are that good of an option the only other hotels are kind of on the outskirts of town which adds to the feeling of isolation. I've found it's a good idea to switch up hotels every three or four days just to keep things fresh. Its also good to not get into a routine. Strange people can be found lurking around hotels, you never know what's going to happen. And, as I implied, I dont like to let the cleaning ladies into my room while Im staying at a place so you need fresh towels and toilet paper after a couple days. Im not staying in town all that often though, most of the time its hotels abroad somewhere in the country or in another country. A new room each night is always exciting, especially when you aren't staying at a chain. Hotels in Europe are the best, I actually really enjoy the communal bathroom style hotels. You never find those in America.

**How many different hotels have you stayed in so far?**

I haven't counted but I have kept tally. I plan on totaling it up at the end of the year. Ive also taken pictures of the majority of rooms/ hotels I've stayed in. I kind of want to do some sort of coffee table book eventually.

**How many different chains vs actual different rooms?**

Well, the majority of them have been Choice Privilege hotels because of the program. Although in Europe and other places abroad alot of times the Choice Privilege hotels are older independent hotels that have become affiliates. Choice Privilege hotels are my favourite chain. I'm a platinum member. I recently became a card carrying member of the Gold Crown Club which is Best Western. My favorite hotel in Gainesville to stay at is The Paramount Plaza Hotel Suites. Which is where I am right now. I fucking love this place. It feels like home.

**How many different states / countries?**

I've stayed in a hotel in every single state in America. Ive stayed in hotels across Canada, Australia, Japan (only Tokyo), and all across Europe (including eastern Europe, Poland, Lithuania, Serbia, Croatia, etc.)

**How many of them are by yourself?**

I'd say somewhere around 40% of this year has been by myself and the rest with my band.

**How many are over the legal capacity?**

A pretty small amount actually. Living a hotel full time its really important to have some kind of semblance of normalcy when your in the hotel. It can't be a constant party, you know.

**How many are for less than 12 hours?**

A lot are for less than 12 hours. Most of the time on the road I check in around 12 or 1am, often later. Check out is at 11, sometimes you can get it pushed to 12, but most of the time we have to wake up to drive earlier anyways.

**More than one night?**

Whenever I'm here in Gainesville I stay at hotels for 3 to 4 night increments. As I said, I don't like to let the maids into my room so after three or for days you need fresh towels. A freshly made bed is nice too. And as I said it's important to keep the scenery changing to not slip into the pit of despair. Plus when you are staying for free cashing in Choice Privilege points I think it's important to not stay for more than 3 nights in a row as the management will come to hate you. Especially when you're the guy who stays up all night just so he can hit the continental breakfast and stock up on a bunch of food to bring back to his room.

**More than one week?**

I've never stayed in the same hotel for more than a week. I have stayed at the Paramount for a week stretch before. Most hotels have a 14 day limit.

**Have you memorized any chain's interior decor?**

Oh for sure. If you stay at one hotel in a chain you've stayed in them all (in the states). They all have the same shitty art on the walls, the same bedspreads, the same carpet, the same telephones. I'm guessing there's some kind of company that supplies this stuff to hotels. Kind of like the Sysco of the hotel world. When I do get a place of my own I've considered decorating it like a hotel room. I want to find out where they order this stuff from and buy some for myself.

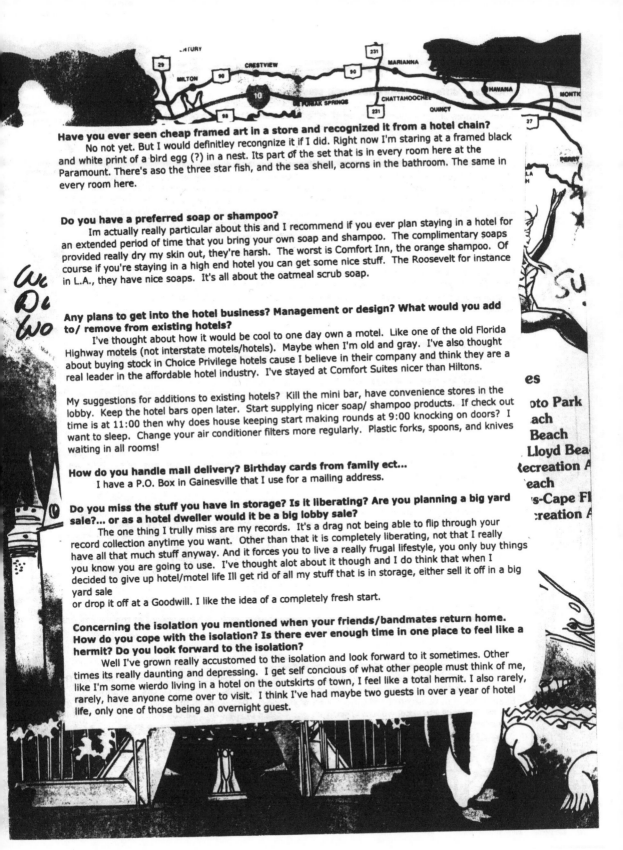

**Have you ever seen cheap framed art in a store and recognized it from a hotel chain?**

No not yet. But I would definitley recongnize it if I did. Right now I'm staring at a framed black and white print of a bird egg (?) in a nest. Its part of the set that is in every room here at the Paramount. There's aso the three star fish, and the sea shell, acorns in the bathroom. The same in every room here.

**Do you have a preferred soap or shampoo?**

Im actually really particular about this and I recommend if you ever plan staying in a hotel for an extended period of time that you bring your own soap and shampoo. The complimentary soaps provided really dry my skin out, they're harsh. The worst is Comfort Inn, the orange shampoo. Of course if you're staying in a high end hotel you can get some nice stuff. The Roosevelt for instance in L.A., they have nice soaps. It's all about the oatmeal scrub soap.

**Any plans to get into the hotel business? Management or design? What would you add to/ remove from existing hotels?**

I've thought about how it would be cool to one day own a motel. Like one of the old Florida Highway motels (not interstate motels/hotels). Maybe when I'm old and gray. I've also thought about buying stock in Choice Privilege hotels cause I believe in their company and think they are a real leader in the affordable hotel industry. I've stayed at Comfort Suites nicer than Hiltons.

My suggestions for additions to existing hotels? Kill the mini bar, have convenience stores in the lobby. Keep the hotel bars open later. Start supplying nicer soap/ shampoo products. If check out time is at 11:00 then why does house keeping start making rounds at 9:00 knocking on doors? I want to sleep. Change your air conditioner filters more regularly. Plastic forks, spoons, and knives waiting in all rooms!

**How do you handle mail delivery? Birthday cards from family ect...**

I have a P.O. Box in Gainesville that I use for a mailing address.

**Do you miss the stuff you have in storage? Is it liberating? Are you planning a big yard sale?... or as a hotel dweller would it be a big lobby sale?**

The one thing I truly miss are my records. It's a drag not being able to flip through your record collection anytime you want. Other than that it is completely liberating, not that I really have all that much stuff anyway. And it forces you to live a really frugal lifestyle, you only buy things you know you are going to use. I've thought alot about it though and I do think that when I decided to give up hotel/motel life Ill get rid of all my stuff that is in storage, either sell it off in a big yard sale
or drop it off at a Goodwill. I like the idea of a completely fresh start.

**Concerning the isolation you mentioned when your friends/bandmates return home. How do you cope with the isolation? Is there ever enough time in one place to feel like a hermit? Do you look forward to the isolation?**

Well I've grown really accustomed to the isolation and look forward to it sometimes. Other times its really daunting and depressing. I get self concious of what other people must think of me, like I'm some wierdo living in a hotel on the outskirts of town, I feel like a total hermit. I also rarely, rarely, have anyone come over to visit. I think I've had maybe two guests in over a year of hotel life, only one of those being an overnight guest.

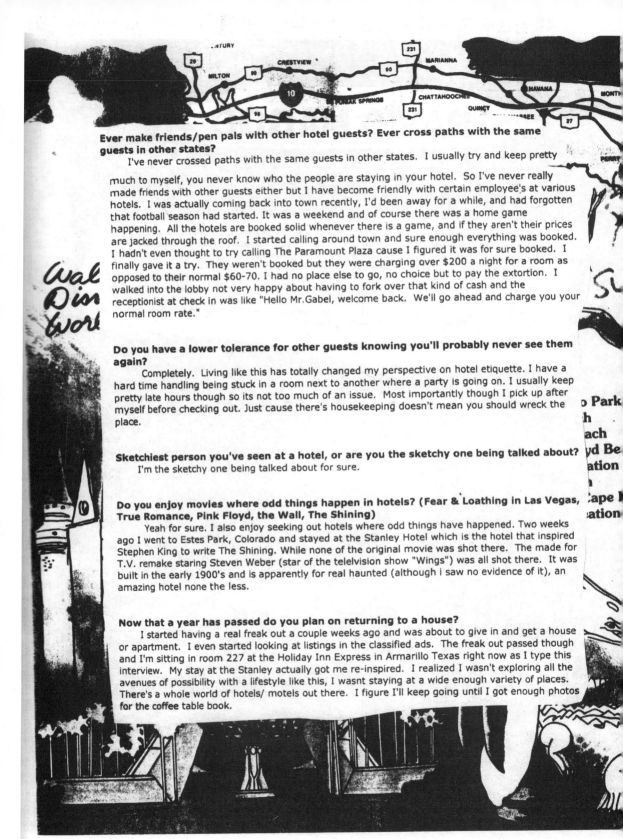

**Ever make friends/pen pals with other hotel guests? Ever cross paths with the same guests in other states?**

I've never crossed paths with the same guests in other states. I usually try and keep pretty much to myself, you never know who the people are staying in your hotel. So I've never really made friends with other guests either but I have become friendly with certain employee's at various hotels. I was actually coming back into town recently, I'd been away for a while, and had forgotten that football season had started. It was a weekend and of course there was a home game happening. All the hotels are booked solid whenever there is a game, and if they aren't their prices are jacked through the roof. I started calling around town and sure enough everything was booked. I hadn't even thought to try calling The Paramount Plaza cause I figured it was for sure booked. I finally gave it a try. They weren't booked but they were charging over $200 a night for a room as opposed to their normal $60-70. I had no place else to go, no choice but to pay the extortion. I walked into the lobby not very happy about having to fork over that kind of cash and the receptionist at check in was like "Hello Mr.Gabel, welcome back. We'll go ahead and charge you your normal room rate."

**Do you have a lower tolerance for other guests knowing you'll probably never see them again?**

Completely. Living like this has totally changed my perspective on hotel etiquette. I have a hard time handling being stuck in a room next to another where a party is going on. I usually keep pretty late hours though so its not too much of an issue. Most importantly though I pick up after myself before checking out. Just cause there's housekeeping doesn't mean you should wreck the place.

**Sketchiest person you've seen at a hotel, or are you the sketchy one being talked about?**

I'm the sketchy one being talked about for sure.

**Do you enjoy movies where odd things happen in hotels? (Fear & Loathing in Las Vegas, True Romance, Pink Floyd, the Wall, The Shining)**

Yeah for sure. I also enjoy seeking out hotels where odd things have happened. Two weeks ago I went to Estes Park, Colorado and stayed at the Stanley Hotel which is the hotel that inspired Stephen King to write The Shining. While none of the original movie was shot there. The made for T.V. remake staring Steven Weber (star of the telelvision show "Wings") was all shot there. It was built in the early 1900's and is apparently for real haunted (although i saw no evidence of it), an amazing hotel none the less.

**Now that a year has passed do you plan on returning to a house?**

I started having a real freak out a couple weeks ago and was about to give in and get a house or apartment. I even started looking at listings in the classified ads. The freak out passed though and I'm sitting in room 227 at the Holiday Inn Express in Armarillo Texas right now as I type this interview. My stay at the Stanley actually got me re-inspired. I realized I wasn't exploring all the avenues of possibility with a lifestyle like this, I wasnt staying at a wide enough variety of places. There's a whole world of hotels/ motels out there. I figure I'll keep going until I got enough photos for the coffee table book.

# East Village Inky #33

Ayun Halliday
PO Box 22754
Brooklyn, NY 11202
ayun@ayunhalliday.com
www.ayunhalliday.com

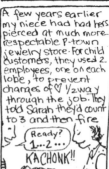

"That's impossible!" said my (unpierced) husband. * "It just fell off!"

Oh yeah? Well then why come I can't pull the earring out? She shrieks bloody murder at the slightest tug!

← Nurse Mary is in her office at school. She, too, thinks the back is in there, but she is much gentler than I. I've raised daughters. We'll get through this.

Nurse Mary gives me alcohol (hooray!) pads (oh... dang.) & some packets of antibiotic cream. We'll fix this kid.

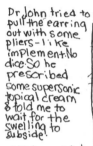
hold still.

I clean the infected ear twice a day, loosing all manner of - brace yourself - crust & ooze. It reminds me of the good ol' days when we had lice (E.V. Inky #22) but still the damn thing wouldn't budge. Father was VERY impatient.

After nearly a week, we go see our pediatrician. My friend, Delta (the 32, remember) had said an antibiotic shot had cured her of a swollen, infected lobe. Can we get some o' that?

Nahhh! The back's not in there! It just fell off!

Dr. John tried to pull the earring out with some pliers - like implement. No dice. So he prescribed some supersonic topical cream & told me to wait for the swelling to subside!

Hey John? It's Ayun Halliday. It's been a week & that earring's still stuck...

rrrnghh... y'know I'm beginning to rethink what I said about the back not being in there.

John gave me the number of his PLASTIC SURGEON friend! ... but that guy didn't take our insurance & his receptionist estimated a starting figure of 300$!

I wish he had better magazines.

I found another one who's in our network, who was seeing new patients, & was open on Columbus Day.

* If I could do just ONE thing to beautify this already gorgeous creature, I would kneel on his chest & pierce BOTH of his ears. I find that a VERY compelling male look.

---

I'm a little leery about blind picks in the health care department, ever since a root canal went horribly awry at the hands of a dentist selected for his convenient East Village location. (see E.V. Inky #11 if you dare!)

It was somewhat reassuring to see the framed certificate identifying Dr. Portnoy as the official Plastic Surgeon of the New York Rangers ...

Though he didn't seem to get what the problem was. Couldn't understand why I was so concerned that the back was in the lobe. I discreetly confirmed his unpierced status (above the neck anyway.)

uh, dr? The "back" is that curlycue thing that keeps the earring from falling off.

Oh. Well what do you call the pin that goes through the lobe?

that's the "post"

Huh. y'learn something new every day.

Once we got that cleared up he was excellent! After applying a powerful topical anesthetic he asked me to assist in pinning back the lobe. My nurse fantasy is indulged w/ increasing frequency. I've held down everyone from Jamba to my mother-in-law *

actual degree is in THEATRE

Ya doin' okay, Mom?

Uh. Sure. Yeah! Fine! Fine!

whooo... she can't feel that! It's g,g,g bloodbath!

LIGHTS! Magnification!

dig dig my probe → slice. my kid.
← powerful nerve block

SUCCESS! CLANK! Ooh Snarly!

Though perhaps not as gnarly as the boob job maintenance I eavesdrop on as Inky recovers by pressing gauze to her ear for 10 minutes.

The patient is rewarded with the title of her choice from Books of Wonder (18 W 18th st) & then we run into everyone we've ever known at the Union, 59 & I must regale them all.

HA!! BIG MOUTH

amazingly there's barely a mark! Ah, the elasticity of youth!

Oh my god, Sean, it was so SICK, but she didn't feel a thing! The doctor's like, "ya doin' okay, Mom?" As if I was going to swoon from the blood! I'm like, Dude, the blood's totally cool, but THAT'S MY KID!!!

It remains to be seen whether she'll reenlist... I thought for sure we'd have gotten 'em punched in a St Mark's street stall by deadline... something to remember.

well... mmmm maybe.

* As she got the inside of her nostril cauterized!!! She was very brave. I don't think she was aware of the smoke. With her other nostril packed with gauze she couldn't smell the burning flesh.

# The Match #105

Fred Woodworth
PO Box 3012
Tucson, AZ 85702

## Crap-Detection Department:

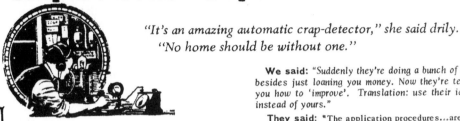

*"It's an amazing automatic crap-detector," she said drily.*
*"No home should be without one."*

IT IS NOW TIME to revisit one of the past installments of this column. In an issue back in 1998 (#93 of The Match), we dissected a promotional mailing from some meteoric outfit newly on the scene, called the Independent Press Association. We warned against it and said it amounted to dangerous centralization that made unbelievable claims. But a lot of publishers didn't heed our warnings, and today they're paying a high price for their obliviousness, as the IPA has plunged to the bottom, taking several zines and non-mainstream magazines with it.

Here's some of the IPA's hype and our responses to it back then:

**They said:** "In its latest and most ambitious effort to nurture and support independent publishing, the Independent Press Association has created a revolving loan program for its members to use to finance direct mail marketing campaigns."

**We said:** *"Wrong. It's a hell of a lot more than that. Further text reveals this as a way by which these people become partners of yours who tell YOU how to run your publication..."*

**They said:** "IPA members can borrow up to $30,000 at a time... 'Magazines that don't invest in serious marketing efforts are usually doomed to slow death,' said IPA Executive Director John Anner..."

**We said:** *"Who is this guy, what track-record has he got in alternative or radical publishing, and how can an outfit that's been operating for 18 months claim to tell magazines like us, who've been going for 30 years, how to avoid 'slow death'?"*

**They said:** "Member publications range from the small and obscure to the icons of progressive independent publishing..."

**We said:** *"If all this hype is true, how come some members remain small and obscure?"*

**They said:** "The Revolving Loan Fund was set up through a $150,000 loan from Working Assets Funding Service..."

**We said:** *"This is a word game that tells us nothing. It's like saying 'Jehovah is Jesus,' or 'Mary Doakes is Jane Roe'. Hoo dat?*

**They said:** "We work to help our members figure out ways to reduce costs, improve the publication, and get their ideas out to a wider audience."

**We said:** *"Suddenly they're doing a bunch of stuff besides just loaning you money. Now they're telling you how to 'improve'. Translation: use their ideas, instead of yours."*

**They said:** "The application procedures...are simple and painless. We will need your completed application form, direct mail campaign marketing plan, financial statements from previous year, and $100 non-refundable application fee. ...To apply, your publication must be a member in good standing, (and) must agree to provide Working Assets with names of respondents to the direct mail campaign. Progress reports must be sent to the IPA..."

**We said:** *"And what do we want those names for? We're not even telling you! So let's see...If you default on the loan, they take your collateral, your publication is finished, they have all your records, and they know the name and address of every reader who might've agreed with what you were saying.*

*"How centralization, control, indebtedness, supervision, and involvement with some big outfit that is vague about where it gets its money, add up to a 'radical' new vision of independence in publishing...*

*"Hey, kids! It's radical! Be the first one on your block!"*

The IPA also attempted to centralize small magazines' printing, mailing, and distribution. Like those giant cable companies which constantly wheedle customers to use their services not only in providing TV signals but also as an internet service, telephone company, direct-deposit bill-paying clearinghouse, etc., the IPA brought with it the dangers of putting all your eggs in one basket. If something happens with the big cable company, *everything* in your life comes to a stop —TV, internet, phone, utilities don't get paid so your gas, electricity and water are turned off, and so on. In the case of the IPA, all kinds of things member magazines had foolishly allotted to the smarmy organization suddenly stopped, not the least being monetary collections from newsstands and stores that had been selling the magazines.

According to the San Francisco Weekly, the IPA owed various lefty magazines about half a million dollars. As in the earlier Fine Print Distribution debacle (which we also warned readers to steer clear of), all kinds of sob stories were rehearsed to explain what happened: "poor accounting systems", "decreases in grant fund ing", and so on. Blame reverberates, but the overall picture is simple: Some previously unknown outfit issues a lot of hyperbolized promotions, draws a lot of foolish people into its web, then goes up in smoke.

When a magazine called Clamor decided it couldn't go on in the absence of IPA's payments, others such as Alternative Press Review (the Anarchy/Journal of "Desire Armed" clone that only pretended to review alternative press anyway) also started whining and issuing emergency appeals because they were, in turn, owed big slugs of money by Clamor.

In one particularly touching plaint (we could almost hear sad violin music), one of the APR crowd sobbed that "when distros go under, magazines can't pay print bills and other expenses." Honestly, what can you expect when you blow a lot of crap into the pipes about "demanding an end to capitalism", but perpetually keep using big-business production services, and never make the slightest effort to own the Means of Production?

Postscript: Desert Moon Distribution, another rotten outfit we had a harsh word or two for in the past, has also gone out of business. Desert Moon was another of these "we are the middleman" usurpers who aggressively interpose themselves between publishers and readers, at the end reportedly owing publishers "hundreds of thousands of dollars". Almost amusingly, considering some of the efforts we here made to get people to boycott such leeches, we now read that at one point late in Desert Moon's history, all its contracts suddenly turned into toilet paper and got flushed. To escape debt, the owner "sold" the thing to one of his employees, and the "new owner" said that he "did not regard himself as responsible" for the debts owed by last guy.

Pretty slick, eh? On the other hand, if people WILL deliberately place themselves at the mercy of con-men after being warned, what can you do? Whether it's aluminum siding, or the old roof racket, or the Pigeon Drop, evolutionary processes have a way of thinning out the herd.

BOMBARDING the mark with unctuous phrases seems to be the con-man s.o.p., and over the years a "ghastly rapid river" of it, in Poe's memorable phrase, has spewed into our mailbox. We got one of the very first Nigerian Letters, when it really was a letter, in about 1986, and wish now that we'd kept it as a collector's item. The following piece, lately received, is in a little different class, much more amateurish, but it has all the familiar odor. (Remarkably, many persons lack, apparently, noses.) For the educational value of this distinctive aroma, presented herewith is a communication which we will cryptically title...

HE WANTS FREE PRINTING.

"Greetings and respects first and foremost! I have waited too long to take the initiative, but then again, that's exactly what this contact is all about. I am eager to take an example from someone that's been in the waters for quite some time. You have my full support as an individual.

"The reason I am talking in terms of individuality is that while my interests are individual, this contact is partially on the behalf of others. I personally want to work with you as a publisher and sometime advisor. I come not as a beggar but as someone seeking mutual benefit. You are my only choice outside of utilizing a local print shop's services. I would much rather cooperate with someone with whom I do share a large majority of ideals.

"Getting to specifics, I am going to be working in association with an organization called the Hakku Ya Aset, or H.Y.A. It is a non-profit corp., centered around Pagan interests, for which I am an acting Agent. We view the term Pagan very broadly, including those of Wiccan and Odinist to Agnostic and Atheist beliefs. And everything in between. We are completely open to other denominations, even if they are not with us. I do realize that you may not wish to have formal associations with this group; that's perfectly fine with everyone concerned."

*(Broad smile appears on recipient's face.)*

"The benefits of this coalition are: We are offering a tax write-off for Services Rendered, PLUS (sic) at least several hours' work with strait (sic) out money. This is as if the whole thing were being paid for normally, except for the equivalent write-off. Of course the Publisher's mention also. Then the constant appearance of your magazine in a resource section— always first in order.

"I view my politics as an evolutionary breed of Anarchy, though I am not shy about using what I believe will work. I know all I say won't jibe with your personal politics but I am a Collectivist and I do practice what I preach, which entails working well with others no matter their affiliations.

"I chose you for many reasons, mainly your experience and obvious intelligence..."

*(Smile now replaced by bursts of laughter.)*

"...However, I have probably made it sound as if we take similar lines on most things. There is one major difference: I am not afraid of computers! Of course, you will not become a Collectivist within the next week or two; but I do respect what you HAVE done, especially the long-term persistence. That, to me, is success. One must look to the successful because they lead by example, by doing.

"So, I would like to hear your thoughts on what has been put on the table. I intend to be ready to go forward on my project soon, and I do admire your awesome work. You can never know what influence you will have on the future. Thank you!

"Most respectfully, etc."

# Paping Teacher's Edition

Shawn Cheng
www.partykausa.com

John Meijas ed.
speedymyshka @aol.com
www.paping.org

THE KID EDITION

I WENT TO 1ST AND 2ND GRADES AT YU-YING ELEMENTARY SCHOOL IN YUANLIN, TAIWAN.

I WENT TO 3RD AND 4TH GRADES AT P.S. 162 IN BAYSIDE, QUEENS, U.S.A.

IT WAS A STANDARD "COURTYARD" LAYOUT, WITH THE CLASSROOMS RINGING THE TRACK AND FIELD.

IT WAS AN IMPOSING BRICK BUILDING, WITH HIGH CHAIN LINK FENCES AND METAL GRATES ON THE WINDOWS.

THE KIDS HAD CHORES EVERY DAY – SWEEPING, MOPPING, AND WIPING DOWN THE DESKS AND BLACKBOARDS.

THE HALLWAYS WERE LIT WITH FLUORESCENTS AND SMELLED FAINTLY OF DETERGENT.

EVERY MORNING THERE WAS A BIG ASSEMBLY WHERE WE STOOD IN FORMATION AND SANG THE NATIONAL ANTHEM AND RAISED THE FLAG.

A-TEN...HUT!!

DURING THE PLEDGE OF ALLEGIANCE I JUST MIMICKED THE SOUNDS. I DIDN'T LEARN THE ACTUAL WORDS TILL YEARS LATER.

I PIGEON KNEE GENTS...

MUMBLE MUMBLE

BETWEEN CLASSES I USED TO BUY PACKS OF RAMEN FROM THE SCHOOL STORE, CRUSH THEM UP, AND EAT THEM AS SNACKS.

MUNCH MUNCH

MY ENTHUSIASM FOR MY BRAND NEW MICKEY MOUSE LUNCH-BOX AND HOMEMADE SANDWICHES QUICKLY WANED.

CHIPS! SODA! SINGLE BOLOGNA SLICE WATER

FOR MISBEHAVIOR AND OTHER INFRACTIONS WE WERE LINED UP IN FRONT OF THE CLASS TO RECEIVE CORPORAL PUNISHMENT.

WHAP! I'M SORRY.

MY BOOKBAG IN AMERICA WAS ACTUALLY HEAVIER, OWING TO THE GIGANTIC HAND-ME-DOWN TEXTBOOKS.

THIS IS BORING!

DIDN'T YOU DO ANYTHING CRAZY OR STUPID?

LIKE WHAT?

PURR

THE BOYS AT MY SCHOOL USED TO FLIP UP OUR SKIRTS.

THEY EVEN PUT MIRRORS ON THEIR SHOES TO LOOK UP OUR SKIRTS.

*20 YEARS LATER  *MY SWEETIE - AIN'T SHE SWEET?

WE USED TO KICK THEM IN THE BALLS

...OR POKE THEM IN THE ASS - "KANCHO!"

NO... I WAS A "GOOD" KID

OH...

NERD!

ANYWAY... DID I MENTION THAT I DIDN'T SPEAK A WORD OF ENGLISH WHEN I STARTED 3RD GRADE AT P.S. 162? IT WAS AWKWARD AND TERRIFYING...

I DIDN'T EVEN REMEMBER MY NEW ENGLISH NAME. DURING ATTENDANCE THEY FIGURED OUT WHO I WAS BY LOOKING AT MY NOTE-BOOKS, WHERE MY MOM HAD WRITTEN MY NAME.

SHAWN CHENG?

SHAWN CHENG??

OH HERE HE IS!

THERE WERE MANY MOMENTS OF CULTURE SHOCK... FOR EXAMPLE, IN TAIWAN, IT WASN'T SUCH A TABOO TO PICK YOUR NOSE IN PUBLIC...

USE A TISSUE!

EW, GROSS

?

MRS. S.

I WAS MORTIFIED BY HAVING TO UNDRESS IN FRONT OF OTHER KIDS FOR GYM CLASS... DON'T EVEN GET ME STARTED ON THAT ANNUAL TEST WHERE THEY GRABBED YOUR CROTCH AND TOLD YOU TO COUGH...

IT TOOK ME A WHILE TO GET USED TO AMERICAN FOOD.

CHOCOLATE MILK

BOILED STRING BEANS

APPLESAUCE

SPORK

"PIZZA" - ON HALF HERO

AND PLAYGROUND POLITICS WERE ALSO FOREIGN TO ME.

YOU WANT FIGHT??

WHAT'S YOUR PROBLEM?

OH!

YOU STUPID!

FIGHT! FIGHT!

SINCE I HAD NO IDEA WHAT WAS GOING ON MOST OF THE TIME, I TOOK TO DOODLING IN CLASS.

WOW! THE TURTLES!

DRAWING BECAME A WAY I COULD RELATE TO THE OTHER BOYS...

DRAW ME THE TURTLES!

OK THEN I READ YOUR NINTENDO POWER?*

*VIDEO GAME MAGAZINE.

I EMBRACED MY MILD CELEBRITY. I WAS LIVING THE "AMERICAN DREAM"!

HEY ARTIST I WANTA PICTURE.

OK!

NO I'M NEXT!

NO ME!

... UNTIL I CAME FACE TO FACE WITH THAT THING THEY CALL THE "ENTREPRENEURIAL SPIRIT"...

TURTLE DRAWINGS!

TEN CENTS EACH!

SUCK YOU!

(I MADE SURE TO INCLUDE COPYRIGHT INFO IN ALL MY DRAWINGS FOR YEARS AFTER)

YEAH... A MIXED BAG ALRIGHT. I THINK MY EXPERIENCES WERE SHAPED BY EQUAL PARTS OF FOREIGNNESS AND CLUELESSNESS. JUST GOES TO SHOW THAT MOST OF WHAT YOU LEARN IN SCHOOL YOU LEARN OUTSIDE OF ACTUAL CLASS, NO MATTER WHERE YOU ARE, I GUESS...

NERD!

SHAWN CHENG 2007

kczines@gmail.com

Written by those who know
(Or those who once were)

About the legislation to ban the thinnest models…

Biba London designer Bella Freud told papers, "I think it's aggressive and repulsive to do this to young people. They are under so much pressure anyway—and now people want to add to it by criticizing them about their weight. Sometimes young girls are just skinny. That's all. And there's a big difference between being skinny and having an eating disorder. Why should they be penalized for being skinny? We have to remember to cherish young people—and not criticize them so much."

Agents constantly criticize their models for weighing too much. Freud displaces a criticism of industry standards to the models themselves.

An **honest model** says: "There most definitely was a lot of pressure from my employers to lose weight… In the beginning, though I was struggling with my ED, I wasn't yet underweight—I was thin but healthy. They measured my waist and it was 27". They told me that I had to lose at least three and get to a 24". They also were encouraging a breast enlargement and I was planning on doing it the minute I graduated from high school but never ended up doing it the minute I graduated from high school but never ended up doing it because I was in the Center at that time. They were "nice" about it, but made it very clear that if I were going to be successful and get any jobs, then weight loss was absolutely mandatory. Especially for what I ended up doing—runway—you absolutely must be at least a size 2, though it's preferable to be a 0. There is no room for negotiation, so that's what I started to do—lose weight, and a lot at that.

I have a couple of model friends that I am close enough to that they will share with me their struggles with ED's. But for every one of them there are probably 10 (that I know) who deny it and probably will until the day they die. It is very un-cool to have an ED in the industry… you more are just expected to put everyone and yourself under the illusion that you are "perfect" by nature, that you are just thin naturally. I myself do not share with others my past struggles with anorexia but not because I am ashamed of it—I do it because I am an intensely personal person and am uncomfortable sharing so much of myself with other people. I pretend just like most of the others that I never struggle.

I'm not sure if it's possible to stay in the industry and stay well… I am underweight (my BMI is 16.6) and my agent is encouraging me to lose another inch on my waist which would require another 4-5 lbs. I am valiantly working with my therapist and dietician to not lose more weight… to just maintain. Of course my treatment team is not happy at all that I have made the decision to go back to modeling and are trying their damndest to get me to quit. I have already said before that I am truly only doing it for how good it pays… we just need it so badly right now. I honestly don't think that it is possible to be healthy

and model. I just don't believe it because I've never seen it. Not once.

My agency does not know that I have an ED or have been treated for it. I don't think I would get a very positive response… and they don't seem very concerned with models having ED's. Like I said—they only care if you are skinny—they don't care and don't want to know how you do it. My agency has given me a personal trainer to "tone up" (in other words lose weight) so they do try to help you exercise and not just completely starve but I would say that in general they just expect you to lose a lot of weight really quickly. I would say that the issue is more ignored than brought to attention.

Cathy Gould, director of New York's Elite modeling agency, told newspapers, "I think it's outrageous. I understand they want to get this tone of healthy beautiful women, but what about discrimination against the model, and what about the freedom of the designer?" She claims that such legislation would put the careers of "naturally gazelle-like" models in detriment.

It is doubtful that any of these human models naturally look like gazelles. Very few might, but those who purport this argument are kidding themselves. Though the fashion industry alone is of course not responsible for eating disorders like anorexia and bulimia, the fact that most agencies refuse to hire models who are not anorexic cannot be overlooked. Steve Bloomfield of the Eating Disorder Association told newspapers, "We do think legislation is needed. This is about protecting the young women and men who work in the fashion industry, as well as those who are at risk of an eating disorder and can be influenced by the pictures that they see. The fashion industry is there to make money and there is no legislation to protect models. It basically exploits people who are underweight and forces others to follow suit."

I have been browsing the magazines lately and they have had a whole novel of eating disorder talk in them. People magazine did a big article on eating disorders and it made me soooo mad because all they talked about was weight and numbers (very triggering… i.e. Sally got to 2 lbs and was about to die… bla bla) and nothing about the psychological aspect of it nor the intense pain that fuel eating disorders. They also discounted bulimia as somewhat "less of an eating disorder" as if anorexia is so dangerous and bulimia has no ill effects…

More than anything else I wish people would get the right information. I'm not a vain person, I want to feel like a capable and worthwhile person, not fit into a certain size.

I was in my physiology class last week and we were talking about how the thyroid reacts during a "starved state" and after lecture was over, the girl next to me was like "I don't get people with eating disorders. They should just stop. I know this girl who has one and she's 30 and on her death bed. My whole family has no pity for her because she did this to herself." GRRRR!

I think the best thing we can do is spread the truth and clear up misconceptions and stereotypes.

# Reclaiming Our Ancient Wisdom

## Catherine Marie Jeunet
### 3527 NE 25th #127
### Portland, OR 97212
### redroserage@yahoo.com
### www.eberhardtpress.org
### Published by Eberhardt Press

HERBAL ABORTION PROCEDURE & PRACTICE
FOR MIDWIVES AND HERBALISTS

BY CATHERINE MARIE JEUNET

*"Herbal abortifacients have been used by women beyond recorded history…
Ancient herbal abortifacients were an integral part of every culture that respected
the woman, the mother earth, and her powers."*

UNI M. TIAMAT

ERBAL ABORTION HAS BEEN WITH WOMEN SINCE THE BEGINNING OF TIME. It has at times been a forbidden wisdom, passed by word of mouth between midwives, herbalists, and women healers. Beginning in the 14th century and through the 17th century, performing or simply knowing how to perform an herbal abortion was a danger. Those who held this information were murdered or frightened into silence. Eventually this knowledge was erased from the memories and lives of nearly all women.[21]

Today, we have only remnants of this once common knowledge. We are left to piece together the clues left behind in an effort to regain the wisdom of our foremothers. With this document, I will compile the currently available information on the subject of herbal abortion. Through examples from research studies, journal articles and written text, I will outline the historic connection between midwifery and the use of abortifacient herbs. I will discuss the use of abortifacient herbs historically and presently, their safety, risk, efficacy and preparation. I will also evaluate their role in today's midwifery practice and how the current-day midwife can implement these herbs and techniques in her own practice.

Women have regulated their fertility for thousands of years. The earliest evidence of fertility control comes from archeological findings from ancient habitation sites in the Mediterranean regions. The female pelvic bones where studied for changes associated with childbirth giving the estimated number of pregnancies a woman had during her lifetime. Paleontologist J. Lawrence Angel estimates that the average woman living around 2000 BC had five childbirths. The number of pregnancies then gradually decreased from 4.7 births circa 1500 BC, 4.1 childbirths circa 1150 BC, 3.6 births circa 300 BC to 3.4 average births circa 120 AD.[19] These findings indicate that during this time women gradually had fewer children throughout their lives. This may indicate the use of some fertility regulation.

Herbal abortion is an ancient method of birth control. The first document of herbal abortions is found in the Ebers Scroll, one of the largest Egyptian papyrus scrolls in existence. This scroll, dated between 1550 and 1500 BCE, contains prescriptions for a variety of ailments and "recipes that are made for women", including an herbal abortion recipe "to cause a woman to stop pregnancy in the first, second and third period."[16] Soranos, an ancient Greek writer on gynecology during the early first century AD, wrote about herbal contraception and birth control, including the use of vaginal suppositories and oral plant based contraceptives.[17]

Herbal abortifacients were an integral part of every matriarchal culture. The use of herbal abortion is directly linked to the role of the midwife throughout history. Midwives did not limit their profession to pregnancy and birth; their care involved issues with menstruation, breast-feeding, infertility, reproductive infections, birth control, abortion and death.[16] Midwives used herbs to regulate, promote and suppress fertility. Women looked to midwives for their specialized knowledge, and midwives

procured abortive herbs for those who desired them.[17]

Midwives were specifically targeted (by patriarchal forces) because of their knowledge and use of herbal birth control and abortion. The witch hunts, spanning more than four centuries, saw an orchestrated campaign by the Christian church and growing scientific and medical professions, which sought to wipe out the women healers.[3] Midwives, herbalists, lay healers and accused "witches" were all targeted. Thousands upon thousands of executions took place; 85% of those executed were women.[5] Henry Boquet's *Examen of Witches* published in 1590, associated many midwives with witchcraft:

> Those midwives and wise women who are witches are in the habit of offering
> to Satan the little children which they deliver, and then killing them…. They
> do even worse; for they kill them while they are yet in their mother's wombs.
> This practice is common to all witches.[16]

An estimated 9,000,000 women, children and men were killed during the witch hunts.[19] By the 1900s most information on herbal abortion was lost, but not all. Never has the old herbal knowledge completely left this world. Women continued to regulate their fertility in secrecy with herbs despite fear of persecution, regulations and laws.

During the last part of the twentieth century ethnobotanists and anthropologists have documented the use of herbal abortives among a wide variety of peoples living traditionally. The use of herbal abortives has been found from among the people of New Guinea to the former Soviet Union as well as in Malaysia, India and Haiti to name only a few. Researchers are beginning to piece together these studies along with the wise woman knowledge passed through generations. These various herbal traditions have been used to regulate fertility for thousands of years.

The first legal restrictions on abortion appeared in the US in the 1820s. By 1900 abortions were banned in most states. Though abortion eventually became illegal across the US, clearly this did not eliminate its need nor stop its practice. Many women successfully aborted without regard for the law. However, thousands upon thousands of women died due to unsafe, illegal abortions.[7] On January 22, 1973 the US Supreme Court, in the famous *Roe vs. Wade* decision, proclaimed abortion legal. Since that landmark decision, anti-abortion forces have been fighting to overturn it. Though abortion remains legal in the US, access to abortion has become increasingly difficult and dangerous due to these efforts.

Even with *Roe vs. Wade*'s protections still in place, 87% of US counties have no abortion provider.[7] According to a 2001 study done by the Alan Guttmacher Institute (AGI), a minority of abortion providers offer services before five weeks of pregnancy; women having abortions in clinic settings travel 50 miles or more for services, and more than half (56%) of providers experienced anti-abortion harassment.[11] Another study done in 2000 by AGI found that abortion incidence and the number of abortion providers continued to decline during the late 1990s.[8] Two decades after *Roe vs. Wade* made abortion legal and safe, many women in the US have already lost access reasonable to safe and legal abortion.

Unsafe abortion is a major cause of illness and death among women. Worldwide, 20 million unsafe abortions are performed annually and 13-20% of all maternal deaths worldwide are due to unsafe abortion.[7]

The need for abortion availability and accessibility is clear. Because conventional abortion access is in danger of becoming less available it is wise to look for additional options for fertility control. We should examine the wealth of knowledge that the history of herbal abortion has to offer. It can be viewed as a resource for women exercising their ability and making safe choices about their reproduction.

*Many poor women imprisoned, and hanged for Witches. Ralph Gardiner, England's Grievance Discovered (1655).*

45

# List #11

**Ramsey Beyer**
ramseybeyer@gmail.com
www.everydaypants.com

[list]#11

the good life.

6/03/07

(A)(A)(A) ways to be an anarchist without interacting with other political punk kids (because, lets face it, sometimes you get burnt out on being around other activists because we don't always agree on everything and we usually think we're right)

-start a garden or work on a farm
-volunteer for community organizations outside of your 'scene'
-work with children or just talk to them
-read a lot, inform yourself and form opinions
-write a zine to vent and maybe re-inspire yourself and others
-think of ways to be more environmentally and economically friendly
-be straightedge or vegan or both
-treat your dog as an equal
-become a big brother or big sister through a mentoring program
-start a distro, maybe a free one
-find ways to resist your urge to buy things or feel like you 'need' things
-do your laundry in the bathtub and hang it on a clothesline to dry
-relax! take a break, do something silly and start to revitalize yourself & your motivation

# Black Carrot #8

Pups
Box 830
Chicago IL 60690
tacolove@gmail.com
www.beetfarm.org

We walked around, talking, and Jon showed me Richmond monuments.. We checked out the tail end of the Richmond Zine Fair. It was sorta cool, and I got rid of all the zines I came with. I met a few people I only knew from the inter'net and saw my 'ol pal Shawn Granton who I've always liked. Me and him and Jon gossiped about the Connecticut Punk Scene (or what's left of it) for a while and we traded some comics. On the way out of the fair, we ran into some hippy girl with a dog who seemed like the average just traveling through your town where ever the spirit of the wind takes me type. I don't have any strong feelings for or against these kids anymore. I used to want to befriend every train hopping dirt bag punk I met, (and hook up with.. which I did my share of) -- but not these days. I'm less apt these days to say "sure you can sleep at my house, borrow my bike, etc etc.." and I'll explain why later, but -- I was on a short trip with my friend and didn't want to listen to someone yammer on and on about where their spirit is going. I gave her a zine, and then she asked for my phone number, and I didn't feel comfortable giving it out. So I said "my contact info is in the zine.." and she put it into her bag. Then she started telling us that Jon and I had really good energies or auroras. And how connected she felt to us. And then at that point, uhh, I'm even less apt to sit and talk about junk like that. We ran into her a few more times that week, (Richmond is small) and we didn't so much feel the same energy she felt for us. Oh well. So a few months ago, I was walking down Milwaukee Avenue, to meet my friend Katherine.. I saw a group of crusty punks sitting on the corner on Milwaukee and Damen Avenue. There was a group of four or five of them, looking the part of the crusty traveler punk, complete with

23

bandanna and dog. I hadn't seen punx in this part of town in a long time. So I went over to go talk to them. Turns out, as I suspected - they were all hopping trains, hitch hiking, traveling.. You know, the punk past-time. I told them I hadn't seem punx around here in a long time. They were spare changing to go buy some wine or (beer). They said they liked it over here (on Milwaukee and Damen) because there were too many homeless people downtown, so it was hard to 'spange - and they can come here and make fun of yuppies. This one guy said that. But then he asked some woman walking by if he can have her leftovers from a dinner. I was thinking how lame it was to go make fun of yuppies but then beg for their change and scraps. Some of the kids were really nice, but some were jerky to me because 1) I wasn't giving them change and, 2) I wasn't a fellow crusty traveler. They asked me why I wasn't out here 'spangin also. I think they read me as one of them at first. But then I told them I live here in Chicago.. and its where I.. you know...

24

live. And then I said I've traveled and hitch hiked and all that crap, but now I have different priorities. I got mixed responses when the first priority I mentioned was bowling.. So, it was just weird. People who I seemed on the surface to have a lot in common with, (you know, liking Doom and Anti Product and Crass) I didn't feel depressed or anything after talking to them, or loosing faith in humanity or punk. I just laughed and said "oh you crazy punks.. what will you think of next?"

# Cashiers Du Cinemart #15

Mike White, editor
Adam Balivet, contributor
PO Box 2401
Riverview, MI 48193
mwhite@impossiblefunky.com
www.impossiblefunky.com

## The (Slow) Killing of Colonialism
by Adam Balivet

Several important years in history:

1521: Ferdinand Magellan lands in the Philippines and claims the region for Spain.

1898: The Spanish-American War leaves the United States with "sovereignty" over the Philippines.

1944: Japan occupies the Philippines during WWII until a U.S.-led force defeats them in the Battle of Leyte Gulf, thus restoring the islands to the U.S.

1946: The Philippines declare independence.

1959: Gerry de Leon and Eddie Romero release TERROR IS A MAN.

1979: Weng Weng appears as Agent 00 in FOR YOUR HEIGHT ONLY.

1983: THE KILLING OF SATAN.

True, that set of islands in the Far East has gone through a lot under the force of colonialism. True, also, that it has responded in kind through the cinema. The low-culture films of a country or region tend to reflect the feelings of the people more accurately than the corresponding high-culture films and the Philippines provides a forceful and subversive model of this trend.

In 1959, Gerry de Leon and his protégé Eddie Romero put Filipino horror on the international map with the ominously titled TERROR IS A MAN. The film serves as a prime example of an appropriation of a Western text, in that it seems largely based on H.G. Wells's The Island of Dr. Moreau (Erle C. Kenton's 1932 ISLAND OF LOST SOULS being the Western film version), telling the story of a doctor performing experiments in turning a panther into a human.

While the film raises questions of morality, science and power, the most important point for this discussion is that all of the main characters come from outside of the Philippines. The fact that the doctor and his wife, the shipwrecked visitor, and even the "animal" come from the U.S. (the doctor's assistant originates from Guatemala), and that all but two of the island's native inhabitants leave the island within the first fifteen minutes of the film indicates a clear awareness of the country's history. This is not to say that the filmmakers have an obvious anti-colonial agenda—or any political agenda, for that matter. Instead, the debate plays out between the doctor, who wants to continue his experiments on the island at all costs, and his wife and Mr. Fitzgerald (the visitor), who wish to leave the island alone. The film differs from later Filipino genre films in that, although the viewer may eventually turn against the doctor (especially when making statements such as, "I can't concern myself with the moral aspects of my

MORE HORRIFYING THAN FRANKENSTEIN!
MORE TERRIFYING THAN DRACULA!

BRING YOUR OWN TRANQUILIZER!

SO TERRIFYING A WARNING BELL SYSTEM Has Been Installed For PUBLIC PROTECTION!

TERROR IS A MAN

work"), the lines between good and evil remain fairly ambiguous until the end. In this way, TERROR IS A MAN distinguishes itself as an early representation of colonialism in Filipino low culture, though without a clear critique of colonialism.

While de Leon and Romero found moderate success in U.S. distribution in the 1960s with films such as BRIDES OF BLOOD ISLAND, U.S. mega-producer Roger Corman found success in shooting in the Philippines in the 1970s. He developed a string of women in prison (WIP) films, directed by Jack Hill and shot on the islands, including THE BIG DOLL HOUSE and THE BIG BIRD CAGE, which have become legendarily successful. In 1971, de Leon made his own unremarkable version of the WIP film with WOMEN IN CAGES. Romero, however, took some aspects of the genre (American women as captives, escape in the jungle) and created his own version of Ernest B. Schoedsack's THE MOST DANGEROUS GAME (1932): WOMAN HUNT. The power struggle between captor and captive is similar to the WIP films, but in this case, the captors are a group of wealthy businessman, led by the evil Spiros, as opposed to a generic prison warden. Recalling the "white slave" films of the early twentieth century in the U.S., WOMAN HUNT does not address a specific colonization issue, but does serve to further polarize the difference between good and evil, as when Spiros explains, "Every man has shown contempt for morality and principle; this is a demonstration."

1979 brought a landmark in Filipino political cinema with Eddie Nicart's FOR YOUR HEIGHT ONLY. Ostensibly a James Bond parody, the film stars Weng Weng as Agent 00 who, standing at 2'9", provides for the title of the film. In representing the Bond character, he plays the hero. His enemies deride him, treat his female associates (equivalent to "Bond girls") poorly, and make attempts on his life. By positing themselves against Weng, they represent the evil against the "good" Weng. FOR YOUR HEIGHT ONLY, thus, serves as another example of the common emphasis in Filipino cinema on a clear division between good and evil. But an additional element exists for the film's foreign audiences who see the English-dubbed version. The bad guys, heretofore referred to as the "crime syndicate" (as they call themselves), have dubbed-in voices replicating those of gangsters and anti-heroes from 1930s and 1940s U.S. films, á la Humphrey Bogart. The accents become especially apparent when one of them says something like, "No one could ever guess about the dough in this dough," referring to drugs hidden in bread dough. The English-speaking viewer would not be out of line in associating the crime syndicate with the United States. Similarly, the viewer might consider Weng, at less than half the size of his typical opponent, as a representative of the Philippines. Therefore, FOR YOUR HEIGHT ONLY tells the story of the heroic Philippines fighting against and completely destroying the evil colonizers—the U.S., in this case, although Spain or Japan could easily serve in its place. And so, when Weng first flies between the bad guy's legs to attack him from behind, we see the beginning of an anti-colonial revolt in Filipino cinema.

When horror and sci-fi films began to wane in popularity in the 1970s, action became the genre of choice in the Philippines. In the 1980s, a wave of violent and mythical action films emerged in the country. These films produced an unusual clash between Christianity and magic and supernatural concepts, such as in

Efren C. Pinon's THE KILLING OF SATAN (1983). Essentially, it tells the story of a man given magical powers to defend a village against Satan. After centuries of Spanish colonialism, the Philippines emerge as the only country in Asia with a predominantly Catholic population, thus making a film about a fight against Satan a popular choice. The country also has a rich and varied history of folklore and supernatural tales. The opening scene of THE KILLING OF SATAN represents both of these facets of Filipino culture with a ritual scene that's part Christian (carrying the cross up a mountain, whippings) and part supernatural (a man cut by a knife remains unscathed). The next scene involves a duel between the Prince of Magic (Satan's disciple) and the local magic man, involving both guns and magic. The rest of the film revels in imagery deriving from both sources. In particular, imagery from Christianity's "Garden of Eden" appears often, with people turning into snakes and snakes turning into people. At one point, one of the Prince of Magic's female assistants takes a bite from an apple after her boss has turned into a snake. On the magic front, many of the film's fight scenes (and there are many to begin with) play out as extended special effects sequences thrown back and forth between magicians. It seems that there may even exist a power hierarchy accordant with visual effects—i.e., certain visuals more powerful than others—but the effects fly by at such a speed that you don't realize who has the upper hand throughout the fight until the end of the fight. In any case, the film provides a battlefield for Christianity and magic.

THE KILLING OF SATAN is unique in its treatment of the concept of master narrative. The traditional Filipino narrative of good versus evil is obviously and repeatedly reinforced in the film. The hero, Lando (Ramon Revilla), simply wants to save his daughter; he has no other agenda. The Prince of Magic, on the other hand, keeps Lando's daughter locked up in a cage with other female slaves with the sole purpose of eventually "setting them free to spread evil." The obviousness of the Christian versus Satan story is underscored by the fact that two elements from different worlds—different master narratives, in fact—co-exist unquestionably: Christianity and magic. This co-existence undermines both as traditional master narratives. To go a step further, the simplicity of the good versus evil plot could be considered a disguise for the subversive treatment of the Christian master narrative.

From TERROR IS A MAN to FOR YOUR HEIGHT ONLY to THE KILLIING OF SATAN, we see a decrease in dependency on the Western narrative, from adaptation to parody to traditional or non-existent narrative, and an evolution in level of colonial criticism, from barely existent to aggressive to subversive. I am now waiting for a documentary in which the government of the Philippines kicks every single Westerner out of the country. Might be a while.

# Panic

Philadelphia, PA
mud@riseup.net

## RECOVERING FROM A PANIC ATTACK
### IN FAR FEWER THAN 12 STEPS

### 1. RECOGNITION

First recognize that what you are experiencing is a panic attack, not a life-threatening emergency. Understand that panic attacks are generally brief, and can be treated and prevented. Fear of the panic itself—the root of all panic disorders—can prolong the attack. Some people are afraid that the symptoms of panic are signs of a more menacing disease. Others feel ashamed and try to deny that they are experiencing panic, which can feed the attack. If your thoughts are spiraling out of control, focus on the factual: This is only a panic attack, not something larger and more terrible. After you make some adjustments the symptoms will quickly subside. It may help to reassure yourself that although you're feeling panic, you can cope with it and it will end quickly. Recognition and confidence will shorten the attack.

### 2. DISTANCE & GROUNDING

Terror and nausea are flooding your body. Your thoughts may be intrusive, negative, and fatalistic. You may feel unreal, weak and incapacitated. Nevertheless, you have the ability to distance yourself from this condition and ground yourself in a broader perspective. Remember your own strength, remember that you have support. A panic attack may dredge up your greatest fears—fears of failing, losing control, loss of love and support, loss of freedom, loss of sanity. Don't let these fatalistic thoughts dominate your thinking. Now is not the time to rationally consider life changes or examine your own failings.

Focus instead on relaxing your breath. This is the fastest way to stop the flood of adrenaline and end the attack. Breathe slowly and calmly, like you would when falling asleep. Try to spread this calm, sleepy feeling to all the muscles in your body. Meanwhile, when either physical terror or intrusive thoughts interrupt you, practice a meditation technique called non-attachment.*

Allow your thoughts and feelings to arise without letting yourself be pulled along by their urgency. Don't try to repress your fears, but don't dwell on them. Watch the anxiety and know that although it is a part of you it doesn't control you. Separate yourself from this temporary state that's happening to you. See yourself on the other side, once the panic has passed.

Keep consciously relaxing your breath and muscles. This kind of detachment becomes easier with practice. You may want to try meditation or relaxation exercises when not experiencing anxiety. Practicing distance and grounding will contain the spread of panic, like white blood cells surrounding and isolating a virus. *see Thich Nhat Hanh's book in Addtl. re

### 3. SCANNING

Identify what triggered this attack. This can be either quite simple or totally baffling. What is happening at the moment the attack hits? Pay close attention to your environment—sights, smells, sounds, people—and what you've been thinking about. Does something around you remind you of something that's been worrying you? Does someone around you make you feel trapped or uncomfortable? Do you feel confined? Have you recently experienced a trauma, or are you trying to ignore a confrontation looming in the future?

With practice you will start to see a pattern in what triggers you. Common triggers include:

- Situations that feel confining: crowded subways, elevators, airplanes, large parties, family gatherings, classrooms, jail cells
- Intimate relationships and the feelings of dependence and responsibility that come with them
- Events where you are the focus of attention: public speaking, performing, birthdays, interviews, tests
- Times of transition such as travel, moving, breaking up, unemployment, illness, recovery
- Encounters with authority figures or dominating personalities
- Being alone at night, trying to fall asleep

In addition to the triggers, there are many possible causes to scan for, which are usually anxious or negative emotions such as:

- Feeling that you cannot meet your own or others' expectations of you
- Feeling powerless to change a bad situation
- Feeling powerless to express anger
- Feeling afraid of losing a loved one
- Feeling incompetent, weak or bad
- Feeling alone and unloved
- Feeling incapable of taking care of yourself or reaching out for support
- Feeling ashamed of your fear or powerlessness

Remember that a number of triggers or causes can contribute to any panic attack.

## 4. ACTION

Acknowledge to yourself the factors that have triggered your attack. This helps contain it. For example, "I feel trapped in this car, and I feel bad I can't pay attention to what my friend is talking about. I'm not sure I really want to go on this trip but it's too late to back out. I haven't eaten a full meal today, and I just quit smoking." In this example several physical triggers—confined space, hunger, and withdrawal—are combined with several psychological causes—feeling pressured to not disappoint a friend, and feeling unable to express fear and need.

Once you've acknowledged what's making you feel bad, immediately change what you can. In the above example, you can tell your friend that you're feeling anxious and ask them to stop somewhere where you can eat and walk around for a minute. Don't be ashamed to ask for what you need. Take care of your physical needs first, then discuss with your friend whether or not you really want to take this trip. Give yourself space and permission to take care of yourself, even if it involves disappointing someone else. Recognize what choices you have to cope with this attack. Once you've eaten and talked out your anxiety, you may feel differently about continuing the trip. The point is to make the decision based on your own desires, not the expectations of others or the fear of panic.

To the extent that you can't change a triggering situation, you can adjust your own response to it. If it's impossible to change your environment—you are under arrest, in an airplane, going through withdrawal, severely ill or otherwise trapped—keep practicing detachment and conscious relaxation. In situations like these, where you must sustain a certain amount of discomfort for a length of time, remember that this is still temporary. Cultivate a protective warmth towards the part of you that is panicking. Acknowledge that what you are undergoing is difficult, and you will have to bear it the best you can. Distract yourself from negative thinking through some kind of activity or reaching out to a friend.

Though some people's attacks are very specifically triggered by external causes—public speaking, airplanes, elevators—other people's arise from internal inhibitions. If your triggers are internal, certain emotions or desires will feel so taboo they'll remain buried from consciousness and only come to light through fearless self-analysis. Immediate actions may lessen an attack, but the panic disorder itself will only fade through a long process of introspection and changing internal beliefs and patterns.

This is especially true if you feel you must be perfect, self-sacrificing and entirely self-sufficient. Any impulse that contradicts this view of yourself will prompt panic and disgust. Panic pushes you to recognize where you're damaging yourself through repression of your own needs. The better you learn how to take care of yourself, the less panic you will suffer. This includes reaching out to others and letting them support you. Listen closely to the strongest fears that arise during an attack for ideas of what you need to change, and don't rule out any options while imagining different futures. Make sure you are in a safe space or with a trusted person when you attempt to confront your fears. Some people may only feel comfortable doing this with a therapist.

With the goal of self-transformation, panic attacks can become a useful tool for probing the darkest places in your psyche. Getting to know your deepest fears lets you look at them rationally and greatly reduces their power.

## 5. PATIENCE & FOCUS

Once you've taken action, you must wait for the chemical reactions in your body to level out to normal before all your symptoms disappear. In the meantime, keep resisting the pull of fear and obsessive thinking. Be patient and stay confident, even light-hearted. At this stage, I sometimes joke with a friend about the remaining intrusive fears that still arise—"Hey, remind me again that my heart's not about to explode...thanks. Ok, what were you saying?"

It's often a good idea to immerse yourself in listening to a friend, watching a movie, or starting a new activity while you wait out the last symptoms of an attack.

## 6. TAKING STOCK

When the attack has subsided, take a moment to appreciate your strength and skill in recovering from it. As your confidence increases, future attacks will be shorter and more easily managed. But also take this time to address whatever were the root causes of the attack—why did these things cause you panic? Were you more prone to panic today than usual? What are the larger patterns in your life right now that could be increasing your anxiety? Do you expect too much from yourself? Do you feel others expect too much from you? Do you have trusted friends to rely on during a crisis? Are you ashamed of showing weakness? Do you find it hard to take care of yourself? What kind of changes could you make to be living a less anxious life—short-term and long-term? What can you change right now that could prevent a future attack from the same cause?

# Carbusters #31

Editors, Kratka 26, Prague 10, 100 00,
Czech Republic AND Pippa Gallop c/o
Zelena akcija, Frankopanska 1 pp.952,
City and zip code: 10 000 Zagreb Croatia

# Steering Zagreb Away from Cars

*by Pippa Gallop; photos courtesy of Zelena-akcija.hr*

**M**ilan Bandic, the mayor of Zagreb, Croatia, is a confident man, and until recently he had good reason to be so. Despite being caught drunk-driving after being involved in an accident, fleeing from the police and having to resign in 2002, the docile citizens of Zagreb (or at least the few who voted) were kind enough to re-elect him in 2005, creating an aura of invincibility, which he has cultivated with the usual populist tactics. When he recently boasted on national television that he will raise household bills in the city again and people will still vote for him, it was hard to be sure if he might be wrong. Yet recent events suggest that the spate of ludicrous transport projects he is unleashing on the city may prove to be clouds with silver linings.

Hardly a fortnight has passed in the last year in Zagreb without some hare-brained transport scheme being announced, not to mention the rash of underground garages already being planned near the city centre. The first reaction was quiet hopelessness — how could we make something as mundane as underground garages into a popular topic? Our first efforts were not encouraging — our CarFree Day action attracted only a little media attention and little interest from passers-by — so we decided to do something that could not be ignored, blocking the street leading towards one of the new garages and sitting on chairs to illustrate the traffic queues expected to form there after the garage opens. The action plan was unfortunately leaked to the police, who turned up with enough vans to arrest all the participants, but at least the media covered the event well.

Then came the Grand Plan for the Northern Bypass and Medvednica Tunnel. It is hard to convey the absurdity of these projects to anyone who has not seen Zagreb, but try to picture a city that is elongated from west to east, with a long mountain on the northern side. The city is doing its best to expand up the mountain, but much of it is still designated as a Nature Park protected area. On the other side is a sparsely populated area known as Zagorje, which is reachable by both road and rail links going around the mountain. But no! Going around the mountain is not good enough. We must go *through* the mountain. And we must build a bypass linked to the tunnel, so that Zagreb has motorways on all four sides. Why should Zagreb city centre be congested from only three sides when it could be from all four?

The sober observer may ask how it is possible to build a motorway in an area where there is no flat land, but gravity never stopped mayor Bandic: We can build it in the sky and in tunnels! For 27 km of bypass, 15 tunnels and 13 viaducts would be needed, costing an extraordinary EUR1.2 billion.

A new rumble of discontent could be heard: in December 2006 an open letter signed by 39 architects, urban planners and academics was published, opposing the bypass and tunnel projects and demanding that the money should be spent on public transport instead. A later public meeting on the subject organised by Green Action was totally packed, and was mentioned by Bandic during an appearance on national television in which he notoriously stated that he would not meet with the opponents of his projects and that if they think they can do better then they should run for election.

Meanwhile, a new front was opening up in the discussion on underground garages in the city centre. "Total Sell-Out! Zagreb Ltd." shouted the massive banner that almost covered a building on Zagreb's central "Flower Square" one morning in December. The "Right to a City" initiative, which started out campaigning on youth cultural issues, had uncovered a project by tycoon Tomo Horvatincic to tear down a block of elegant but neglected old houses on one side of the square, and replace them with glass-and-steel luxury apartments, a shopping mall and an underground garage for 700 cars.

At first Horvatincic's proposal received almost universal praise from the media, with features such as "This man wants to beautify Zagreb" and other thinly-disguised PR. However, Right to a City's dramatic banner action and repeated protests of the secrecy surrounding the project attracted massive attention and the Flower Square project soon became a hot topic.

A group of actors joined in, protesting the destruction of a house in the block where famous Croatian poet Vladimir Vidric was born, by holding a reading of his poetry on the square — over 1,000 people attended, making it one of the largest protest gatherings in Zagreb in recent years. The media debate heated up further, with numerous talk shows devoted to the topic in which Horvatincic showed himself to be more interested in insulting his opponents than addressing their arguments. In early 2007, over 50,000 signatures were gathered against the project, and discussions showed that surprisingly, compared with the apparent apathy of less than one year ago, the underground garage and loss of part of the pedestrian zone at its entrance featured heavily in people's opposition to the project.

Most recently, the Earth Day activities of Green Action and Right to a City were devoted to opposing the project and getting citizens involved in having a say on the city they want to see. Besides the traditional concerts and street stalls, this year's Zagreb Earth Day also took an unexpected twist on April 22...

An unlucky policeman on his quiet Sunday shift who had just popped off for some doughnuts (no, really!) returned to his post in Gunduliceva street to find that it had been suddenly transformed into a pedestrian zone by 150 people who had placed flowerpots and barriers across the street, and were enjoying their newly reclaimed public space, playing ping-pong, badminton, football, listening to music, reading newspapers, chatting with friends, and drinking free tea. The pedestrian zone in the centre of the city hadn't been expanded for 30 years, and people felt it was about time, not to mention that pedestrianising Gunduliceva street would halt the Horvatincic project by blocking the entrance to the planned garage. Reclaiming streets may not be a new idea elsewhere, but it was the first time that it had ever happened in Croatia and the atmosphere was scintillating.

Bemused police tried to figure out what to do but the best they could come up with was bringing in the mobile crane normally used to remove (a few) illegally parked cars. It didn't work — it was hardly suitable for lifting large flowerpots and the driver, finding the whole thing entertaining, wasn't too keen to help. The young police officers threatened to arrest the person appointed for police liaison, at which point she dropped to the floor to make it more difficult. The cops looked at each other and then asked, "Are you alright, ma'am?"

The action ended at the pre-arranged time, just as the riot police started to arrive, and the police liaison was taken to the police station for questioning. Later, out of the glare of the media, a call from above caused her to be formally arrested and she was held overnight, as if she would repeat the offence if let out. An appearance at the court the next morning brought sympathy from the judge, who said that there would have to be a fine, but that it would be as low as possible, and the action also earned unexpected praise from staff at the detention centre, who thought it was great.

There is still a long way to go. New underground garage projects in the centre are still being announced with alarming frequency, and there are wacky plans to lift a railway line into the sky to make more room for offices and car parks. It is already too late to stop some of the garages near the centre, but the massive growth in transport activism in Zagreb gives reason to be hopeful.

The first results are already starting to show: Horvatincic recently announced that the Flower Square project could be modified to move the entrance to the garage away from the pedestrian zone and make the underground garage just for residents — not good enough, but at least an admission that public opinion cannot be completely ignored. Bandic has also recently failed by a wide margin to be chosen as chairman of the SDP, Croatia's main opposition party, and was beaten by a relatively unknown newcomer. It's a race against time to see how much damage to Zagreb can be avoided, but the authorities have got the message that they can no longer act with impunity — Zagreb belongs to its citizens. ✖

# I'em Sorry But I Love You Both #1

**Katie and Stewart**
imsorrybut@gmail.com

One morning in April 2007, tucked away under the stairs of our apartment complex, was a trash bag filled with notebooks that hadn't been there the previous day. Never to be ones to let other peoples' secrets go to waste we quickly brought them back to our apartment. Inside were the journals of a group of five to eight year olds from the summer of 2000. More volumes to come.

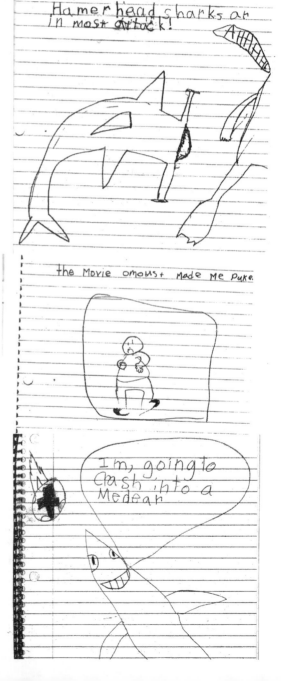

# The DIY Guide to Drums

Portland, OR 97217
drummer@riseup.net
www.myspace.com/kickball
www.myspace.com/explodeintocolors

# WHAT AM I GOING TO BANG ON?

Buy a drum kit. You can get one for $300-400. The brand isn't real important— just put good heads on yr drums! But if you have the $$ old 60s & 70s Ludwig & Gretsch kits are sweet. A snare drum, bass drum and cymbal is more than enough to start with. Or use some buckets! Get a practice pad — they are awesome for working on right-left coordination, speed, & bounce. Build one like in the illustration below... the sole of your sneaker is also a great bouncy practice pad! Get some good drum heads. Take the head out of its box in the store and tap it. Do you like its tone? White (coated) heads are great for brush work... or anything really. Aquarian & Evans heads are sweet.

rubber

wood

# HOW DO I ADJUST THE SOUND OF MY DRUMS?

First off, get a drum key and keep it handy. To tune, you must adjust the lugs, ever so slightly at a time. Pick a lug to start with. Tap with your finger about 1 inch from the lug. Compare this pitch with that of the lug straight across the head until they are in tune with each other. Then tune the lug adjacent to one of the tuned lugs, and then tune the lug opposite...and so on & so forth. Tune your bottom head to an interval that compliments the top head; don't tune either too tight.

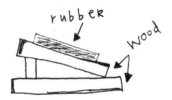

drum key

muffler & dial

lugs

You can minimize how much your drums & cymbals resonate by muffling them with tape or with a plastic ring around the circumference.

Try different bass drum beaters [wood, felt] for different sounds.

Add a chain or other metal object to a cymbal.

Put a pillow in your bass drum; try it with & without the front head.

# RUDIMENTS

RUDIMENTS are drumming exercises. They can be applied to all sorts of drumming. Practicing rudiments will help you develop your left-hand/right hand coordination, control of dynamics [volume], and speed. Practicing YOUR RUDIMENTS first thing each time you play your kit is a GOOD IDEA. All of the rudiments in this book are in one section... So skip back and forth between the rudiments and beats sections, rather than focusing on just rudiments or just beats.

PRACTICE YR rudiments on YOUR practice pad and also on the snare drum. Once you get each rudiment down, also try it on the hihat and toms.

USE A METRONOME while practicing to stay on beat [sometimes]. A metronome is a mechanical timekeeper. I have an old one that looks like [illustration] but the new digital ones are also great. Practicing with a metro- -nome will give you an idea of how consistent a tempo you're keeping. But of course some fluctuation in speed is natural. [unless you are a robot]

# I LOVE ME SOME RUDIMENTS.

PLAY each rudiment with these variations:

[1] start with the right hand  [2] start with the left hand

[3] vary tempo. Try faster + faster tempos, mastering each on its own. Next, try a gradual increase in tempo — and make sure to maintain one volume throughout.

[4] vary dynamics. Start quiet (noted as "p", for piano, in music) and gradually get louder (noted as "f", for forte). Maintain the same speed throughout.

★ REMEMBER, just cuz you are playing louder does not mean you should be playing faster (& vice versa).

★ An increase in volume is called a crescendo and is represented by "⟨——" A decrease in volume is called a diminuendo and is represented by "——⟩" ☆

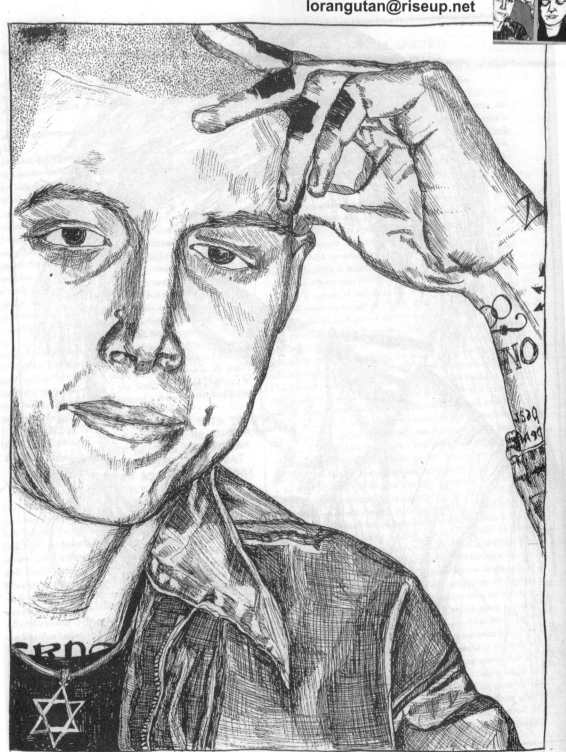

# ASH

A. I'm an idealistic person. I am looking for other idealistic people who are trying to live by their beliefs and do something special with their lives. Truthfully, I thought I had that in punk but it turned out to be pretty much bullshit. Everyone seems to be pretty much as self-serving and hypocritical as society at large. It really got to me. I quit and went back to being skinhead, which is what I was originally, since I was 13. It is definitely the thing I feel most comfortable in. I feel like it is much more real. People are not trying to be something they're not, even though there are problems in that subculture too...

JL. How did that transition happen?

A. Originally I was into Ska and became skinhead at 13. Eventually Skinhead contradicted what I was though. I felt contradicted in my anarchist beliefs. I was realizing how queer I was, that was the biggest one. It was also just a lifestyle thing. I was homeless and started squatting, I started traveling and riding trains and I was getting more queer. It just wasn't fitting; I stopped claiming skinhead when I was around 20. I started living in punk houses, squats and whatever. It felt much more open. A more diverse set of lifestyle and beliefs - or so I thought. But really it is all just an act to me. People front a lot about things they have nothing to do with and know nothing about. I think a lot of people are just trying to be something they're not and it's a real big turnoff. I think a lot of people don't try and it's just posture. Really extreme ideas as a joke. If someone had no idea what punk was, came from a far away isolated country or something and saw punk, they would think, These are the most extreme, bad-ass people that there are! But really they're not at all and it felt kind of ridiculous to me. I didn't want to be a part of it anymore. The thing about skinhead is, it's less about trying to be something specific and something you're not, and more about defiantly being who you are. That goes back to the whole queer thing, both people in and out of the scene say things like, skinheads can't do this, skinheads can't be gay, skinheads can't ride trains, but what it really is is - a skinhead can do whatever they want. Basically anybody who has what it takes to do it can do it. There are gay skins, there are strong women skins, gay women skins. Maybe a lot of skinheads don't like them but they're not going anywhere. The punk scene has this false inclusiveness. Where in the skinhead scene there is NO inclusiveness. Anybody who gets into it has to force him or herself into it. You get tested on it, which can be this violent thing but... [Ash talks in length about the fighting initiation into skinhead, it not being official, keeping yourself in, proving yourself.]

**IN PUNK YOU CAN JUST SAY, OH I AM PUNK, WHEN YOU COULD HAVE BEEN THIS ASSHOLE YESTERDAY! THE MINUTE YOU SAY YOU'RE PUNK, OH IT'S GREAT, EVERYONE ACCEPTS YOU, YOU CAN DO WHATEVER YOU WANT, WHEN YOU COULD BE A TOTAL SLEAZEBAG SHIT. I THINK PUNK ATTRACTS A LOT OF PEOPLE FOR THAT REASON.**

JL. How did you feel your queer identity was represented in the punk subculture?

A. I didn't really feel that queer or gay in the punk scene because it's so queer in this sense of "everybody is." It is weird because I was misled. It really pissed me off.

**THERE ARE ALL THESE EFFEMINATE PUNK BOYS RUNNING AROUND WHO ARE REALLY JUST SLEAZY DUDES HIDING BEHIND THIS FALSE QUEERNESS.**

I feel way more queer in skinhead subculture because your not gonna act queer if you're not because it's not a plus. It is not necessarily a minus, but it's not a plus. People don't try to front. It's just who I am. The people here haven't had a problem with it yet. If there is a problem, it's still who I am. I felt like in punk, people were always talking about empowering people, but in skinhead people don't empower you, you empower yourself. Down in South Florida where I'm from, it is way more diverse. There are way more nonwhite people in the Skinhead scene than in the punk scene. It is much more diverse racially, class wise, and it is like half men and half women. Those are some of the things that got me to it. The punk scene, for all the inclusion it talks about, doesn't really live up to that.

JL. Why do you think there is more diversity in the skinhead scene than in punk?

A. It might me because the skinhead scene has always been more working class oriented. Maybe there is something about the aesthetic and lifestyle that attracts more diversity, I don't know. The biggest thing about skinhead is pride. Whatever you are, you're proud of it. You're not trying to hide it or change it. You are defiantly proud. It's more about what is going on in your life and neighborhood - the politics of the streets and everyday life and so it might resonate more with those who are from the streets and the ghetto. Most skinheads are from an urban background.

It sucks being looked upon as a Nazi, when I am pretty much the opposite of that, especially being Jewish. I know who I am and the difference between Nazi skinheads and others. I'm at the point of not really caring what the general public thinks anymore. I don't want to scare a little old black lady on the bus, that sucks. But at the same time I think people would accuse me of doing that anyway. People have accused me my whole life of being a Nazi, which is really weird.

I was talking to my friend about how the punk aesthetic and even punk band names might look to certain people. For example, that little old black lady on the bus, she sees somebody dressed all in black with crazy metal stuff hanging all over them with a t-shirt that says something like Brother Inferior or some indecipherable symbol. Even the Crass symbol. People who are not white punks think you are some crazy Satan worshiping Nazis. It is so easy to be mistaken for someone you are not. I know who I am, my friends know who I am, I try to an extent not have people think I am a not Nazi.

JL. How do you do that?

A. I am a big guy. I will cross the street so people don't think I am following them. I wear this out all the time (his Jewish necklace). If people come up to me respectfully I will talk to them about it. Actively working against Racism is an everyday-life type thing. I try to limit things to real interactions and things that are naturally part of my life. I just have sincere conscious interactions with people. I don't identify as white by the way. I'm very conscious of the fact that I look white to a certain degree to some people. Well, some people don't consider Jews white. I think most of America, some people more than others, don't consider Jews white on some level. I think I am definitely considered an "Other" by most white people. Most definitely by most punk people I know. I am half North African, Algerian and Moroccan and my dad is Scottish and Irish. It is funny because certain Middle Eastern people and North African people catch that. Most of the time, white people consider me white and non-white people will see the non-white side of me - it is weird.

**JL.** I have friends who because sometimes they can pass as white, while they are bi-racial or personally identify as different races, will identify as white because they pass as white and therefore receive many of the privileges of having white skin because of that perception. People who are white see your whiteness.

**A.** I identify as mixed-race. First off as Jewish. The thing is, I don't know my dad's family, I never lived with my dad. I grew up with my mom's side of the family. We were strictly Jewish and moved back and forth from Israel to here when I was younger, so I am very culturally Jewish and also very culturally North African. It is a huge part of my history. I was very light.

## IT USED TO DRIVE ME CRAZY THAT I LOOKED SO WHITE. I HATED LOOKING IN THE MIRROR. I WOULD CURSE MY DAD FOR POLLUTING ME.

That's a whole other story. I had a lot of crazy ideals back then. I am pretty much proud of everything I am now; it doesn't bother me as much. Honestly, I even like passing as white because it truthfully is a benefit to look more white, obviously. It is a privilege and I am not going to beat myself up over it anymore. I am just going to live my life in a good way. I like the fact that I get benefits from it. I like the fact that police believe me when I say something, to a certain extent. Which is not always the case. In south Florida, it doesn't matter what race you are, you are fucked. If you live in a shitty neighborhood, everyone is harassed. But from what I have learned in most every other part in America and I have learned this by traveling and now being here - it is clearly a benefit to be perceived as white. You are not going to get fucked with hitchhiking or when you are riding trains. You are less likely to get arrested when you are caught if something happens, if you get into a fight with somebody, you are less likely to get arrested. When they are not like you are, well you know I am gonna get off. That's unjust but that's the truth. Like the other day I was walking down the street trying to catch the bus to go to work. This dude attacked me who wasn't white. He attacked me with a bottle and I fought back. The cops showed up, and they just ran right to him and cuffed him and just started talking to me and asked me what happened! You know what I mean? What if I was a black guy walking down the street and some white guy attacked me with a bottle? That would suck, the cops would run up and cuff me and get his side of the story. So I am not gonna beat myself up about it anymore. I like the fact that I can pass for white when I want to. I say, be proud of what you are and work with what you got. Go out and get and achieve what you want. It may be easy for me to say that because I *do* pass and I am a large male and I do pass as hetero and all this stuff, but I just got to be myself. That's a big thing in the skinhead scene, non-white people in the skin head scene don't complain about what they are, they don't try to hide it like in punk. They are defiantly proud about what and who they are.

## GUILT IS TOTALLY NON-PRODUCTIVE. MOST PEOPLE HAVE THAT PROBLEM. I THINK A LOT OF NON-WHITE PEOPLE WISH THEY WERE BORN WHITE AND A LOT OF WHITE PEOPLE WISH THEY WEREN'T BORN WHITE.

A lot of people have wishes. I used to not pass for heterosexual at all. I used to be a sissy boy, really effeminate. That did not serve me well down in the south. I think in a certain respect I have repressed that and gone to the complete other side of the spectrum.

As I get older I see myself getting prouder, as far as gender identity goes. This is who I am now, and we change through our lives. I am just trying to do it well. Less and less trying to fight against everything and more and more just live my own life well within the context of everything around me. I am just trying to do everything naturally and not hide or repress any parts of myself. I am trying to consciously choose who I interact with and be really conscious when I interact with them.

1435 W. Sherwin Ave. #3
Chicago, IL 60626
lewispants@gmail.com

### Don't pimp New Orleans

In a workshop I was in at the United States Social Forum this year, Mama D., an elder and community leader from New Orleans said something I can't get out of my head— "Don't pimp New Orleans". From my understanding her grief was towards activists who are not from New Orleans who make New Orleans their issue or project or subject, and override the voices and work of the people from there—black people in particular—who are struggling to survive and to be leaders in their own struggle.

I have questions about what it means for anyone from outside of that city to make media, to host events, to claim Katrina or New Orleans as "our" issue. I have questions about my own motivation to go to New Orleans as a volunteer—what did I think I would see, learn or accomplish that was so different from what might be seen, learned or accomplished here in Chicago, where the plagues of racist displacement and capitalism are the same song to a different tune? Too many white folks like myself skip in and out of New Orleans gaining "activist credit" and stories to tell without stopping to really ask where and how we are needed in a struggle which is the struggle of people of color and poor people in the South. I want to hold that while it is important to talk about New Orleans, to push for the national and global support that the communities there need, it is also important to follow Mama D.'s directive not to pimp the city, not to idealize or use the struggle there. More and more I hear college graduates and activists with relative amounts of access and mobility talking about how "cool" it would be to move to New Orleans. I love that city in my bones, but I question whether it is respectful at this point to go there and inhabit the homes and communities of those who could not return. I question the grounding beneath walking on graves, beneath contributing to the gentrification project that is attacking the city since Katrina. I don't know—these are questions.

If we see Katrina's effect on New Orleans as an isolated incident, it's also possible to believe that "recovery" will happen with enough money, time and charitable volunteerism. Whereas if we see New Orleans as a dynamic, historic black city in the context of a racist nation-state built on slavery and stolen land, all "outsiders" to the city are faced with different questions about the stakes of a struggle for recovery. I imagine Chicago's South Side flooding—who would suffer, who would recover, what would follow. New Orleans is a special place, but it is not an exception.

I hope that anything I share about New Orleans, about racism, about my own role in the city as a volunteer and love for the city as an outsider, will translate as an inspiration to keep struggling wherever you are, and whatever struggle is immediate to you. To keep "being humble, and as fierce as possible" as my friend Ingrid Chapman said in a US Social Forum workshop. To honor those who came before, and not claim ownership over others' lives.

60

# Morgenmuffel #16

Isy Morgenmuffel
PO Box 74
Brighton, UK BN1 4ZQ
morningmuffel@yahoo.co

## the annual swaffham horticultural show

A MONK GNOME? HOW ODD.

SATURDAY WAS SUNNY AND WE CYCLED TO THE CONVENT (!) WHERE THE SHOW WAS.

IT WAS IN THE GYM, AND KINDA INDESCRIBABLE

LOOK AT THE SIZE OF ME MARROW*

OOH ARR

SWAFFHAM AND DIS HORTICULTURAL S

HEY, MY BREAD CAME 1ST! YES!

THIS IS AWESOME!

OH NO THE ICING WENT RUNNY IN THE PLASTIC!

IT CAME 3RD! LOOK- THE JUDGES SAY IT WAS 'UNUSUAL'!

* IT WAS THE LAW THAT YOU SUBMIT YOUR ENTRY ON A PAPER PLATE, WRAPPED IN A PLASTIC BAG!

LOTS OF THE WINNERS WERE ALLOTMENT HOLDERS CURRENTLY DEFENDING THEIR PLOTS FROM PROPOSED DEVELOPMENTS. THE MAYOR WAS PRESENTING THE AWARDS..

#SORRY, COULDN'T RESIST

YOU KNOW WHERE THESE WERE GROWN? YOU'LL KNOW SOON ENOUGH!

FIGHTIN' TALK!

CONGRATU-LATIONS

REFUSING TO SHAKE HANDS!

HO

SOME PRODUCE WAS THEN AUCTIONED

50p.. DO I HEAR 50p...

WE WENT BACK AND PLAYED CROQUET IN THE GARDEN.

CAN SOMEONE EXPLAIN THE RULES TO ME AGAIN?

WHEN DID MY LIFE GET THIS WEIRD?

# Kissoff #12

**Chris Landry**
**1048 Dovercourt Rd Unit 1**
**Toronto, ON M6H 2X8**
**CANADA**
pierrot_mon_ami@hotmail.com
www.kissoff.officialfindingjesus.com

A New Kind of Music

ights were quiet where I lived and on some nights I
ouldn't sleep. Outside my bedroom window I could
ear the breeze through the evergreen tree and
ometimes a car would pass panning its headlights
cross my bedroom walls, giving me a start.

he neighbourhood kids, the ones in their teens and
lder than me, would hop over the fence at the park
t the end of the street. There was a swimming pool
t the park and I could hear them splashing and
houting in the middle of the night.

en I was old enough, I would escape my room on
leepless nights, but I didn't go to the pool.
ere was a place downtown where bands from across
e continent were playing a new kind of music.
he admission was next to nothing and they even
ncouraged you to write on the walls.

e police said that the place was run by gangs and
rug pushers and the local papers printed these
cusations. But all I remember were Jeff's pink
oes, dancing and the time when a band from the
was playing and someone brought a baby pig that
n giddily up and down the club.

fore the place closed forever, there were times
en I missed the last bus home. It would take more
an a couple hours to walk. Mary was younger than
, but seemed tougher and more experienced because
e grew up and lived in the city. Together we
lked across the bridge to the east side of the
ver and stayed up all night in her living room.

Sometimes I wouldn't be home for days - I had
nothing but time - I didn't want to go back to my
room with the evergreen tree and the headlights.

One time we begged in the street. I thought it was
strange and told her so, but she said it was just
for fun, just an excuse to talk to people. And we
talked to a lot of people. Some told us stories and
some of them offered us jobs.

We decided that the city was full of lonely people
who just wanted to tell stories.

We didn't accept any job offer because if we had
jobs we could no longer stay up all night exploring
streets we've never been on or tell secrets on the
living room floor. And besides, we were 15 and 17
and we sort of thought work was for suckers. We
didn't need money to do any of the things we did.

When we hitchhiked west to go to a music festival
we got in an argument and went our separate ways.
She said that I was just like the others and a fake.

It was a little while before I could resume a
normal sleep pattern again.

**Keith Rosson**
**Portland, OR**
**keithrosson.com**
**keith@keithrosson.com**

# WELCOME TO FUCKEDVILLE

There are defining moments that choose *us*.

We know this: moments that gather themselves around us, that mark a particular chapter or change in our lives. They are small events or monumental ones – a lot of times it doesn't necessarily seem like it's got to be a huge, consequential thing (though, yeah, oftentimes it is) but rather just a small blip that passes across the geography of your life where you're, like, *present* for it – able to see and feel it – and can recognize how it marks a new high or low in the landscape of your time here, of your inner life. You understand? They're just these moments that smack you in the chops with their clarity, their ache – sweet or not – of your living. These moments that bring us right back into ourselves, our place in life, what we have gathered about us, what we have lost. I've had dozens, hundreds:

The night that the man I consider, for better or worse, to be my father left a series of drunken, increasingly incoherent messages on my answering machine after he'd been totally sober for nearly fifteen years.

Tanya and I on a weekend trip once. A beach trip, flying a ninety-nine cent sweet-ass Strawberry Shortcake kite, the two of us totally alone on the sand while rain-flecked wind lashed us, the sky up above the color of stone. Me, smiling like a fucking maniac.

My grandfather, small and yellowed on his deathbed. This man – who was never once unkind or unjust to me, who was in a war but did not have to kill men, who once had a multi-barbed fishhook punch entirely through the webbing between his thumb and forefinger, who flattened the barbs with a pair of pliers in his free hand and pulled the hook free, doing it without so much as a hiss of pain – now lay there unintentionally groaning in quiet, nameless agony, his eyes searching the room when my grandmother leaned down close to him and said, "Keith has to go now. He wants to say goodbye." How I touched him so lightly on the hand, afraid that any contact would somehow hurt him more, his eyes finally settling on me, the blank pain in them not changing at all. But he said, almost sounding surprised, "I can *see* Keith." They were the last words I ever heard him speak. I said to him quietly, my hand so gently on his, this yawning hurt for him hammered and centered somewhere between my stomach and my throat, "Goodbye, grandpa. I'll see you later." I left to get on the Greyhound home and he died three hours later.

Neckties Make Me Nervous playing a show in which the music we made seemed to not be just five dudes screaming and pounding away at shit separately, haphazardly, so afraid of failing, but instead locking into this brief moment of time, fifteen or twenty minutes tops, in which we were seamed and stitched together so *good*. Cohesive, with hands so *sure* of themselves, those chords I played cementing themselves to the bass and drums and tearing throats, all of it soaring into something so much bigger and stronger and more beautiful and angry and sad than anything we could have done alone, than anything I

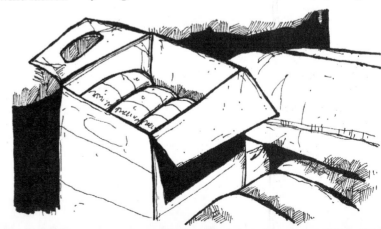

ould have done without them.

Nineteen and blackly hungover and reaching, reaching inside the cooler of a convenience store for a small bottle of orange juice. My hand grasping it, those cooled ridges of glass, that hangover wracking me, my hands riddled with tremors. And the bottle falling from my hand, shattering on the floor, juice and glass shards arcing and fanning outwards and what was left of my life seeming to grind to a stop at that exact moment. As if a page of my life had turned forever, somehow. I didn't take a drink of alcohol for nearly five years after that.

Waiting for a bus some hot summer night, maybe nineteen, some older dude swaggers around the bus stop, loudly belittling his girlfriend, *bitch* and *cunt* reverberating off the pavement. She stands there mute, her head down, just the three of us there. I give him a look and he says, "You want some too, bitch?" and swings, stopping just short of actually hitting me. I flinch anyway. "What I thought," he says, smiling. I say nothing back, afraid.

Locked in my own constraints, my inability to see beyond myself, we are arguing. We have argued and I have made Tanya cry while the night presses in on the cracked skylight above us, both of us laying there in bed. Her voice is thick with tears when she says, "Don't you get it? It's just that you're my *best friend*. I just want you to be fucking *nice* to me." And there are knives everywhere for weeks after that, sharpened by shame and honed by guilt that I have done this to the one person who knows me better than anyone, the one person who knows me so well and still covets me in spite of it.

And I had one today – just one of those brief flashes of recognition that pull you back into your station and placement in life. I have been drinking every night for the past few weeks; drinking hard, barely eating, rarely sleeping, just slammed up again and again against those questions of *What? When? Where? How did it start between them? Did we ever really know each other at all?* These are nights that stretch their arms wide and last forever. I cannot stop thinking, cannot find closure for this. It's a metronome that lessens when I'm among friends but never entirely goes away. I have begun dry-heaving at bus stops from dehydration and lack of sleep, lack of food, everything spinning to the point where I lean against a utility pole so I don't fall down. Lawyers have begun calling me regarding debts that I owe. I do not know where next month's rent will come from. I've got the most

hilariously, insanely raging case of hemorrhoids I've ever had in my life – all drink and no food, right – to the point where it feels like someone's cheerfully driven and then parallel parked a Honda Civic up my asshole. Due to lack of Federal funding in a particular school district, I no longer have a job. My mother has fallen down at work and broken both of her ankles and one of her wrists and is just now beginning to heal. Her vulnerability, her mortality, weighs on me.

I've made the trek from my apartment to the Safeway ten, fifteen blocks away, me and the aching Honda I'm carrying around in my fucking drawers and I just want to get in, buy some groceries and get out. I've got my little basket and fully recognize that things are going south, things are slipping away from me hard and fast, that I need to get it together. It is the first day or night I haven't drank in some time and I put bananas, soup, carrots in the basket. I think, *I will come away from this somehow, I will make it through. I will begin treating myself better.* It is the first sliver of hope that I've felt in some time.

And when I am leaning over the green peppers there in Safeway – fragilely adamant that I will make it through all of this wreckage somehow – my nose just begins to gush blood, like someone twisted a spigot. I drop the basket, my hand over my nose, my head raised, warm copper etching the back of my throat. I walk out of the store, begin stork-walking my way home and after a few blocks it's stopped. I spit thick wads of blood onto the ground, that electric taste of batteries in the back of my throat, hope dismantled fast.

One of those moments that just carves itself into you and brings you right back to exactly where you are, you know?

Spitting blood, I just kept thinking, *How did I wind up here? Was there a specific instant that brought me here? What choices have I made that took me right to this moment: in my early thirties, jobless, heart-busted, spitting blood on the sidewalk and stumbling around like an assfucked penguin because I've got Gwar-sized hemorrhoids, which has got to be the uncoolest bodily misfunction short of the Weeping Penis? How did this happen? With no real future and a history that it now seems was not what I thought it was at all? How in the* shit *did this happen?*

And all that came back was my own voice, resigned and oddly jubilant:
*Welcome to Fuckedville, man. This is where you live now.*

# Sugar Needle #32

**Cathy Camper**
**PO Box 66835**
**Portland, OR 97290**

**Sugar Needle**

Inside:

Dishwasher Pete Comes Clean About Candy

# Dishwasher Pete Comes Clean about Candy

For those of us that have been doing zines forever, *Dishwasher*, along with zines like *Ben is Dead*, *Cometbus*, *Beer Frame*, and *Thrift Score* was one of those nationally available zines that put zine-ography on the map. Pete Jordan, who is Dishwasher Pete recently published a book, *Dishwasher,* which talks about his quest to wash dishes in all 50 states AND an oil rig, as well as his exploits fooling David Letterman, and publishing 10,000 copies of his zine while sofa surfing with all his possessions crammed in a garbage bag.

Although his book is great, *Sugar Needle* editors still had a few unanswered questions after reading it. Pete was gracious enough to answer them in the interview below.

**SN:** Any thoughts about the differences between self-publishing your own zine, and having a book published with a major publisher?

**DP:** The major difference between the two is that I don't have to do any of the physical distribution of the book. I could just focus on the writing and then let the publisher print it and ship it off to bookstores. With my zine, publishing and distributing 10,000 copies of each issue got to be too much for me to handle while washing dishes and living out of a duffle bag. I couldn't meet the demand and thus the zine sorta stopped without me admitting that it had stopped.

**SN:** Just wondering, for those of us who do zines, what are the pluses and minuses you've experienced?

**DP:** The major plus is, again, not having to deal with the physical aspects of the production/distribution. There is no great minus though. I don't have any horror stories about heavy handed demands from my publisher. The book was written exactly as I envisioned it and my editor was happy with it. Well, the publisher's lawyer did ask me to change three names (because of the illegal activities I describe those characters doing) and he also had me remove the word "thieving" from one passage. Out of 93,000 words that I wrote, it wasn't too big of a deal to excise one of them.

**SN:** Do you think you're reaching a different audience with the book?

Hopefully I'm reaching the same audience as the zine plus folks who never had even heard of the zine (or of zines in general).

**SN:** When you were doing your zine, I was amazed you were able to self-publish it and distribute it, at the same time you were traveling AND washing dishes. Any tips for what made it work?

**DP:** Well, in the end it didn't work. But when it was working, I suppose what helped was that I had so many friends working in photocopy shops who either did favors for me or who looked the other way while I did favors for myself. A tip? Befriend photocopy shop employees.

**SN:** Sometimes when people make candy, they screw up and cook the sugar syrup too long, and it burns and bonds onto the pan creating a carbony mess. Any dishwasher suggestions for how to clean a pan like that?

**DP:** Two things: First, a good soaking. Pour hot, soapy water on the pan and let it sit for a few days. Second, if the first step didn't help, then chuck the pan. Actually, step two doesn't necessarily have to come second. (Note: these are tips for the professional dishwasher where chucking burnt cookware is part of the job. If this is pan-burning is done in the home, then one must flagellate themselves for burning perfectly good sugar! Then toss the pan and don't burn sugar again!)

**SN:** Unlike a lot of people today, you seem to have a healthy disinterest in fame. What advantages do you see in being an ordinary guy?

**DP:** I just like keeping to myself, doing my own thing, not being bothered... At a dinner party or something, I have no qualms about being the quietest person in the room since I'm never seeking a stage. Plus I enjoy observing other

**DP:** I once got a fan letter from somebody who had a candy factory in Connecticut. I lobbied her to let me come wash whatever they needed washing in their factory. But I never heard back from her.

**SN:** And what's your favorite candy, and why?

**DP:** Living here in Holland, I'm in black licorice heaven. The great variety of flavors available is mind boggling. At some outdoor markets, there are vendors who sell nothing but licorice—40 or 50 different types. During my first year here, I tasted as many different kinds of licorice as I could get my hands on. Eventually, I settled on picking up *dubbelzout* each time I needed a licorice fix. *Dubbelzout* translates literally as "double salt" and is enjoyed via an acquired taste. It's hardcore sour. Nearly every American guest that I give it to spits it out immediately, claiming I tried to pass off on them some kind of novelty fake candy.

For more info about Pete and his book, check his website;
www.dishwasherpete.com

Choose Your Chocolate

The chocolate industry wants to change the standards chocolate, allowing manufacturers to use vegetable oil instead of cocoa butter and still call it chocolate. But cocoa butter is what gives chocolate that "melt in your mouth" quality that makes it so good. Unlike other US companies, Mars has sworn to continue using 100% cocoa butter. That means M&Ms, Snickers, Dove, 3 Musketeers and Twix will have the real deal. With candy companies looking for ways to lower cost and calories, expect a lot of American chocolate to end up tasting more like chalk-lite.

**Diane and Katin Imes**
16055 SW Walker Rd. #406
Beaverton, OR 9706
citizeen@deepideas.com

CITIZEEN
How to Make Community

All (Grouped) Together Now

# To Flake or Not to Flake?
## *Thoughts on the power of Showing Up.*

**H**as this ever happened to you . . . you've found a new group, and it looks really interesting. You send an email, find out when the next meeting is, and tell them, "I'll be there!" You put it on your calendar. You look forward to it.

. . . Then, the day of the meeting approaches. Suddenly, you're not so sure you want to go after all. You feel nervous. You 're not sure you can face a bunch of strangers. Besides, you've got a big day tomorrow, and you need rest. And perhaps you're just beginning to come down with something . . . yeah, that's it. Maybe it's best not to go. OK, you're definitely not going. You sigh with relief, and flip on the TV.

You, my friend, have just flaked out.

Not that you're alone in this – the "flake factor" is rampant in our culture. Consider this incredible statistic: political campaign and charity group organizers commonly experience a 30-50% flake factor when rounding up volunteers. As in, 30-50% of the people who commit to helping out, never show up.

Now granted, sometimes you have to cancel a commitment at the last minute. Things come up, or you get legitimately sick. This is fine. But if your goal is to find community, then you need do battle with your flaking-impulses. We're here to help you.

## Why do people flake out?

We believe people flake for two reasons: the first being simple social anxiety. Everyone experiences it to some degree, but in this age, where we all do so much of our communicating online, our face-to-face social skills are getting rustier and rustier. We may love the idea of joining a knitting group or a book club, but when the moment comes where we'll have to actually leave our homes and talk to live people, many of us run for cover.

The second factor is this: the costs of flaking out are too invisible in our culture. So, let's look at those more deeply. . .

## What flaking costs you

Remember that at heart, most of us are yearning for a wide circle of supportive friends. And, remember what we wrote in Citizen #1: building friendships takes time . . . and a little initial awkwardness. Every time you flake out on a social commitment, you're extending the your time in the awkward phase. If you flake out all the time, you may never build close bonds with anyone, and you'll certainly never feel like part of a supportive circle of friends. Seems like a big price to pay down the road for saving yourself a little social anxiety today.

## What flaking costs others

Flake-outs can also hurt other people, and this is especially true for groups. If you flake out on group meetings a lot, it's possible that you've never organized a group yourself. Try putting yourself in an organizer's shoes for a moment. Imagine that you've decided you want to meet some new people, and build a supportive group. So you take the risk, and invite a bunch of strangers to meet with you. You answer emails, and coordinate everyone's schedules to set a meeting date. You look around your area for a suitable location. You make sure there's food and drink. You're all excited, and looking

"In all things that involve social pressures, if we want to see change..."

forward to seeing who shows up. The big day arrives . . . and out of the 20 people who told you, "I'll be there!" only two show up. Imagine your disappointment.

The same scenario applies to parties, dates, family dinners . . . . The next time you're considering flaking out, remember that your actions will definitely disappoint the other people involved Your decision to let yourself off the hook definitely hurts someone else.

## *Overcoming the urge to flake*

So, when you're in that moment, and flaking out seems like the most attractive thing in the world, how do you keep yourself from flaking?

Well, this is indeed a challenge. But you can do it! We'd like to offer a few tactics.

One great tactic is this: every time you start thinking maybe you won't go after all, you need to visualize, clearly and in detail, the potential benefits of showing up. Why did you join this group in the first place? Write the reasons down on post-it notes, and stick them everywhere. Keep the bigger picture very clear in your mind, so you'll have the strength to push through your last-minute anxiety.
On a related note, if you're on the verge of flaking, remember what flaking costs. Do you really want to disappoint other people? Do you really want to be alone and unconnected?

A second tactic: prepare yourself to socialize. Many of us feel social anxiety because we're not sure what to talk about with new people. If that's what makes you flake, then arm yourself for conversation. Scan the headlines for conversation topics. If you're going to a book club or discussion group, make sure you've studied the subject matter so you're very comfortable with it. Make a list of

friendly questions you could ask a new acquaintance if you ran out of things to say.

Lastly, put the whole thing in perspective. If you're feeling scared about facing a group of strangers, consider this: it's just a couple hours out of your life. It's just a few butterflies in your stomach. It's just a conversation. It's just a group of fellow human beings. And everyone's there for the same reason you are: to meet new people and make friends. How bad can it be?

Leave your house, feel the anxiety, and show up anyway. Your efforts are always rewarded.

# Rad Dad #7

**Tomas Moniz**
**1636 Fairview St.**
**Berkeley, CA 94793**
**tomasmoniz@gmail.com**

## gangsta father                              by tomas

rad dad is not cool; it's not about being hip, not about trying to be in style, not a trend. rad dad is for radical parenting. The uncomfortable kind. The difficult kind. Radical as in not complacent, as in conscious and conscientious of our impact on our children, our partners, our environment. Radical as in taking responsibility for the privileges some of us have, whether we want those privileges or not. Radical as in being cognizant of how we challenge patriarchy (or not), how we participate in capitalism, how we depend on unquestioned roles of authority and hierarchy. And then, radical as in having the courage to consider ways of changing these aspects of fathering.

Lately, I've seen numerous new books or web sites that clearly are trying to profit off of or benefit from or create a market for hip fathering, talking about how men can still remain men (whatever that means) and be a cool dad as well. What so many of these books or sites lack is a social critique, an understanding that for so long fathering has been intimately connected to patriarchy, to violence, to capitalism. Unless we as fathers do something to change that, no amount of coolness, no amount of humor, no amount of hip papa clothes can cover it. So my new mantra: We need radical change, not radical baby accessories.

For me, rad dad is about reaching out to community. It's not a place to provide excuses for some of the fucked up ways fathering is manifested by some men in our society nor about absolving ourselves of our complicity in the ugly history of Traditional Fathering. We gotta own up to it. And that's why I know I need other radical parents, both mamas and papas, to help me see how I am caught up in this history. Especially, when I'm unaware of it which happens all the time. I need them to show me how myths of fathering are perpetuated in the media or to help me see when fathering is being used as a marketing ploy or is being packaged for consumer convenience.

rad dad for me is recognizing how I need help.

I can't do it alone because I already know I'm a sucker; I'm a fool. I laugh like hell during Shrek and his silliness, and my kids love him, so he's gotta be a good model for fathering, right? And I'll admit I was the first one at the bar getting all stupid when the Warriors were in the playoffs. Don't get me wrong. We as people can and should have our own interests outside of parenting, enjoy the company of other adults in places that perhaps aren't super kid friendly. But we are straight up wrong if we think that the word father means to be cool, to be part time, or that it's temporal, ending when we are not with our kids, or that it's limited to the realm of the house.

I want the word father to mean: warrior, to be synonymous with dedicated; I want it to be analogous to activist, environmentalist, feminist, gangsta, anarchist. I want people to step back when we announce we're fathers and that we're here and we ain't leaving until some things change.

Starting with ourselves.

rad dad is as much about radical parenting as it is about fighting patriarchy in all aspects of our society. I believe actually that to reclaim fathering, it will be contingent upon men to work diligently for equal access and rights for women in the world outside parenting. We can't expect to be equal partners in parenting and not have women be equal partners in the rest of society. To reclaim fathering we will need to reconsider intimately what it means to be successful and how capitalist notions of success are tied to the construction of male identity. To reclaim fathering we will need to question the social stereotypes of fathering that for so long have been used to justify gender specific parental roles.

> I want the word *father* to mean: warrior, dedicated, feminist, anarchist

Now I also wanna recognize that how we individually manifest our parenting and our relationships is up to us. There is nothing inherently wrong with a man providing the main income for a family and a woman being the primary caretaker. But it needs to be transparent, needs to be a choice and not the default. Fathers need to actively consider what might be the underlying reasons for their decisions about how they father and what they give priority to.

And, most importantly, fathers will need to actively, vocally, publicly support and speak up for other fathers.

So let me give a shout out to the amazing fathers and mothers and other parental allies that I had the pleasure to meet and depend on as I ventured out on the Kerbloom/rad dad speaking tour of the Pacific Northwest. It was so inspiring to realize that there are people I can call up and say, *I need a place to stay* or *can you help me out* or *come to our event*, and they are there lending you a pillow, offering what they can, bringing their kids and neighbors to see you read. So that is what rad dad is about, what Kerbloom is about, what creating radical community is all about. There are so many people doing so many different, cool things that every time I feel slightly exhausted or overwhelmed, I just need to look around me or think of those that have helped me, and feel

reinspired, rejuvenated. You all rock.

I hope you enjoy rad dad 7 and tell other people about it. I am not sure what the future is for rad dad, but I am trying to imagine other things it can do, can become, can transform into like the children we all love and rear: from a baby to toddler and on. Part of this growth has been the tour of the Pacific Northwest that just passed. I'd like to do more tours, meet other parents, help organize a radical parents conferenece, so if you are interested in doing something like that, or have any other ideas about where you see a zine like rad dad going, let me know;  I am asking for help and guidance.

With love and respect coming outta the East Bay where the younsters get hyphy... tomas

# Biff #5

Bill and Allie Donahue
biffmagazine@hotmail.com

## The Editors (Junior Editor) Weighs In

biff
editor
Allie
Donahue

I was eight years old when my dad and I started *biff*. At first, it was a simple production: silly stories about my grandparents, lists of top tens, and drawings of our beloved mascot.

I sat dutifully at our grimy kitchen table in brightly colored Hannah Andersson dresses gripping my pencil tightly and biting my lip while I scratched away until I got the drawing just right. I was usually pleased with the outcome. I was always showered with praise. "biffing" was something my dad and I did for hours.

But now the joyous feeling I had when I was eight isn't there. Now that I'm older I feel like our readers expect *biff* to be good. They want the writing to make sense, the drawings to be detailed. But to me my drawings look dumb and bland. My writing never sounds right. Dad's editing makes me angry; his praise seems false. And instead of brightening me it magnifies my anger and I retreat into a shell. I sit in my bedroom and escape into my iPod and the phone. It's so much easier that way. Writing takes work and energy, and my energy has slipped away as I've grown. As it's slipped, so has my interest.

Dad's watched it slip. He asked me if I still even wanted to do *biff* again.

I knew somewhere deep inside of me I did. *biff* was a part of my childhood—the childhood I'm still clinging to. I realized that I need to keep that childhood alive and that doing *biff* could help keep it alive. And so to make this issue, I dove down into myself and rekindled my joy and love, my energy and interest.

In this issue we are looking at a very tender subject—religion. In my seventh grade class, it has been an ongoing debate whether God exists or not. Dad and I decided to embrace this subject and look at people's many different views on religion. We have an interview with one of my great friends, Claire, a young atheist, and an essay my pen pal wrote about her bat mitzvah. Dad and I ourselves visited four different evangelical churches, all just blocks from biff world headquarters. Religion being such a vast subject, we are only able to give you a peek of it here, but in that peek we've tried to give you variety.

I was talking a lot about "childhood" up there. I think we all know that childhood is the time in your life to get out there and try new things. *biff* is something I've tried, something I've loved. But there are other things just as marvelous as *biff* that wait—my writing club, raising my two fluffy chicks, Willoughby and Gwendolyn, and growing tomatoes in a homemade miniature greenhouse to make salsa from scratch. I want to learn as much as I can and see as much as I can before this childhood morphs into teenhood and then into adulthood. So, ladies and gentlemen, it is with great sadness that I tell you that biff 5 will be the last issue.   Enjoy.

Allie Donahue
Allie Donahue

Bill Donahue
Bill Donahue

biff's editors in 2003...

...and four years, 43 stories, and 837 editorial skirmishes later, in 2007.

**Nicole Georges**
**PO Box 12763**
**Portland, OR 97212**
**nicole@nicolejgeorges.com**
**nicolejgeorges.blogspot.com**

# Clutch #18

Clutch McBastard
PO Box 12409
Portland, OR 97212
info@tugboatpress.com
www.tugboatpress.com

May 14, 2007

TODAY I AWOKE WITH A CRUSHING REALIZATION of the MEANINGlessNESS of life.

That this existANCE is Nothing but A torturous void filled only with suffering ANd loneliness.

That we ARE All doomed to empty lives, PAiNful deAths, ANd A quick fAde iNto obliviON.

ANd then I sAt ARouNd ReAdiNg comic books All dAy.

hee hee

SNOOPY

# QSL USA

**mm cross**
**5152 Verdun Ave.**
**Montreal PQ H4G 1N6**
**Canada**

These are QSL cards, the (card!-)stock in trade of the 1960s-70s CB radio craze. 4 years ago I found a couple in a box in a shop. Now I have 130,000 & counting, & a project called myQSL.org, all about them. Along the way I've learned a lot about what makes them so weird and amazing. I've been wanting/trying to make a zine with/about them since about 2 secs after finding one, but in this TENTH month of the FOURTH year of myQSL.org, it seemed like the universe was finally saying "10-4 good buddy!!!" So here we are!!!

I called the zine QSL USA because not everyone can remember the letters QSL that easy, unless they get the play on mySQL. Maybe the esses in "QSL USA" will keep it straight for you! Also, putting USA in the title of things is kind of retro sounding. It's not a diss Canada! You are just as awesome and instrumental to this collection, ol' home + native land!

With millions of cards flapping around the world, you could start anywhere, but it never hurts to start with introductions, so this issue is just the plainest examples of CBers themselves, nothing but humans with radios, as seen on their cards. We're not even scratching the surface! In future issues you'll see them at home, on the road, as ladies, animals, at work, at play, and all their other various & sundry interests.

**350097: Doc & Stinger**

OK well, before they started giving out the K callsigns, the FCC used to give out, like, ##@-####. You feel me? But the letters would only be A, B, Q or W. So these guys were EARLY ADOPTERS and got an old one at home, but by the time they souped up their "wagon" they got the new kind.

**160272: The Rupperts**

This is an example of what I file under "Base & Mobile" cards, where the CBer shows you the home (base) and car (mobile) they're broadcasting from. Maybe they should be called American Dream cards... But as some Canadian seventies EZ listening song sez, "ain't nothin better in the world you know, than lying in the sun with your radio…"

**400546: The Shapes**

OK I was unsure about including this one because this issue is all about CBers at their simplest. I thought Mr.Shape was holding a mic but now I think maybe he's admiring himself in the mirror! And what is that flatulent bird doing flying over him!? And is his toe OK or is that his sock!?

**380165: Jules Auge**

Well, given the rubber stamp/penmarks, this elaborate work of art was for temporary or cheapo use I guess, if you were waiting for your new QSL cards or too put out to pay for personalized ones. Am I right, Jules Auge of Niobe New York?

# Hungover Gourmet #10

Dan Taylor ed.
Written by Bryan Senn

PO Box 5531
Lutherville, MD 21094-5531
editor@hungovergourmet.com
www.hungovergourmet.com
hungovergourmet.blogspot.com

## Jackie Chan: SUPER*CHEF?*

**WHO GOES TO** the *mall* to eat while vacationing in Hawaii? Amazingly enough, I do – despite the fact that I'd sooner stuff red hot peppers into orifices I'd rather not think about than visit one of those soul-sucking monuments to consumerism. But this was different, since said shopping center houses the one and only food palace owned by my (and millions of others') favorite Asian action star – Jackie Chan.

*Jackie's Kitchen* (open for about a year now), located in the Alamoana Shopping Center just West of Waikiki in Honolulu, is the first (and only, to date) of a proposed chain of restaurants around the globe. Its fairly extensive Asian-flavored (naturally) menu offers everything from smoked duck (a whole half-duck, with excellent seasoning and a tangy plum sauce) and noodles to steaks and local seafood dishes.

But for me it wasn't the (surprisingly good) food that was the main draw – it was the All-Things-Jackie ambiance generated by the framed photos, movie posters and plasma TV screens (showing a Jackie Chan movie) that studded the walls. That's right, while you eat you can watch Chan-the-Man in action all around you (sans sound, but with helpful subtitles).

The first night we ate there (yes, we returned to the scene of the *Crime [Story]* several days later) the film du jour was the newest *Police Story* movie (*San ging Chaat goo si*, or *New Police Story*), which wasn't even available in the West yet. The snippets I saw looked intense and brutal and well up to Chan's high action standards. The second go-round had us watching the *Around the World in 80 Days* remake (which, thanks to Jackie's acrobatic turn and comedic charm, isn't half-bad – silly gadgets, love story and all) in between courses.

The restaurant also sports an inviting flair bar, where the bartenders flip, spin and toss the glasses and bottles in an amazing display worthy of a scene in Jackie's next opus. As I whiled away some time at the bar waiting for the wife and kid to finish their shopping, one of the bartenders (from Liverpool, no less) told me that on opening day, when Chan himself was there to christen Jackie's Kitchen, the place was mobbed by thousands of fans. Fortunately, the screaming hordes were long gone, and, though the establishment was fairly busy, it only took a matter of minutes to get seated. For good food and fun, Asian action-style, Jackie's Kitchen earns a *(Project) A*.

Oh, and like all good (or not-so-good; re: Planet Hollywood) celebrity eateries, Jackie's Kitchen has its own (tastefully limited) line of merchandise, including various shirts, dvds and magnets. And yes, I had to take home a couple of pilsner glasses (hey, for only two bucks more you get to keep the big glass after draining it of such amber ambrosia as the refreshing Hawaiian Longboard Lager, Oregon's well-balanced Drop Top Ale, and the classic British Newcastle Brown Ale).

# Angry Black-White Girl

Nia Oxette King
30 Ox Bow Rd.
Canton, MA 02021
oxette@riseup.net

### Ethnic, or something

I am light-skinned, Black, white, Middle Eastern and Jewish. I grew up in a predominantly white, Irish and Roman Catholic middle-class town where I knew no other mixed race people except my sister.

I wish my parents raised me around more Black people and culture. Claiming any part of Blackness now feels to me like the cultural appropriation it appears as to others. I feel conspicuously like a suburban white girl among the Black, urban members of my family. Yet, I feel distinctly like the only person of color in a room of whites when they are making racist jokes or being entertained by racist stereotypes.

I want to be part of a more racially diverse community, but I fear that my presence in people-of-color-only spaces will be seen as intrusive. I want to disassociate myself from whiteness and the history of white oppression, but have the privilege of being seen and treated as white and need to be accountable for my own racism. I sometimes question whether my choice not to identify as white provides a convenient escape from having to own up to my privilege and prejudices.

I have to "out" myself to negate the assumption that I am white, and even then my self-identification is sometimes ignored. When I make my heritage known, I am often invalidated with "you don't look Black." Failure to explain my ethnicity to new acquaintances merits remarks like, "I've never seen a white girl with hair like that before. Are you ethnic or something?" The second person who asked this, a customer at the coffee shop where I worked, added, "Or are you one of those people who doesn't like to talk about [your ethnicity]?"

I'm talking about it. I am African-American, Lebanese and Hungarian and the following experiences illustrate just a few of the challenges I face as a light-skinned Black-and-white mixed race person in predominantly white environments:

Before I was born, my maternal grandmother disowned my mother for marrying my father. She only started talking to my mom again, 10 years later, after my grandfather died. Every year to this day, my parents fight about spending Thanksgiving with my mom's family, because my father still, understandably, feels unwelcome and uncomfortable among them.

My father instilled a lot of Black pride in me early on in life. I identified as Black when I was young, but was eventually worn down by people telling me I wasn't. I now identify as mixed race.

On another shift, one of my co-workers had made a game of trying to guess my ethnicity. "You're not any kind of Spanish?...Brazilian then! Italian?...Irish?..." She keeps going. I shake my head no to her guesses and stare at the floor, hoping that somewhere along the line she learned this is a sign of discomfort, a sign that means stop. But she keeps going.

Finally, "I really don't appreciate being interrogated about my ethnicity." This is the first time I have stood up for myself and refused to answer. After the fact I feel proud.

"Geesh," she says, no longer talking to me, but to a white coworker standing alongside her, one of three other caterers who witnessed her game, my cross-examination. Maybe they would have got in on it themselves if I hadn't cut her fun short. "I was just wondering. I like to learn about other people's cultures." I was raised in a white suburb, I don't have any culture to give you. Go find someone else to exploit for your cultural enrichment.

I am riding home from a shift in a car full of caterers. Naomi asks the only male in the car to not speak while she calls her husband, so he doesn't get jealous. "He's Lebanese," she explains, "they like to keep their women on lock." I think of my Lebanese grandfather. I never met him, but all the stories I've heard are about how he let my grandmother walk all over him. I feel defensive, but don't have the knowledge of Lebanese culture or acquaintances to back up anything I might want to say.

I quit my job. I've gotten a ride off Craigslist to visit a friend in Western Mass. The driver is a forty-five year old white woman who also lives in JP and sports a "tree-hugging dirt worshipper" bumper sticker. She spent most of the westward journey talking with other aged hippy riding with us about her guilt over driving a car, her Buddhism and her acupuncture practice. She mentions that the woman she studied acupuncture under helped a skilled Chinese acupuncturist come to States to work for her and made all this money off of him. "I'd like to do the same...if you hire somebody in the States they might leave you to start a private practice, but if you bring them here on a work visa they can't leave you." This scenario sounds too much like slavery to me, I want someone to validate my sentiments. So appropriating Eastern religions you're down with, but importing brown people and keeping them you think is ok? I dread the ride home, without the hippy dude to keep her occupied. We make small talk.

"Have you traveled much?" she asks. I mention having gone to Uganda. She asks why Uganda, and try to explain my dad's desire to see the Black motherland.

"Your dad is African-American?!" Yes.

"Is he your biological father?" Yes, he's my goddamn biological father.

"You don't look Black." REALLY? I kind of smirk it off, like it's no big deal, instead of letting out the anger I am feeling since I don't want to end of up on the side of the road.

"Can I touch your ha- Do you have African hair?"

"NO. YOU CANNOT TOUCH MY HAIR."

"I didn't ask, I only half-asked," she says, laughing, and then tells me how on good days people sometimes ask her if she has some Black in her, trying to regain lost ground. "Sicily is just a piece of Africa that floated away. That's what a friend of mine who is African-American says."

# Ghostpine #11: Crows

PO BOX 42017
RPO Jeanne-Mance Montreal, QC
H2W-2T3
CANADA
http://ghostpine.wordpress.com/

THE FIRST
MEETING
OF

# THE SOCIAL JUSTICE CLUB

NOTE:
IN THE PREVIOUS EPISODE OUR NARRATOR (ME) WAS ASKED TO HELP RECRUIT A NEW CLUB AT HIS HIGH SCHOOL BY HIS ENGLISH TEACHER, MR. MICHEL. INSTEAD OF BEING ABOUT DEBATING OR PLAYING CHESS THIS CLUB WAS TO BE ABOUT SAVING THE FRICKIN' WORLD. LETS SEE WHAT HAPPENS NEXT!

I ate my bag lunch in three minutes flat, staring at the hands of the clock. Nothing happened. Mr. Michel sat at his desk leafing through the newspaper. He unscrewed the top of his thermos and poured soup into a mug.

"I told everybody," I confessed.

"Sure," he said casually.

"Everybody."

He only acknowledged the empty class room a few minutes later, looking up from his paper and joking nonchalantly "Pretty small club, eh?"

I nodded and managed a small smile, but "Fuck you," was what I thought. My brain whirred with despair. After all the running around I did to start this club, it's not my fault that no one showed up, I thought. Fuck. That's what I get for getting involved with this shit.

Yes. Fuck extra-curriculars, fuck high school, and fuck me for a being fool enough to believe, in my most optimistic moments, that my fellow students could be united into the vanguard of a suburban revolutionary congress. No one was coming. Fuck.

Then Sundar walked in. His shoulder length curls bobbed as he greeted me. "Uh, hi," he said.

"No one's here," I said. "No one's coming." If people hadn't come in the first ten minutes of lunch break I figured they were obviously never going to come. I was ready to throw in the towel and go back to sitting in front of my locker, being laughed at by my friends.

But the sun was out. Maybe I would walk out past the football field, instead. Slipping through the gate that opened onto the soccer fields next to the industrial park I could sit there in silence, stare at the clouds and wonder yet again how the fuck I was going to survive two and a half more years of high school.

"I just talked to some people in the hall. They said they were coming. People are coming," Sundar said, completely sure. He sat down at the desk next to mine and pulled a package of sesame snaps from his pocket, offering me one after he tore open the plastic.

---

Each minute following brought a few people through the classroom door, and then more, until groups of four and five were clamoring for the few remaining seats. Some sat on the floor while others stood or leaned against the walls. The room filled with the great excited chatter of people arriving on the threshold of something unknown together. We chatted as if attending some teen cocktail hour and all the while people I hadn't told about the meeting arrived with others I had never even seen before. The ugly room that housed hours of sedate pedagogy was alive in a way I never imagined it could be.

Oh, and then the goths arrived. The goths! Really. I hardly knew them, but had guessed their wardrobe of black nihilism and eyeliner was just a costume. They arrived in black capes of gloom and pants stitched with graveyard mist, but I knew with their arrival that they loved, not hated, the world.

The room twittered with the excitement of individuals realizing that maybe, unexpectedly-- although they had hoped, always hoped-- they had found a fellowship, a step above a gang, mightier than a clique. And into all of this joy came the punks, dark clouds tied to their mohawks. They sat in the aisles between desks, crossing their legs like oversized kindergarteners. Alex stood next to me in front of the blackboard, detailing his latest encounter with the school administration, only to be interrupted by a throat-clearing that cut through the room's conversations.

"It's twenty past," Mr. Michel said. "I think you'd better get started."

"Okay." I said. And then, all confidence suddenly drained, asked "How do we do that?"

"However you want. It's your guys's club, I'm just the supervisor."

"Uh," I said. As much work as I had put into recruiting, I never for a moment considered what I would say if people actually showed up at the meeting.

"Okay," I said, "Welcome to the first meeting of the Social Justice Club."

"Yeah, *welcome*," Alex parroted.

"I guess we're all here because we believe that the world is a pretty messed up place. The idea behind this club, I guess, is that we can somehow make a difference for the better.

"So to begin, I guess I would just like to know what, uh, everyone is interested in working on." I was overwhelmed. "There are a lot of issues, but I think we should work on the one's that we can all agree on. A democracy . . ."

"So call 'em out and we'll write them down on the board" Alex said, handing me some chalk.

"Okay, I'll write down a political issue I'm concerned about for a start." I brushed off the remnants of white from the board and then wrote 'East Timor,' the nation illegally occupied by Indonesia, on the board in the clearest script I could manage.

As I wrote the 'i' of Timor Sundar suggested we look into native land claims and before I had enough time to write that out in full someone else called out "Women's issues," and so it went. After five minutes of writing on the black board, the suggestions slowly came to an end. My hand was cramped and the board was covered with problems. Stepping back and looking at all the white chalk lines, I was amazed at the breadth of our grievances. Every problem we could think of was up there; an alphabet of dissent from Animal Rights to Women's Issues.

"Okay," I said. I took a deep breath, letting it sink it. The world was fucked. "Maybe we could divide into small groups that work on an issue that's important to us. Then each committee can bring their ideas to the rest of the club and we can talk about what to do. And then we'll do it."

Desks creaked as they merged into clumps of three or four, small islands of talk.

In fifteen minutes Sundar had already planned our first action, brought it to the group and had it approved unanimously. In fourteen days we were going to sell Fair Trade coffee and chocolate in the foyer.

We were running out of time. As the electronic bell sounded, final questions were asked.

"Can we be me on more than one committee?"

"Yes!" Alex called.

"Do we need a leader?"

"No! We're Anarchists!" he pronounced.

Mr. Michel looked up from his from his paper, after sitting in disinterested silence for the last half hour. "Oh, that reminds me, you need to elect two leaders to represent you."

Alex sneered.

"It's policy," Mr. Michel shrugged.

"I nominate Jeff," Sundar called.

"Alex!" a voice called.

I wrote both Alex's and my name in the small space on the board that wasn't covered in scrawl. "Okay, who else?" I asked, prepared for a deluge similar to our rapid diagnosis the world's ills.

The class was silent. I looked to Sundar, he was probably the smartest person in the room, but he was staring out the window, suddenly entranced by the birds flitting outside.

"Well, I guess we don't need to have a vote," Mr. Michel said, wrapping things up. "Congratulations to club presidents Alex and Jeff!"

"Co-coordinators, maybe?" I suggested, uncomfortable with my new tile.

"Four more years! Four more years!" Alex yelled, holding his arms over his head in celebration. The punks howled their approval. Alex ran to Tops, his right arm outstretched for a high five. Instead of congratulating his friend, Tops simply picked him up, hung him over his shoulder and carried him out of the room.

*. . . to be continued*

# Keep Loving, Keep Fighting / I Hate This Part of Texas

**Hope Amico/John Gerkin**
**P.O. Box 791639**
**New Orleans, LA 70179**

"You tell yourself the waters will recede, and when they don't one day you say maybe they will the next."  Lionel Petrie, resident of the 9th Ward, September 6, 2005 (from New Yorker Magazine Sept 19 2005)

So Why Do You Stay?

Dead friends and fear, shootings of strangers, despair and poverty, limited resources and I could go anywhere...

But where would I go?

Could I make it through winter anywhere colder without the jasmine under my window for the brief spring nights before the morning wakes me blazing and sweating already?  The long hot summer has been shaping my way of working through the year—manic in the spring, calmer when the rains start. The people who can leave town go to California or Europe and I nap on the floor under the ceiling fan every day. The quiet is addictive, especially to someone who simultaneously loves cities and solitude.  Summer is for storms that could wreck us, but usually bring a rainy night then beautiful clear day.  Summer is for cold treats and having lots of time for your friends who have also stayed in town. Iced tea and biking slowly.   In the fall, your friends return and the dancing starts again.  There is native music, born in this town and there is what is created and inspired by it.  Where else can we block the streets for a parade because we are celebrating or mourning?

A city that has so little to lose offers everything it has.

When the recklessness is too much and the damp soaks through our thin walls, I leave for somewhere warmer or better insulated. And then I come home.

My blood family is in New England and South Carolina but parties this winter were all about what John calls "family time".  There are more people here that I feel close to and responsible to than any where I've called home.  It is partly the shared history, the recent losses and trials, but also the brilliance and love.  It is because they still answer the door after so many sleepless sad nights.  We continue to adapt to whatever circumstances we are offered.  It is stubbornness and refusal to give up. Maybe stupidity.  Maybe we are all clinging to the last bits of a bad relationship, remembering the romance of the beginning, waiting for the waters to go down tomorrow.

So maybe the question should be:  *how do you stay?*

I have said that what I love about this city is that anything can happen.  For better or worse anything  does happen.  Your friends start their own Mardi Gras parade.  Now three years later they have enlisted thirty people to play in the marching band for it.  You could have lost it all here, and folks have, still some return to rebuild their front porches to be here because they don't know where else to go.  Some scrappy kids start a bike shop in the dark corner of a warehouse and six years later there are classes for kids and adults, open shop hours, a night for women and transgenered people.  For every few dudes I have to ask to come back another night, someone tells me how good it is to be able to work in the shop, how different those nights feel.  A kid from class is in the park showing other people how to patch a flat tire.  He was once asked to leave the shop for shouting at volunteers, now he helps with classes.

I wake early every Saturday to go to the farmer's market for good bread and tamales and broccoli before I go to work. There is a new coffee shop with good coffee and really good food.  My friends started a band a year ago that makes me cry sometimes and dance like celebrating every small victory. Sometimes, I ride home along Frenchmen Street, a block out of the way to wave hello to Arthur.  He remembers me from the first days the bike shop  re-opened after the hurricane.  I biked around my neighborhood looking for anyone who might be back who might need a bike.  He still waves hello, often a defiant fist in the air and shouts ALLRIGHT! at me.

There is joy here.

On Saturday afternoons in April, as the sun is getting ready to give up and the air is cool and calm and quiet, I believe in all the possibilities of beginnings, of sprouts and stubborn plants and resilient people. Because the water went down and our hearts are sad but not hard. Because we hesitate with strangers but show that much more love for our friends.

Things are difficult and you have to know that. You have to know what will be terrible in some situations but not let that kill you. You have to take what is good about it all, and let it inspire you. And then try harder. And when it seems like too much, rest.

"For the world is as glorious as ever, and exalting, but for credibility's sake let's start with the bad news."    Annie Dillard

SEPTEMBER 2005. NEW ORLEANS

Helicopters chop-chop-chop non-stop. I can hear the sound of water running, a broken main pulled up by a falling tree. Military transport trucks growl past every once in a while. A breeze stirs the dry branches left on the still-standing trees. Mostly, though, what is noticeable is the silence; these sounds are enormously loud because there are no other sounds. There are no cars, no music, no voices. The constant whine of air-conditioners, the background white noise of summer, is not to be heard. A city of silence, bereft of its populace. Our footsteps echo as they crunch on the dead grass, or rattling the corrugated tin strewn everywhere, or slipping on the wet muck inside of houses.

Have you ever seen a dead dog laying on the street where you live, and its stomach has exploded from bloating in the heat for days? And the dog is laying not far from a house that has collapsed, kind of just imploded into a pile of wood and broken furniture with a roof atop the heap? And all around the dog and the rubble-pile house and the knocked-down trees laying in the street, all the vegetation and plant life is withered and grey. Actually everything is this ashen, mud-washed hue

below the watermark, which stands at about six feet, just over your head. The watermark is a greasy black smudge, a line everywhere you look, like someone power-washed the contents of a bottomless septic tank across everything you can see, or like a giant doo-doo crayon was dragged along and it looks like you are standing in an altered photograph. And that line is above your head.

Everywhere you go it is desolate and dusted, a desert, sun-bleached and baking. Acrid, rotten, rotting. Death a specific stench here and there, but more constant is the malodorous toxic mud and decomposing vegetation. The city mummified. You turn the corner and that woman who lives at the corner of Broad and Canal, usually with two shopping carts full of stuff and always so many layers of clothes, she's sitting there at the bus stop. Dressed for winter in Wisconsin, or a moon landing perhaps. There is not another person around, perhaps even for miles.

She is sitting there in front of the Whitney bank, a cardboard box full of MRE's next to her, rubbing cream onto one bare foot. Shoe and sock on the bench. Hot sun and the surroundings blasted, all grey-brown, like a bomb had gone off or everything covered in ash. Then, a group of marines comes walking down the street, the deserted empty street save for you and this woman. They're so orderly in camo and their red berets are the only color in the entire scene. Fresh-faced, like dressed up school kids but carrying guns as long as your leg.

In another moment of surreality, one of many, the silence of a deserted neighborhood perforated by approaching calls of "here kitty kitty," and "good boy, good dog," as SPCA volunteers walk the barren landscape feeding animals and spraypainting houses with notes, creatures for which to return. "Dog, fed 9/8. Cute puppy." "One fish, Sep. 13." These mimic the spraypaint markings on houses which denote, among other things, the number of living or dead found by search and rescue groups.

And you go from friend's house to friend's house, collecting unflooded items and whatever can be salvaged, later calling folks to tell them how it looks, ask if there's anything to search for. The places we have built up, collected, nested, loved and lived in. They are archaeological mudpits, stinking and ravaged, desecrated.

# Next Stop Adventure #2

**Matt Gauck**
**Somewhere in Portland, OR**
nextstopadventure@gmail.com
http://www.thedreamerandthefool.com

However, i rely on happenstance frequently enough that i know SOMETHING will work itself out, and sure enough, after some phone card usage, and a little map debating, my brother Zack agreed to drive and come get me and take me to iowa city with him to help move into his new apartment. What followed was a lot of not bending my knee, but rather, hanging out with my brother, dumpstering all the furniture we could find, and then just enjoying the small town that is iowa city. This went on for awhile. Long enough for an intermission...

## SOMETHING TOTALLY DIFFERENT

I'll get back to the whole 'bike trip' thing in a moment, but i have another story worth telling. Besides, the concept of 'next stop adventure' was just an adventure-esque text, which generally happens to relate to biking. Keeping with the theme, this next tale involves me riding my bike, doing something illegal, and centers around the concept of adventure. I think i've learned that adventure is when you stop thinking in 'normal modes', and switch to the 'i wonder...' or 'what if?' types of thought. Largely, this type of living and planning is just plain ridiculous. But it IS fun. And i love fun.

I also love Rainer Maria. Hands down, they were and are the best band of all time. Reversal of Man, Good Clean Fun, Pg.99, Bad Brains...they all take a back seat to Rainer Maria. Yeah, i know, some list to compete with, huh? This is the only band i have gone out of my way to get all the recorded material of, including the split 7", the old direction LP comp, as well as the 1955 record AND cd. That's just sad. The songs are identical, it's strictly a format difference...Anyway, it takes an unbridled love such as this, to kick one's mind into "all or nothing" mode. Oh, and it certainly helps if you don't want to pay 65 dollars to see them play a 20 minute set at Lollapalooza...

The news was in place - Rainer Maria was playing Lollapalooza, in Chicago, where i had recently relocated to, and it was incredibly expensive. There are two things i hate in that last sentence, one of them is Lollapalooza, and the other one, well, i'll let you gue$$. The stakes were set - Saturday, noon, at the small stage near Lakeshore Drive. I studied the map on the Lollapalooza website, and thought it was close enough to the barrier, i could probably just listen from the sidewalk, then throw a zine at them as they were leaving, yelling "i met you in austin, at south by southwest..." Seemed like a decent plan; heck, maybe i could pull the old "i'll help you carry that amp in, if you want" routine. I mean, i've seen 'catch me if you can' like 20 times, it can't be THAT hard. I set my watch alarm, fell asleep on my floor, and dreamed of Caithlin asking me on stage to help with backup vocals. Preferably on 'atlantic'...

Next thing you know, i'm looking at my bike, my phone, and my total lack of a real plan, save a map drawn on the back of a receipt - and it occurs to me, that maybe i should grab one more thing. The whole night before, i had also been pouring over my old issues of heartattack, specifically those where mack evasion had written columns, one of which is expressly about gate-crashing. I didn't learn anything too new, but left it all with a good feeling, that maybe it IS possible. One way to find out, huh? Oh, and that last thing i grabbed - that was my old tour pass from the last Circle Takes the Square tour i had roadied on. A small, shiny, laminated card with dates on the back, and a key ring hole at the top. It probably measures about 4 inches by 5 inches. Small. But extremely powerful, it turns out...

...Because next thing you know, i've biked downtown, locked up across the street, did some 'talking on the phone and wandering around the back fence' routine for a second, and then decided i'd give it a shot. My first plan had actually been to just jump the fence somewhere, but there really were a lot of guards, and the fence would have shaken in 50 feet in either direction. It would've been obvious something was going on. I needed to be obvious for a different reason. I was important. I was a roadie for a band playing Lollapalooza...just repeat the lie enough and you will believe it, seriously. That's what i learned when i took my keys from my pocket, and attached them, with a caribiner (a touring essential) to the front of my shorts, which was polished off by my "real-yet-fake" tour badge, shining proudly at the front of this loud, jingling mass. At this point, i was supposed to be inside, so, naturally, i just started walking there. There was one guard right in front of me, so i acted like i'd been awake for too long, like it took an extra three hours to drive the van here, and like i had to hurry back to a merch table i shouldn't have left in the first place - so i didn't even break stride when i flashed my tour badge at him. He waved me in with an "ok".

ME, LONG KNIVES DRAWN

The SECOND i got beyond that fence, i had all the 'band cred' in the world. I walked out from the area i was in, to the main courtyard thing, sat under a tree, and waited about twenty minutes for Rainer Maria to set up and go on. In this span of time, nothing

really happened. Specifically, no one came up to me, looked funny at me, or, well, paid attention to me. It's almost like it worked, huh? I noted not to finger point too much while singing along, as i didn't have a wristband, which was one of about four million differences between me and the surrounding crowd. Twenty minutes later, after knowing all the words among a sea of people who may have all been either deaf or asleep, i figured i'd press my luck until it backfired. The least i could do was get kicked out, now. I didn't care to see Nada Surf, so i had nothing to lose! Besides, i had to at least say hi to Caithlin again - mostly to give her a zine, but also, there was the off chance that she'd been trying to call me over the past 8 months, since we last met. I mean, it IS possible. Not probable, but who cares - i just saw Rainer Maria for free, right? As it turned out, there was a guard blocking the entrance to the 'backstage' area, and i managed to hang out there long enough for kyle, the guitarist, to come up and thank me for singing along. We talked for a moment, ending with me asking if i could say hi to the rest of the band. "Well, yeah, but i think you have to have a pass to get back here", at which point i replied, loudly, so the guard could hear "oh, yeah, i got one", and showed kyle. "Oh, cool, yeah, they're right back there..." I fooled kyle, i fooled another guard, and as i crossed that second 'audience / performer' barrier, Caithlin turned her head right towards me, as if to say "...finally."

Or, realistically, just to say 'hi'. In the end, i gave away a zine, talked to the whole band, offered my services as a pro merch guy, (with references to boot!) and exchanged some emails and phone numbers. My "touring with Rainer Maria" dream would ultimately never quite work out, because they broke up, however, i am confident in saying that had they toured again after i saw them, i would've been on it. I'm serious. I have phone numbers and emails, people. Heck, the next time i saw them was in milwaukee, after a bus ride and

hanging out on a playground for nearly 4 hours, when Caithlin walks by, recognizes me, and invites me to dinner with her, Kyle, and their merch guy, a 'just out of high school kid' that Kyle's family knew. Purely situational, that merch guy...shoulda been me. They even paid for my dinner! Keep in mind, this is my favorite band of ALL TIME, and they recognize me in a different state, dedicated a song to me, AND bought me dinner, at a 'sit down' thai restaurant. Yeah, exactly. When i get 'in' with a band, i get IN with a band. (Writers note - i am always happy to sell merch, so if you're in a band, and need to get rid of 10 shirts to an audience of 5, get in touch! seriously!)

I left Lollapalooza that day, sitting on top of the world - well, biking, actually - thanking myself for never ebaying that tour badge. I probably would've made six or so dollars off of it. Funny how useful things like that can turn out to be, huh? One of the last things i heard, as i was leaving, was "excuse me, can i see that badge again?" Huh. Time to put confidence mode back on. "Sure, i'm just taking a little walk, i'm with Circle, (as i motioned towards the big stage)"..."oh, i'm sorry". Sorry? A guard apologizing? I knew there was some way this could get better, and that was it.

## A POST-SCRIPT NOTE TO RANIER MARIA

If i haven't said it enough, or ended this movie on the proper 'outro' speech, i'll do it again here. Your band, the creative force that it is and was, stands as the most inspirational, groundbreaking music i have ever heard. A flurry of compliments will surely fall into a well-worn path of positive reviews over your eleven year career, so i will state it simply - thank you. I love Rainer Maria.

"i am not a traveler, nor an adventurer. things happen to me in my search for a way out."

—henry miller (black spring)

# You Don't Get There From Here #5

YOU
DON'T
GET
THERE
FROM
HERE
#5

Carrie McNinch
PO Box 49403
Los Angeles, CA 90049
cmcninch@gmail.com

# Adventures in Menstruating #

Chella Quint
chartyourcycle@gmail.com
www.chartyourcycle.co.uk
www.myspace.com/chartyourcycle
www.chartyourcycle.blogspot.com

In the spirit of 'Make Do and Mend' for our wartime theme, we present...

## Tampon Crafts

Tampon Crafts is an almost completely anonymous website full of...tampon crafts. They did have an email address though, and when I asked, this is what they had to say about their inspiration: "As far as why we created the site, we just wanted to have fun with something that people have such silly hang-ups about. Liberate tampons, so to speak." I love this website. There are crafts for several holidays throughout the year, including a Valentine bouquet, fairy lights that I really want to make, and a Chanukah menorah that would have come in handy last year when I left mine at work after a library Chanukah party. It would have been awesome to make it out of tampons. The one I improvised out of tin foil and play-do didn't have crazy self-lighting action! This craft was meant to be an Easter Bunny, but I think bunnies are cool all year round, so you can subversively craft with confidence! Hell, have a tampon bee!

### Tampon Easter Bunny

What's fluffy and white and cottony soft? Tampons! And bunnies! That's why this tampon Easter Bunny was such a natural. If he sticks around for your period, he'll bring you some unfertilized eggs.

**Materials**
Playtex tampon with pink plastic applicator
Two Tampax tampons
Hot glue gun
Utility knife or scissors
Wiggly eyes
Pipe cleaners

**Instructions**
Remove Playtex tampon from applicator. Moisten slightly to expand and let dry. Save pink plastic applicator. Remove Tampax tampons from applicators. Hold tampon, pinching at each end, and pull to expand. Widen in the middle to create an "ear" shape. The string side should be on the back, while the "furrow" side should be on the front. Trim strings off bottom and top if necessary.

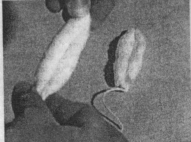

To make the inside of the ears, take the plastic applicator from the Playtex tampon and use scissors or a utility knife to slice it into vertical strips. The tip of each strip should be one of the applicator "petals"; continue cutting till you reach the ridged base of the tube, then cut across. Round off the square bottom of each strip.

Fill the length of each rabbit ear tampon with hot glue and press a plastic applicator strip into place, with the pointed end up and the curved part pointing out.

Remove string from Playtex tampon and set it aside. Set the tampon "point" up. Use a generous amount of hot glue to attach ears, placing them inside the "creases" or folds of the tampon.

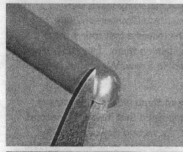

Cut off the tip of one of the remaining pink plastic applicator "petals." This triangular piece will be the nose. Hot glue it to the tip of the Playtex tampon.

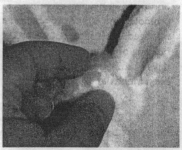

Hot glue the eyes in place. Cut the pipe cleaners into four two-inch pieces and hot glue into place on either side of the nose.

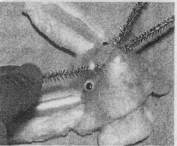

If you wish to hang the bunny as an ornament, hot glue the reserved string onto the back.

So if you've recently given up tampons, but still have some lying around, or are ever struck by a crafting urge and have no supplies to had, try tampon crafts today! If you do, please send in a photo of your tampon craft creation!

**BIG HANDS**

# Big Hands #5

Aaron Lake Smith
1104 Imperial Rd.
Cary, NC 27511

Now there I was, a young and desperate young bachelor, sitting alone in my apartment, having reached a new alien lows, fearing all social interactions other than the kind mediated by paper brusquely tossed over a counter in exchange for coffee or gasoline. It was in this kryptonite-weakened state that I spied an advertisement on the back of the local alternative weekly for a free local phone dateline.

"Why not?" I think, "What more do I have left to lose?"

I realize that this is how it ends—marooned, isolated in our apartments and condos, sending out smoke signals over fiber optic wiring, screaming into the abyss for a human connection. I lower the blinds on all my windows and pace the floor, and then dial. The phone rings. A sexy female computer voice picks up, sopping with innuendo, backed by primal thump of some lustful techno dance-beats

*Welcome to Quest Personals. Raleigh's HOTTEST local dateline. Your choice for Raleigh's HOTTEST local singles. Men press one.*

I gulp and press one, wrapping the cord around my fingers.

*Now you will record your personal greeting* the digitized single prepares me to record my paragon of personality to sell myself, an attempt to convince others that I am worth wasting precious free trial minutes with. I clear my throat and lower my voice, attempting to sound older than I am.

"Hey, Aaron here. I'm in the Raleigh area and uhhh, just bored, looking for someone to hang out with."

It fell a bit short on describing the idiosyncrasies of my personality, in detailing the vast, unconquerable snow-covered peaks of my towering intellect. This is why I don't do well in cities, finding myself sweating when accosted with questions like "What's so unique about you?" Sure, I can hula-hoop, and have broken my nose a couple times, but my existence really boils down to a few standard universal processes—Work a boring job, produce largely pointless commodities, eat, breathe, make excrement, and if lucky, copulate, for pleasure or progeny. But thanks to the pleasantly-engineered voice of my A.I. guide through the singles netherworld, I am ushered from these dark nether

regions of my subconscious. I click through the greetings, aghast at the bruised, unabashed world-weariness of these advertisements

"This is Angela. I'm a grown forty five year old widow from Durham. Look guys, I'm just looking for a good man; A man who doesn't play games. A man who doesn't CHEAT on his woman, because Guys listen, I'm the real deal...and I know how to *treat* my man. I will *cook* for my man. But guys, *do not fuck with me.*

America, America, this is you—huddled in the corner on the portable, mashing the keypad through the sorrowful soliloquies of your neighbors, looking for love in all the wrong places.

I breeze through the husky, unapologetic voices of men who've infiltrated the "women" greetings to offer clandestine, no-strings-attached blowjobs to lonely straight guys. Wow, starting to be genuinely depressing. That is until I come to one greeting,

"Hey, this is Janet. I'm here in Raleigh for a job. Pretty lonely here, just looking for someone to hang out with. I like driving around, reading, punk music."

I send her a message and we connect to "chat". It's a little bit awkward at first, but soon a rapport forms naturally. She's twenty-seven, and works traveling around the country with a roving computer tech support team, living in rent-by-the-week hotels in exchange for salaried pay. And just like that, she invites me to come out to her place and hang out.

I drive out past the RDU airport on the tangled, tentacled-mass that is the Beltline, the landscape flattening out into an orderly symmetry of wealth; shiny fake Thai restaurants, gas stations with equipped with televisions at the pumps, an Extended Stay America looming behind the well-manicured lawns. I park and jingle my keys; the only sound in the sapling-tree silence other than the distant, oceanic whoosh of the highway. I walk up a couple of flights of stairs and knock on her door. A severe, plainly dressed woman answers the door, looking kind of like Janis Joplin.

"Aaron? Hey there, pad'nah" she rasps, smiling, smelling of week old kitty-litter and stale nicotine.

"Hey Janet" I grin.

"Well, what are you waiting for? Come on in!" She leads me into her dimly lit, otherwise nondescript hotel room: low-pile carpet, a TV, bed, bath, and a bible. Just a place to exist for a little while. She lights a cigarette.

"Well, wait a minute. Let's go around the corner and see my friend Bill." We step out onto the carpeted open-air landing and walk around the corner to a different room, where Janet knocks, and barges in without waiting for a response.

"Bill!" she waves her arms in the air, dangling her cigarette

"Look at what I found", she singsongs, cackling and pointing at me demurely. I stand there awkwardly, dangling my hands out of my pockets. Hi there Bill, I'm, uh, seventeen, lying and saying I'm twenty-one, and I met Janet on a telephone dateline. Bill is in the corner tapping away at a keyboard in a tangle of cords and computer monitors and barely glances back, rolling his eyes

"Oh Jesus, Janet, can't you see I'm busy? Hi, nice to meet you—Goodbye!" Janet laughs and drags me back to her lair. I sit on the bed while she nests on the chair, lighting another cigarette.

"Well, well, well—-What are we going to do now? You want a beer?" she grins.

"I don't know" I mumble, looking down at my shoes.

"So you like punk rock, huh? How about this?" She laughs, digging through her CDs and throwing on the Misfits Collection I. She cackles maniacally and points her finger at the stucco ceiling, screaming along:

DEMON I AM AND FACE I PEEL!

TO SEE YOUR SKIN TURNED INSIDE OUT, CAUSE

GOTTA HAVE YOU ON MY WALL!

GOTTA HAVE YOU ON MY WALL, 'CAUSE

I WANT YOUR SKULL

## I NEED YOUR SKULL

I suppose this could be construed as a real creepy thing for someone you didn't know to sing alone to you in a nowhere hotel room, but I didn't seem to mind at the time.

"So you want to kiss or what?" she rasps, nicotine-addled, eyes at lustful half-mast.

"Sure." I say. We move towards each other, my awkward, fumbling lips finding hers and sharing a long, blissful moment. We continue pecking, intermittently. Then she begins to steadily devour. Her teeth gnashing against my lips and then, all at once, biting down

"OUCH!" I yell, drawing back, putting my hand up to feel the hot rush of blood to my mouth.

"Oh sorry, I'm not really the gentle type." She flashes her fangs predatorily. She leans forward to suck the blood off my lips. Bataille would have been proud. We kiss some more, and I'm trying to fend off her Sadist onslaught, but it's an uphill battle.

"OW FUCK!" I scream.

"Oh, you like that, huh?" she smiles at me toothily.

"You know, I have to go to work tommorow. I should really get going." I lie, muttering sheepishly

"HA! Well, sweetie—no use in hanging around if you're in a rush. I like to take it slow. You should come back when you have some time." she cajoles me, stroking my arm.

"Alright, well—see you later, Janet." I glance back at her as I walk out into the glaring daylight, lying there, smoking on the bed of some dim hotel room, staring at a muted TV, the Misfits Collection CD still skipping on the night stand. I start the car, rejoining an empty stretch of fresh Beltway. We're just a few lonely people, mashing down on the accelerator. Satellites fallen out of orbit, drifting through an unfathomable nether, all the while hoping, praying for a crash.

# Hirsteria #1

Justinn/Greanne
PO Box 365
Flagstaff, AZ 85002

HEY QUEER---

SO YOU WANNA GET MARRIED COULD HOLD YR BREATH THRU THE AND PRAY TO A GOD THAT HATES THE DAY THAT THE STATE IN A SYSTEM CLASSISM, -ETC PHOBIA QUEER TO EXTENT--- A SOLDIER HETEROSEXIST IS LESS JOIN THE BEFORE IT'S

AND JOIN THE ARMY? SURE, YOU GRUELING PROCESS OF REFORM YOU THAT YOU'LL LIVE TO SEE ALLOWS US TO FULLY PARTICIPATE THAT PERPETUATES SEXISM, RACISM, FAT-HOMO-TRANS-INDIGINOUS FOR THE COMPLACENCY OF YER DOLLAR OR YOU COULD LIVE LIFE A FULLER, MORE FULFILLING MARRY THE MOVEMENT, BE IN THE WAR AGAINST OPPRESSION THIS SOCIETY THAN SUSTAINABLE MUTINY TOO LATE.

THIS ONES FER THE FAGS: A CALL TO ACTION

We're being pulled under and swept away by the surge of gay male socializationthat's flooding our tv screens under the guise of progressive social change. we're solidifying the division between dyke and fag. where do we as queer people stand on border issues, literal and figurative? are we arming the border or uprooting its foundation? are we be begging at the gates of the mainstream to open up just long enough to let our child free double incomes in and shut our allies out? are we being swallowed whole and losing ourselves in the process?? ①

it's time that gay men took a stand against sexism, against racism, classism and fat phobia. ③

i was reading an essay in one of my favorite books, Against Violence, it was written from the perspective of a butch dykewho had experienced a lot of pain and shame. she was talking about how it felt for her to walk down the street, comparing men to packs of dogsand concluded that, 'even faggots piss on trees.' it was really hard for me to read but i had to admit she had a point. i just wish her analysis had gone deeper. ②

dykes had our backs in the ACT UP! days marched against the epidemic and fought for all of our visibility. i'm sure i'm not the only one who's had a dyke come to my rescue in the event of street harrassment, weneed to educate ourselves on womyn's issues and shut the fuck up about some girl needing to cover up her fat rolls and get off the stage of the ricki lake show. we need to finally fuken figure out that fat is more then tolerable that it can be healthy and hott. we need to come to a consensus that rape is wrong and intolerable in all of its forms. we need to wake up and realizem that we're more powerful united and that queer solidarity needs to take a precedence over our allegiance to the patriarchy. ④

# Warmer

**Toronto, ON**
**Canada**
**www.birdandmoon.com**

The **Intergovernmental Panel on Climate Change** (IPCC) considers two degrees warming to be the maximum permissable change.
By 2100 we are likely to reach 3.5 degrees. CO2 persists for decades in the atmosphere, continuing to heat the planet and glaciers. The [...] never experien[...] befo[...] planet's histor[...] Warming will b[...]gr[...]ver[...] causing famine [...]os[...]f [...]e, a[...]

**CROP YIELDS TO FALL BY A THIR[...]**

The Great Barrier reef will lose 95% of coral by 2050 in the best case scena[...]

One million species [...] extinct by 2050

drought ha[...]taken ho[...] in Amazon [...]asin as [...] record high[...]

another po[...]ib[...]fe[...]ba[...] exponentia[...]i[...]re[...]se a[...]

Nov. 16, 2006

Dear Mr. Prime Minister,
I am still pretty worried about this climate change thing. I know you are busy but could you please

# Unleashing the Imagination

Allan Antliff and "Bones"
allan@uvic.ca
bones@mutualaid.org

## Robert Henri (June 25, 1865 - July 12, 1929)

American artist Robert Henri (b. 1865) was a close friend of Emma Goldman and an anti-academic artist in his own right, who, in 1908, organized the first in a series of independent art exhibitions that

Robert Henri, by Gertrude Kasebier (1900)

successfully challenged the power of America's conservative art academies. The National Gallery collection includes a portrait by Henri of George Luks, a newspaper illustrator turned painter who participated in the 1908 exhibit. Note the looseness of Henri's brush and the hurried rendering of details, such as Luk's hands. This slapdash style was a deliberate affront to academic values. Henri would go on to teach a free art class at an anarchist center in New York (The Ferrer Center) from 1912-1918. He was also outspoken in his opposition to World War 1 and a stanch supporter of Emma Goldman until his death in 1929.

### FROM LIVING MY LIFE: VOLUME TWO, BY EMMA GOLDMAN

"At a lecture in Toledo a visiting-card had been left on my table. It was from Robert Henri, who had requested that I let him know what lectures I was planning to deliver in New York. I had heard of Henri, had seen his exhibitions, and had been told that he was a man of advanced social views. Subsequently, at a Sunday lecture in New York, a tall, well-built man came up and introduced himself as Robert Henri. "I enjoy your magazine," he said, "especially the articles on Walt Whitman. I love Walt, and I follow everything that is written about him." I learned to know Henri as an exceptional personality, a free and generous nature. He was in fact an anarchist in his conception of art and its relation to life. When we started the Ferrer evening classes, he quickly responded to the invitation to instruct our art students."

Robert Henri, George Luks

Robert Henri, *Emma Goldman* 1935. Painting destroyed in 1935.

for a detailed account of Robert Henri's work, see: Antliff, *Anarchist Modernism: Art, Politics, And The First American Avant-garde* (2001).

# Marcel Duchamp
## (1887-1968)

Upon arriving in New York in the summer of 1915, Duchamp was asked by a newspaper reporter what he thought of the war. He replied that he had "greeted the war with his arms folded"– the stance anarchists and socialists had urged the working class to take during the years leading up to the conflict (sadly, when the time came, anti-war solidarity fell apart).

Duchamp's contribution to the disruption of the American art market was the provocative idea of the ready-made. The ready-made was any mass produced product Duchamp selected to serve as an art object. One of Duchamp's earliest selections was chosen in 1915--a "ready-made" snow shovel which he picked up at a hardware store. The name he appended to it–In Advance of the Broken Arm –poked fun at the importance avant-garde artists gave to titles, which were an important factor in the marketing of their increasingly abstract paintings. The National Gallery has on display a "replica" of this shovel (the original disappeared) which Duchamp "authorized" in 1964. Another ready-made preserved in "replica", (the entire Duchamp room in the National Gallery is nothing but replicas) from this period took a more pointed aim at American nationalism.

Marcel Duchamp, In Advance of the Broken Arm (1915) 4th version 1964

Society of Independent Artists Exhibition, New York, April, 1917

On the eve of America's entry into World War 1, Duchamp anonymously (under the name "R. Mutt") submitted a urinal, titled Fountain, to the first exhibition of the "Society of Independents". This organization had been formed in 1916 by a group of American artists and art collectors to stage a 'block-buster' exhibition of contemporary art, the only stipulation being that exhibitors were to pay a nominal entrance fee.

The submission of the urinal threw the organisers into complete confusion. When they opened up the crate and saw what was to be exhibited they held a special meeting and, after arguing at length, decided by majority vote to refuse it, on the grounds that it was not a work of art at all.

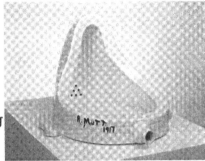

Marcel Duchamp Fountain 1917, 5th version 1964

In fact, Duchamp was not only challenging the conventional notion of what an art work was. He was also attacking the pro-war attitude of the exhibition organizers. When the exhibition opened in early April, 1917, the United States had just entered World War 1 on the side of France and its allies. Sensing an opportunity as the war grew closer, the organizers of the Independents Exhibition took to promoting their event as a pro-American embodiment of democracy in art. During the exhibition they hung American flags from the ceiling and staged an American Red Cross benefit. Duchamp, who was in the United States because he opposed the war, was disgusted by their attitude. And so he submitted the urinal to test the "democratic" waters. The organizers, as we have seen, responded by violating their own rules and refusing the exhibit –so much for democracy.

Marcel Duchamp, Duchamp's pissoir

Duchamp's contempt for the American's eagerness to market modern art as "democratic" went hand in hand with contempt for the war and the cultural and political values that sustained it. His response to a questionaire sent to a select group of modern artists in 1919 sums up his attitude. Asked if he thought the war had influenced the development of the arts he responded "I don't weigh potatoes with shit."

# Criminally Yours

Megan Hamilton
3134 Eastern Ave
Baltimore, MD 21224
megan@creativealliance.org

Benn Ray, editor
Eight Stone Press
PO Box 11064
Baltimore, MD 21212

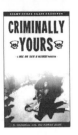

## BALTIMORE CRIME MAKING ME PROUD

 Benn Ray

**We were in a Dick's sporting goods** in Bloomington, Indiana, and the cashier was giving us a hard sell on some bonus card crapola.

"You sure you don't want to buy a bonus card," he asked.

I said no.

He was just this close to saying, "What, you don't like to save money," which really drives me crazy. I mean it's true, there's nothing funny about savings and one should never laugh them, but I've been getting a lot of hard sells from business service people, and I swear to hell the only thing they must have taken away from whatever bullshit business school they went to is, "When losing a potential sale, always ask the mark, 'what, you don't like to save money?'"

So I cut him off.

Instead of saying, "I loathe Dick's. I loathe sports culture. I loathe you and all the customers in the store. And the only reason we're in here is to get a gift for someone back home," I said, "We're not from here, so no thanks."

"Oh, where you from?" he inquired.

And I said "Baltimore."

"I'm pretty sure we have Dick's there too," he quipped.

And I assured him he did, but that I never shop at Dick's, I most likely never will again, and I am here specifically for this one item we are purchasing which is  not available at the Dick's in Baltimore (a Hoosiers sweatshirt since, we were, like, in Bloomington) and which we will be giving to someone.

"Baltimore, huh," he snorted, realizing his defeat. "My car was broken into in Baltimore. I didn't like it. I liked DC though, but not Baltimore."

I guess since I wasn't going to buy his bonus card, he was trying to offend me. But it didn't work. Here Baltimore made me proud.

Just 2 nights before, we were in a cafe (called Atomix) in Chicago talking to some friends, and one who works at Quimby's (a bookstore there kind of like a sister store to Atomic Books) was telling us about her experiences the one time she came to Baltimore to do a reading at our store.

"As we were driving through the city, we happened to go past a drug store," she said. "There was a security guard out front. We looked over and noticed someone sneak up behind the guard and steal his gun and run off with it."

This is what she remembers of Baltimore. When she thinks of our city, this is what comes to mind.

As far as crimes go, it's more of a caper than anything. And it is kind of a funny caper at that.

Then she says, "And as were leaving the city, these drivers of two different cars were cruising down the road and having an argument at the same time. We got stuck at a stop light, with our car between the 2 other cars, and the drivers were yelling at us to roll down our windows so they could continue their argument

through our car."

And while that may be weird (or to some potentially scary), it's certainly not a crime. But these are 2 examples of how people view our city based on their experiences here. Not only that, but the way they respond to these experiences also reveals something about their character.

Our Chicago friend is cool, so her crime story will be an amusing anecdote. The Bloomington Dick's cashier is not cool, so his crime story will be an indictment of 700,000+ people.

While my friend from the bookstore was never a victim of a crime in Baltimore, she did see one crime involving a gun and almost get caught in a fight between other people. But the way she told these stories, these events almost seemed to endear the city to her. And I thought this was especially odd since she lives in Chicago, a much larger city. I assumed there would be much more crime - but I guess not.

Now the Bloomington guy, well, he left shit out in his car and parked in Mt. Vernon, went to see some festival and then got drunk at the Brewer's Art (an area bar). Having his car broken into was enough a crime for him to never want to come back to Baltimore again… but really, it was partially his own fault. You never leave anything even remotely valuable visible in your car when parking in the city And whoever his city friends were should have told him as much (thinking a rube from Indiana might not be familiar with the strange customs of a big city is a customary assumption).

And since this guy was pretty much a hard-selling sports Dick, I felt proud of Baltimore for breaking into his car. In fact, I was most likely grinning with inappropriate pride as he was telling his little tale. "That's Baltimore," I said. "It's an acquired taste." But what I really meant was, "And don't come back.

## THE CRIME THAT WASN'T

 Megan Hamilton

**It happened (didn't happen?)** right in Glamden.

My buddy Susan and I were off on some fun day trip somewhere. So I parked my beat Honda in the alley behind her house at the bottom of Chestnut.

I had tons of stuff in there including a Walkman on the back seat. Parked early AM. Came back late. Can't remember if my ADD-self noticed I had left the car unlocked or not but everything was there. I split and didn't think more of it until....

My buddy Susan was talking to her little old lady "Hampden hon" neighbor. Apparently while I was away, said hon saw a local kid she knew scope out the Walkman, try the door, and grab it. Super senior gal, of course, knew all players.

She jumped on the horn and called the kid and told him to put it back. He said no. Not taking "no," she called the restaurant where he worked as a busboy (I can't think of the name

– it was buried amid all the houses, kinda off the beaten track.) and talked to his boss, who of course she knew, and told the boss to tell him to put it back.

Boss did. Kid did. All before I even got back! So... moral of the story? Sure - Baltimore can be a pretty bad ass place, but I got other stories like this one. It can be a nice ass place too.

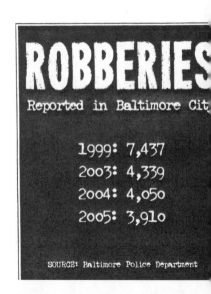

ROBBERIES

Reported in Baltimore Cit

1999: 7,437
2003: 4,339
2004: 4,050
2005: 3,910

SOURCE: Baltimore Police Department

# Bony Landmarks #3

## The American Book Pirate

By Andrew Coltrin

**Andrew Coltrin**
**PO Box 42181**
**Tucson, AZ 85733**
**look_for_signage@yahoo.com**

Portland, Maine
THOMAS B. MOSHER
Mdccccij

Two-thirty in the afternoon on the Bookmans trade counter has the potential for being either a rare and magical moment or a total crap fest. For a couple months I had been in the middle of a bad string of crap fests. Tantrums and communication breakdowns had been plaguing my book buying shifts. Some days I would blame the coffee. Other days I would determine that it was just human nature in general that was at fault.

That Thursday I was totally at acceptance, if not peace, with the idea that the trade counter was how the store got both customers and merchandise into the store. And with no merchandise or customers, there would be no paycheck. I was ready to eat whatever surprise or aggravation might come my way. I would eat it, smile, and do whatever I could to put saleable goods onto the incoming carts and in-store credit into our customers' pockets.

At this moment of ease and resale clarity, up came a retired couple looking to cash in on something that had been sitting around their house for entirely too many decades. They were excited. They knew that they had something golden.

They asked to speak to someone who knew rare books.

Rare books. Sometimes I am reminded of how much I actually have forgotten about the rare book trade. The specific knowledge of bibliographic terms and condition states has atrophied with disuse since my days of generating catalogue entries for online booksellers. Even without all that readily at hand, there's something about the feel of a truly rare book, an uncanny aura that makes me want to put it somewhere safe, where people won't accidentally breathe on it. A book that calls to mind words and publishing terms that nobody actually uses anymore: three-quarters bound in leather; marbled boards and endpapers; uncut pages; quarto, octavo, duodecimo.

So I smiled and took their treasure into my hands. I liked the feel. I opened to the title page and had a pretty good idea how much what I was holding was worth. It was a little over a hundred years old, with some slight edge-wear to the boards. The paper was nice, white paper, un-yellowed by time and the acidity of cheaper paper stock. The chain lines of the screen the paper was made on were present in its texture. The title page was printed in

two colors, red for the title and date, black for the author and publisher. The book, an anthology of old French poetry in English translation, though small, and a fairly minor entry in the cannon of literature, was a pleasure just to hold.

"Really cool!" I said. "Published by Thomas B. Mosher, the American Book Pirate! We would sell it for about twenty-five dollars. I could offer you half that in trade." A quick bit of research showed I was actually being a bit generous, but I wanted that book in the store. To be honest, I wanted a chance to buy it for myself.

I'm not generally a book collector. After moving every year for five years, I've gotten used to purging my library. But some books are special. Some hit you in a personal way. Books are artifacts that work on many levels. There's the physical thing of it. There's the narrative within. And there's the meta-narrative, the story of what was going on in your life when this book came into it. The Mosher book was resonating deeply with the meta-narrative.

My first real encounter with the Book Pirate was when I worked in the Labyrinth in downtown Portland, Oregon. It was my job to check the orders and e-mail inquiries every morning. One day there was an e-mail from a John Lovell Beddoes asking about an issue of Mosher's literary magazine, the *Bibelot*, we had listed in our online catalogue. He wanted to know if it indeed carried some poems by one Thomas Lovell Beddoes. If so, he wished to acquire our copy for the library of the Thomas Lovell Beddoes Society in England.

It was very strange. I'd never heard of Beddoes, the poet, but it had a feel of obscured familiarity. I had to know more.

I started with the copy of the *Bibelot* issue in the Labyrinth warehouse, located in the basement of the four-plex where my boss' mother lived. The tiny, unassuming pamphlet with the blue cover was beautifully printed. The letters and engraved designs pressed deeply into the paper. The words had the depth that belied the metal type they were printed off of.

It thrilled the zinester in me. It was definitely an artifact made by hand. And there was some twinge of synchronicity as I read the publisher information: Thomas B. Mosher, Portland, Maine. After all, was I not living in the city that was named after the city this magazine was published in?

I had to find out why someone named Beddoes was looking for Poems. I had to find out more about this publisher. I turned to the mighty river of information Dubya calls 'the internets.'

Beddoes was relatively straightforward. He was a 19th century poet, all but forgotten when his relatives suppressed his work after his suicide. But what about Mosher?

Thomas Bird Mosher is some kind of internet folk hero. There are several biographical articles as well as documents related to his publishing practices. Among them is the text of a 1909 advertisement taken out as a warning to English booksellers not to carry Mosher's editions of English authors. It was in these documents that he is decried as "the American Book Pirate."

This is probably why he's a hero. Because pirates are cool and books are nerdy. Anything that makes a nerd look cool is destined to find heavy representation on the internet.

Unfortunately for the internet, he wasn't all that exciting of a pirate. Rather than flagrantly defying the law, Mosher merely took advantage of a fairly large legal loophole. According to the American copyright laws of the day, any works in English that had not been issued in an American edition were fair game for American publishers. While technically unethical, and upsetting to the Brits, there was no action that could be taken in American courts against Mosher's piracy.

Looking closer at Mosher we find neither eye-patches nor pitched battles on the high seas. Although he was the son of a sea captain, and in his youth he had spent almost three years traveling the world at sea with his family, he spent most of that time below decks, reading. When he did go ashore, it was to visit booksellers and graveyards (he liked to make rubbings of old epitaphs). He spent 20 years in various careers, running various businesses into bankruptcy before he turned to publishing in 1891. During his two decades of failure, his love of books remained. He acquired an in-depth understanding of printing and book-making, and eventually hit upon success with his publishing venture.

His piracy was more of an injury to English publishers than to the actual authors whose works Mosher used. In many cases the authors were like Beddoes, already deceased and otherwise condemned to obscurity. Other authors were glad to be given some American exposure they otherwise wouldn't have had. Some were even quite pleased to be presented with the editions Mosher made of their writing.

In the end, the controversy from the advertisements denouncing Mosher's piracy only served to increase awareness of, and demand for, his books. And eventually he was successful enough at his business to observe proper publishing conventions... like paying authors.

It's hard for me to judge whether Mosher's sidestepping English copyright law was right or wrong. I have trouble criticizing a man for doing something he obviously loved and doing it so well. Mosher was an artisan bookmaker who had an interesting way of selecting the text he worked with. I suspect his choice of material was much less to do with merit or legality, than it was about being something he was excited about setting in type and giving a nice, hand-sewn binding to. I take pleasure in knowing that he existed, and I really enjoy the production values of his publications.

To hold a Mosher book is to hold something that turns the contemporary notion of media piracy on its head. Today it is so easy to burn a bootleg disk of a movie or an album, or to download it onto a hard drive. And never mind the debate over where intellectual property lines should be drawn, what about the esthetics? Is that shiny disk of metalized plastic labeled with a magic marker something that looks nice in your living room? Probably not. But an edition published by Thomas Mosher looks fabulous and is most likely in better shape than most books of its vintage.

Which brings me back to that moment on the trade counter.

I really wanted that Mosher book that the retired couple was trying to sell. I wanted it because it was a good buy for the store. And I wanted it for my personal meta-narrative. Unfortunately, what the couple really wanted was to hear that it was worth a couple hundred dollars. That's pushing it for meta-narrative.

The couple left with their book, but I wasn't that let down. If there's one thing I've learned from working the Bookmans trade counter, it's that if somebody's looking for something, it will show up eventually (often at the most ironic moment possible). About a week after writing the first draft of this piece, I found another Mosher book already priced and sorted onto the poetry cart.

**The American Book Pirate** *originally appeared on*
a website I may or may not be supposed to be hyping. Google my name and you'll find it.

100

# Listy #2

**Maria Goodman**
**PMB #303, 2000 NE 42nd Ave, Ste D**
**Portland, OR 97213**

## Vince's Vocab Virtues

My sister used to work in an office where this
guy Vince would always call and rant in her
ear for up to an hour at a time, using these
same esoteric phrases over and over:

Chicken with teeth
Since Jesus was a corporal
Low-hanging fruit
THAT SAID
Skin in the game
Up to the butt in alligators
Thrice
How many angels on the head of a pin
Button, button, who has the button?
Bells on our toes
Just for giggles
Give her a Cupie doll
Systemic Snafoo
It looks like this "lion" is being "bearded."

# Corrupt Corvids #1

**San Diego, CA**
**Email: kczines@gmail.com**
**Website: kcelaine.blogspot.com**

We're fighting fundamentalism!

Dear celebrity magazines,

I hate how you follow every female celebrity's weight like it's groundbreaking news – how last month you were calling Angelina Jolie anorexic and this week you're suggesting she's pregnant (even though anoretics can't menstruate), probably because she ate a meal.

But what I hate more is how I gravitate toward all your stupid weight stories even though I know you're a sleezy tabloid with cheap "journalism."

Which leads me to...

♡ KC Elaine

Dear Lindsay Lohan,

I've never paid much attention to you because you're a kid star who grew up without much talent, but I can't blame you for that. Then you lost weight, and you had the audacity to glamorize it like you were this saint who "nearly died" and it was, like, so dramatic and exciting and stuff. Then you were outraged because the headlines said you were bulimic. Well duh, I'd be mad too. They simplified everything. But your backlash was very hurtful.

First off, I know your secret. I know you can't be medically bulimic if you also meet criteria for anorexia. Me too! I stuck my fingers down my throat all the time and I wasn't bulimic. Most people don't know what eating disorders are[1] let alone how one receives a "bulimia nervosa" diagnosis. But what pissed me off is when you said that was "DISGUSTING." How could you shame so many women like that, especially when you shared so much in common?? How could you? Then you said you could help girls with anorexia! What???? That convinced me that you wanted to represent the glamorous portrayal of eating disorders. And there's no excusing that, unless you apologize.

♡ KC Elaine

---

[1] I used to be one of these people. I thought that anorexia meant losing a gross amount of weight and bulimia meant puking. I had no idea that eating disorders are more like a spectrum, that they are real and complicated mental illnesses, that individuals can't just stop, and what hell they feel like. I didn't understand until I was sick.

Dear Mary-Kate,

Listen, I don't mean to judge you when I say I know that you didn't go to rehab for your eating disorder. There's nothing to be ashamed of in getting help for a drug problem. I know you had to tell something to the press, so you took the "good girl's" route, and that's okay - because it's none of their damn business. What makes me sad is that we live in a culture that says eating disorders are pretty and drug abusers are evil. Neither is true.

I'm sorry that you grew up under the eye of cameras that told you YOU MUST BE THIN THIN THINNER. That, as a celebrity, you can't really recover from an eating disorder without sleezy tabloids calling you fat. Your career depends on it, and that's tragic. I'm not saying you're not anorexic. I don't really know, but I'm guessing you needed help for that on top of your drug treatment (I stayed where the press waited for you, where all the new admits said, "Is this where Mary-Kate went?")

I wish you could get help for your eating disorder too. I wish the press wouldn't call you recovered and shapely after you gained a measly 6 lbs (so they say) and came out of treatment still underweight. At an eating disorder center they'd make you gain a healthy amount - but the cameras make that so hard for you to do. How is Ashley doing? She's very thin too, but it's probably good the press hasn't noticed. Look out for her, k?

There's something important I need to tell you - recovery really IS possible. Your dad told the press that anorexia is something no one can ever recover from. Doctors used to teach that, but no professional believes that anymore, and people HAVE recovered. Having a parent who is misinformed or doesn't know how to support you is so hard. But don't listen to him. If you want to, you can recover.

Big hug. I don't know much about you, I just think that the media sucks. Thank you for not making any lame statements about eating disorders. If you don't want to talk about it, you don't have to -I really respect that you didn't say degrading or simplistic things about EDs.

♥ KC Elaine

*Dear Kelly Clarkson,*

*I didn't think I liked you until I rocked out to your album in rehab. God those were tough months, but Breakaway was such a "recovery" song for us. I don't even know if you wrote it, but I have to say I loved it.*

*But I'm not sure what your point is with the bulimia story. I'm not sure whether I should only blame the media for what it selected from your interview, or if it's also your fault and the journalist (gasp) gave an accurate portrayal of your words. I dunno, maybe you don't know enough about your own disorder to be ready to talk about it yet. And I respect that, until it starts stereotyping.*

*Here's the deal. You became bulimic for 6 months because you didn't make an audition, and then you snapped out of it cold turkey?? It ain't that simple. Maybe you're one of the rare ones who fits the stereotype, I can't be sure, but eating disorders start from a lot more than not making the stage - self hatred, perfectionism, anxiety, etc etc etc, and I'm VERY happy for you for stopping cold turkey, but for the rest of us it's much, much harder. And now you're one more simple example for people to quote when they say, "Just eat" or, "Snap out of it!"*

*This is tough to write and keep a clear conscience, because I want to validate everyone's experiences. On the other hand, I don't buy that it was so simple, and I hate how the simple examples are exemplified.*

♡ *KC Elaine*

*Alanis*

Dear Kate Winslet,

What can I say, you are my hero! One of many, but you're a big one. You're my ex-Hollywood frontierswoman - you didn't sell your soul. You could have had any role you wanted after Titanic, and you publicly announced that you refuse to starve yourself for a role like that ever again! Thank you for being frank about weight and your eating disorder in the media, for not glamorizing it, for being real, for refusing to lose weight, for stating your disgust at how the media won't stop talking about your weight, for trying to sue when some magazine airbrushed you into someone else (I'm sorry you didn't win!). And you know what? You are BEAUTIFUL. I look at you and starving myself seems crazy. It sounds crazy fan talk, but as a public figure I love you. You take your fame, know that people listen to you, and then use that advantage to say something positive, something constructive, and against what everyone else in your field is doing. That takes courage. Thank you, Kate.

Dear Alanis Morrisette,

Thank you for not being afraid to show your emotions, for being a strong, angry, sensitive, and talented woman, and for not apologizing about that. For not bragging about your eating disorder! I found in an ancient interview how you have suffered from eating disorders - and you were frank, and you said you went to therapy for it. You don't use your weight or your disorder as the selling point for papers. Thanks for not making that the forefront of your career. After all, we're more than our eating disorders. As someone who's been there and knows it hurts - I hope you're recovered.

PS - I saw you with the Barenaked Ladies in LA.
                              You rocked!!!

Love,

                    ♥KC Elaine

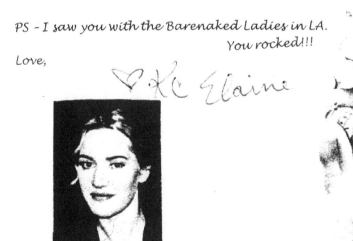

# Mamaphiles #3

PO Box 4803
Baltimore, MD 21211
www.mamaphiles.com
Kate Haas
www.irandazine.com

### I've Earned It
Kate Haas

A couple of weeks before my oldest son started school, we attended a playground get-together for incoming kindergarteners and their parents. After speculation about the teacher and the usual grousing over district enrollment policies, conversation turned toward the momentous step kindergarten represented.

"This is my last kid to start school, " one mother announced, mournfully. "They'll both be gone all day now, and the house will seem so empty. I don't know what I'll do with myself."

I regarded her with envy and some astonishment. "All that time to yourself? To do anything you want? Ooh, you'll find *something* to do," I chortled, giving her the comradely grin of one mother-in-the-trenches to another.

She looked at me as if I'd insinuated that she might take up exotic dancing. "Yeah, I'll find something," she said, stiffly. "I'll keep busy." She moved hastily away.

Clearly I had made a major faux pas. But how?

I have one child in half-day kindergarten and a three-year-old at home who no longer naps. There is rarely a moment in the day when I am not with one or both of them. Although I chose to stay home with my kids and don't regret that choice, I've always treasured solitude, and I never really made my peace with the loss of it that motherhood so abruptly imposes.

My husband and I do our best to spell each other: evenings after supper the boys go to the park with him; some afternoons the three of them set out on a bike ride together, leaving me alone. I savor every moment of these interludes. Finally, a breather. A chance to shed the ever-present parental sense of responsibility and simply exist by myself. My husband knows how precious solitude is to me, and he's generous about making sure I get it. Still, with two active kids and a slew of home improvement projects on the agenda, time alone these days is mostly like bad, teenage sex: unplanned, unpredictable, and it doesn't last long enough.

But this will change. For so long, my youngest boy had been a wispy-haired baby, bouncing along in the backpack while I walked his big brother to school. Then, when Nate turned two, it hit me: eighteen months from now, at three and a half, my baby would start preschool. Eighteen months is a long time, true. But it wasn't beyond the reach of my imagination. He would be in school for three mornings a week. *Let's see, that's ten and a half hours* – I stopped, astonished. Ten and a half hours of free time. Every week! The thought of it made me giddy.

It made my close friends giddy, as well. Their kids are slightly younger than mine, and they've watched me hit the significant milestones first. I've sent back dispatches from the frontiers of weaning, potty-training, big beds, and kindergarten; but nothing looks to provide more vicarious thrills than the scenario of one child in school all day, one in preschool – and no baby at home.

"Just think: you'll be able to take a really long nap, three days in a row!" says the stressed-out mother of a wakeful toddler. "Or go to the library without chasing anyone around," another adds, enviously. "You could watch a movie *all at once*," chimes in a third. We silently contemplate these luxurious scenarios.

For years now, we've been in the thick of hands-on, day-in, day-out mothering. A break in the intensity, even one represented by a few mornings of preschool, has long seemed to all of us like some sort of Holy Grail. Like everyone else, we have ambitions. Some that have long simmered on the back burner, others born more recently out of our experience as mothers. Those hotly anticipated free hours represent a breathing space in which to reconnect with old goals or to embark on newly-planned projects. Until my conversation with the woman at the playground, it had never occurred to me that not all at-home mothers contemplate this stage of life with the same degree of excitement I feel. That there are those who mourn the end of the daily round my friends and I are beginning to chafe under.

A few days later, I encountered another

mother, an older woman whose third and last child was also starting kindergarten this year. Tentatively, I asked whether she had any misgivings about all of her children being in school. She looked at me as if I was crazy.

"Are you kidding? I work part-time from home and now I'll be able to get more done – plus have time for myself." She sized up my three-year-old in his stroller. "Preschool next year?" she asked.

"Yeah. Three mornings. I'll have ten and a half hours a week of free time! Not that I'm counting or anything," I laughed, a bit uneasily.

My new acquaintance looked me in the eye, then leaned closer, as if to impart a hard-won secret. "Listen. You might want to look into part-time work when your baby starts school. And that's fine later on, if you want to. If you need to." Her voice took on the cadence of a preacher or a politician. "But not right away. That first month, enjoy yourself. Watch a movie, go to a bookstore; whatever you want. As long as it's something *just for you*. Because after all these years of changing diapers and cleaning up after those kids, you've earned it. *You've earned it."*

I continued my walk, her words echoing in my ears. Earned it. Have I? Thanks to a combination of luck, location, and frugality, our family can live on one modest income. I do plan to return to work, but not until the boys are a bit older. Theoretically, I could use my free time to eat bonbons and take bubble baths. Have I earned *that*?

More to the point, do I regard the work of motherhood this way? As labor for which I'm racking up invisible points? For which I deserve some compensation beyond that of seeing my children grow up to be decent human beings?

It feels petty to admit, but there's a part of me that does believe a reward is in order. Sure, I do this job for love. But it's work, all the same. I'm not getting a salary for it. Social Security won't credit me for these years at home. Neither am I likely to land a meaningful part-time job during those preschool mornings. Time to myself is the only payment I can expect to receive at this stage. And frankly, from where I stand, time alone ranks right up there with gold.

As a parent, I've put my children's needs before my own, wholeheartedly, day after day, discovering in the process a capacity for acting unselfishly that still surprises me. I don't like to think about how often, lately, it's just an act. After six years, stay-at-home parenting is wearing me down. I love my children dearly, but I don't mind admitting it: not only will my eyes be dry on the first day of preschool, they'll be alive with excitement.

I look forward to coming home from preschool by myself. To going up the steps and opening my front door in thirty seconds, instead of spending five minutes coaxing a toddler into dropping the big stick and coming inside. I want those soul-restoring hours in a quiet house, regularly, day after day. Not with one ear on alert during the unpredictable span of a child's nap. Not hours scrounged at the expense of my partner's need for solitude. Time for me. Time to dig into long, complex novels; to compose that letter to my senator; to write. Time to come home and assess who I am, now that the intensity of the early years has lifted.

Sure, I've earned that.

# Am I Mad...or has the whole world gone crazy?

**850 north 41st street**
**Philadelphia, PA 19104**
**weissman42@gmail.com**
**www.dhruva.vesana.com**

It is not always constructive to obsess
over things that we cannot change.
It is easy to internalize the suffering of
our fellow humans and to be overwhelmed by it.
Yet, on the other hand, ignoring the
results of our actions is no solution.

we have witnessed before the results
of our willing ignorance.

The health of a society--its degree of social well-being--can be gauged best
by observing the condition of its most marginalized and maltreated members.
Holistic health means nothing if all are not well; mind freedom means
nothing if all of us are not free.
Social justice and its pursuit are a pillar of our mental health.
To paraphrase Hellen Keller, happiness is dedication to a worthy cause.

108

# Urban Adventure League

Shawn Granton
PO Box 14185
Portland, OR 97293
tfrindustries@scribble.com

## here is South Portland?

e area once commonly referred to as South Portland is one of
tland's oldest settled districts. Developing along a narrow strip
land hemmed in by the West Hills (Tualatin Mountains) on the
st and the Willamette River on the east, South Portland went
far north as approximately SW Market Street (the 1950-era
uthern limit of the Central Business District), connected to
wntown. The furthest southern extent of the district is the
lwood Bridge, though it could be argued that SW Hamilton
eet was the southern border of the densely populated area.

uth Portland is dominated by its natural features: the hills and
e river. Its area is divided into three zones: the hills; the
rshy river lowlands, or floodplain; and the upland river terrace
tween both, interspersed with little ravines (gulches) where
all brooks flowed from hills to river.

uth Portland was at one time one of the most vital neighborhoods
the city, as vital as anything on the east side is these days.
rough the years, the vitality of this 'hood was sapped due to
rious factors: neglect and neighborhood flight started the process,
d highway building and the ever ubiquitous "urban renewal"
ished the job. By 1970 the integrated urban district of old was no
re.

contemporary times the area between SW Market south to I-405
considered part of downtown. The area south of that is called
ir Hill, and southeast of that (where the Ross Island Bridge on-
mps meet Front Ave.) is called Corbett. The area south of SW
amilton St, where Corbett Av crosses I-5 and drops steeply, is
metimes referred to by its historic name of Terwilliger or Fulton.
e area to the east of that around SW Macadam Ave is known as
hn's Landing. For many years the neighborhood association for
e entire era was known as Lair Hill-Corbett-Terwilliger, but in
06 the association renamed itself South Portland. The name lives
ain.

## The Early Years of South Portland

When the city of Portland was founded in the mid-nineteenth
century, the natural features of the Willamette Valley steered the
direction of its development. The West Hills posed a formidable
barrier to western expansion, and before the bridges and
streetcars opened up the land in East Portland and Albina (now
parts of SE, NE, and North Portland), it was not practical to
expand eastward. The early city expanded laterally along the
west bank of the Willamette, allowing easy access to the river, the
area's main mode of travel.

South Portland was first settled in 1847 by the Caruthers family,
mother Elizabeth and son Finice. The family set up Donation
Land Claims to farm on around what is now the west approach to
the Ross Island Bridge. As young Portland expanded, the
Caruthers found it more profitable to plat the land for
development. Their land was platted in the familiar Portland grid:
200 foot by 200 foot blocks with 60 foot streets. Homes began
to be built in the areas upland while industry took over the
riverbanks.

The area has always been dominated by transportation, starting
in the 1860's when the County Road was "macadamized", or
paved, to allow improved access to Lake Oswego and points
south. The first railroad, the Oregon Central, came in 1868 along
what is now Barbur Blvd. to connect the farmlands of the
Tualitin Valley to the waterfront wharves. This line later became
the Southern Pacific "Red Electric" interurban line. Another
railroad, the Oregon Railroad and Navigation Co., came in 1887,
closer to the river (and paralleling Macadam Ave.) This railroad
still exists, though it is only used for an excursion trolley
(Southern Pacific discontinued freight delivery on the road
around 1984.)

Transportation between South Portland and downtown improved
even more in 1872 when a horse-drawn streetcar travelled south
down SW 1st Avenue to SW Porter St. Another line went in
around 1882 along SW 3rd. Eventually the lines were electrified
in the last decade of the 1800's, and in the early twentieth

century the First Avenue line was extended southward along Corbett Ave. Commercial growth centered around First since it had the best transportation.

The period from roughly 1880 to 1920 was the golden years of South Portland. The transcontinental railroad came to town around 1883, which opened the floodgates to settlement in the metropolitan area. South Portland attracted great numbers of European immigrants, most notably Italians and East European Jews. Many of the new settlers started gardens in the "unusable" areas of the neighborhood (the steep hillsides) and sold the produce in downtown's markets. A community support infrastructure developed to help the new inhabitants cope with this alien land. The churches, synagogues, worker's clubs, and most notably Neighborhood House provided English language and citizenship classes, recreation and care of the children, and a sense of community for the residents.

## Decline and "Renewal"

South Portand's decline (or when South Portland went south, bad pun intended) started right before the Great Depression. The mass influx of European immigration slowed to a trickle, cutting off new settlement in the neighborhood. The children of the foreign-born South Portlanders, instilled with that sense of "upward mobility" that's tied to the American Dream, moved away to nicer suburban neighborhoods. Then came highway building.

The first major project to start dividing and fragmenting the neighborhood was the Ross Island Bridge. Built in 1927, the initial impact to the area was minimal, as the bridge only connected to Corbett Ave and had no other ramps. In 1935, the Southern Pacific "Red Electric" line was abandoned and purchased by the state. The right-of-way became Barbur Blvd, part of the federal highway system (U.S. 99W) and Portland's main artery to Salem and points south. Ross Island Bridge's west approach was modified to allow for increased traffic.

The next step was Harbor Drive (1943), the divided highway where Waterfront Park currently sits. To make a seamless connection to Barbur-US 99W, Front Ave through South Portland was widened and made into a high-speed corridor. This permanently divided Lair Hill from the Corbett district, destroyed buildings, took away the streetcar lines, and hastened the neighborhood decline. To make matters worse, a series of ramps were constructed between Front Ave and the Ross Island Bridge in the early 1950's, clearing away several

blocks and isolating the community more.

The 1950's saw South Portland in sad shape. The southern ha was being divided and decimated by the road construction, whil the northern part was "blighted". The densely packe neighborhood was not desirable to new home buyers, who woul prefer the newer houses and bigger lots in outlying suburba areas. The population that remained was primarily the foreign born immigrants from the turn of the century. Lonely hote housed single elderly folk, and the commercial concerns locate throughout were the type that relied on the area's cheap rent t survive.

Around this time the idea of urban renewal was brought to th table. Mayor Terry Schrunk was elected in 1957 and made it high-priority during his sixteen-year term to improve th condition of the city. South Portland, like Albina i North/Northeast Portland was considered by the powers-that-b to be "hopelessly beyond repair", and he thought only way t solve the problem and stave off further decline was to clea everything away and start anew. This line of thinking wa further encouraged by federal incentives, as there was plenty o money flowing from Washington towards urban renewal, an further distilled by people like Ira Keller, high-powered Portlan businessman and eventual head of the Portland Developmen Commission.

In 1956 the city designated 54 blocks of land in South Portland from SW Market in the north to SW Arthur in the south, betwee SW 4th Ave and Harbor Drive, as an "urban renewal district". I May of that year, money for renewal was awarded by the federa government, and the project moved ahead.

Named the "South Auditorium" Urban Renewal District due t the fact Civic (Keller) Auditorium was located just to its nort at Market and 3rd, Schrunk, Keller, and the council went to se the project to the city. The district's poor shape was over emphasized through brochures photographing some of th worst-off buildings. Knowing that not all the buildings wer dilapidated, South Auditorium's boosters noted that even th best were from an earlier era, "some even fifty or more year old", appealing to the Postwar citizen's obsession wit modernity. To further dissipate lingering doubt (and to remin Portlanders of the city's stodgy reputation and its perennia "second-banana" ranking next to Seattle), the boosters warned *"Portland can't afford to be a horse-and-buggy city in this atomi age."* (actual quote from the literature) The project won th approval of the city at large, overcome with the urge to "Perk U

rtland". In May 1958, a vote (Proposition 52) to authorize
e district and the creation of the Portland Development
mmission passed.

e residents of the South Auditorium district were not
eased, however. There was little chance for public input
ring the planning stages of the project, and by the time the
sidents realized what was happening it was too late. Some
uth Portlandites organized under the banner of the Property
vners Committee and attempted to find relief from the plan.
ayor Schrunk bluntly told them their plan was "a backward
ep." The City government was not to be swayed. "Progress"
on out.

1963 all of the land within the urban renewal district had
en purchased, the residents relocated, and the structures
eared. On August 20, 1964, groundbreaking ceremonies were
ld for the new development, and construction began
ereafter. The design for South Auditorium was a mix of high-
se apartments, hotels, and office towers. Most of the streets
the project area were vacated, leaving only SW Harrison and
ncoln to traverse the zone. However, tree-lined pedestrian
alks cut through the blocks, following the rights-of-way of
e old streets and leading to well-hidden parks. The area is
ean and sterile, lacking the vitality of a true neighborhood,
neighborhood like the one it replaced. Oregon's largest
ewish and Italian district was forever erased from the map.
rban renewal did not stop there. While construction of South
uditorium was progressing, the PDC designated the areas just
orth of the district as urban renewal zones as well. The low-
se structures gave way to the sparkling "new downtown" we
now today. Portland State College (now University), to the
est of South Auditorium, expanded from its Lincoln Hall
cation in the later 1960's. Its growth spread southward along
e park blocks and westward into Goose Hollow, razing houses
nd small buildings for larger campus structures.

The last piece of the puzzle for the transformation of South
Portland was the construction of the Interstate Highway system.
I-405, the Stadium Freeway, was completed in the mid-1960's.
Its route, looping around downtown from the west, cut through
the South Auditorium district (its route planned into the
construction), and displaced more buildings to the west
(including two blocks worth of the South Park Blocks). The
segment of I-5 known as the Baldock (or Salem) Freeway was also
built around this time, using another old rail alignment that cut
through South Portland near Hamilton St. The Marquam Bridge
was completed in 1966, adding to the hopeless tangle of ramps
that came to define the area.

As the sixties drew to a close, the public began to realize that
mass-renewal projects and freeway building could do more harm
than good. Yet the government infrastructure—and money—to
keep on steaming ahead with renewal was still in place. In 1968
Lair Hill came into the radar of the renewal machine. It was
deemed as unsatisfactory in its current state, and the city decided
the neighborhood should be cleared and rebuilt with low-density
apartments or high-rises for students and/or elderly. When the
residents found out, they blew up. Determined to not have their
neighborhood go down the same road as South Auditorium, they
effectively organized and stopped the project from coming to
fruition. In 1977, the city council named Lair Hill a "historic
conservation district". The tide had turned, and preservation and
rehabilitation of a district was valued more than clearance and
reconstruction.

South Portland is still seeing its share of new development,
however. The South Waterfront Project looks to repeat the Pearl
District along the long-ignored riverfront. Oregon Health
Sciences University is expanding, the arial tram over the
neighborhood connecting it to the new waterfront.

# One Way Ticket #5

Julian Evans
1610 Rue Notre-Dame
Ouest, Suite 119
Montreal, QC H3J 1M1

# Mathematicians.

Alexander Grothendieck, one of the most influential mathematicians of the twentieth century, lives in a remote hamlet somewhere in the south of France, enjoying his solitude and entertaining no visitors. He was born in 1928, in Berlin, to Hanka Grothendieck and Alexander Shapiro, both anarchists. His father, a Russian Jew, participated in uprisings against the Czar at the turn of the century. He was in and out of prison, narrowly escaped a death sentence, and had only one arm due to a failed suicide attempt. He tried to kill himself in order to avoid being arrested, but failed and instead cut off his own arm. Around 1921 he escaped prison again and fled from Russia, spending time in France, Belgium and Germany associating with many different anarchist groups. He met Hanka Grothendieck in the mid 1920s in Berlin, as they were both part of the same radical and anarchist circles. Hanka was born in 1900 to a bourgeois family of Lutherans in Hamburg, and she rebelled against her parents by moving to Berlin to become active in avant-guard and revolutionary social

movements. She wrote many articles for anarchist newspapers including a piece that defended the rights of prostitutes. In 1933, both of Alexander Grothendieck's parents went to fight in the Spanish Civil War, and so they placed him with a foster family. They fled Spain when Franco came to power, settling in Paris. Upon arrival they sent for their son, who met them by train. After only three years living together, France was occupied by the Nazis during World War II and the family was placed into internment camps, Hanka Grothendieck and her son separated from Alexander Shapiro. He was deported in 1942 to Auschwitz by the French authorities, where he was killed.

Hanka Grothendieck and her son were eventually also separated, the young Alexander being sent to a school in Chambon-sur-Lignon. Lucky for him, a Protestant pastor in charge of the school resisted the Nazis by protecting Jews. During Nazi raids, Alexander had to hide out in the surrounding wilderness with his fellow Jewish students, sometimes for days at a time. When the war ended in 1945, he was reunited with his mother and at the age of seventeen enrolled in the University of Montpelier, where he began studying mathematics. He went on to study in Paris and make significant contributions to the field, first becoming an expert in the theory of "topological vector spaces." He then began work on algebraic geometry and homological algebra, work that would gain him widespread notoriety, some comparing his advancements in mathematics to Einstein's work in physics.

He inherited the radicalism of his parents somewhat, and became known as an eccentric character in the scientific community, prompting wild rumors concerning his personal life. During this early time in the university, a colleague commented

on how he made a point of not having any rugs in his house because they were "unnecessary." He was also said to wear sandals made out of tires, and a close friend noted he was "always an anarchist at heart." Later on, he gave lectures in Hanoi, the capital of Vietnam, as it was being bombarded during the Vietnam War, in an act of protest. Around this time, influenced in part by the massive social upheaval in Paris, May '68, he started a group of politically engaged scientists who published a journal concerning the pressing dangers of nuclear annihilation and ecological destruction. In 1970 he largely withdrew from the university as a protest of the growing role of military funding in the academy, continuing his work in mathematics on an individual basis. He refused the prestigious Crafoord Prize in 1988 on ethical grounds, saying in a letter that the rising militarization of the scientific community might well lead to the destruction of civilization.

In 1991, rumor has it, he left his house and disappeared. He is said to live an isolated existence, completely withdrawn from public life, while still being widely regarded as one of the most influential mathematicians of modern times. He wrote in his autobiography:

"And every science, when we understand it not as an instrument of power and domination but as an adventure in knowledge pursued by our species across the ages, is nothing but this harmony, more or less vast, more or less rich from one epoch to another, which unfurls over the course of generations and centuries, by the delicate counterpoint of all the themes appearing in turn, as if summoned from the void."

\* \* \*

Mirrors in strange places. Upstate New York. Another highway onramp. Another cardboard sign. A sunny September day, my steady smile working its magic on my outstretched thumb. That moment of eye contact. A pause, a projection of hope, a rising internal expectation most often crushed. But this time, someone actually stops. I run up and get in.

"Where you headed," I ask, like a ritual. We're already speeding down the interstate.

"I'm going to the casino. I have a gambling problem." I'm a little startled by this little confession, relayed without a moment's hesitation. I find out that we're almost the exact same age, born within a few months of each other. He's already graduated from some military mechanics school, and has just started a job where he makes sixty thousand dollars a year. He's married and expecting a child. Our close proximity of age makes me think about how our lives measure up. I've just dropped out of university for the second time, have worked only a few months in the last few years, and am moving across the country just to be with someone who makes me feel happy and alive. A lot is up in the air for me, to say the least, and this guy appears to have it all figured out. At least I'm not addicted to gambling—just hitchhiking.

He drops me off at a "really good spot" somewhere outside Albany, once again proving the golden rule—never trust anyone who picks you up to be an accurate judge of the highly sought after and always illusive "good spot." This spot was by no stretch of the imagination "good," there was a concrete wall where the shoulder should have been, and all the traffic was coming from another highway and going way too fast. I hop some fences and walk across a field to the interstate, bushwhacking through some brambles and bushes to make it there. Now, the "interstate vs. onramp" controversy is one of my favorite examples of the widely divergent opinions on what is the best strategy for hitchhiking. I'm a firm believer in the onramp, and it's usually the best way to not get hassled by the cops, but I have definitely met a few devote believers who maintain hitching directly on the interstate is the way to go. Honestly, it just sort of freaks me out to be standing beside so many cars going so fast. So when there's no onramp to speak of, like in my present situation, I try to walk along the interstate to the next exit with my thumb out, hoping that there will be a better spot up ahead, but open to the minute possibility someone might stop right on the freeway. I've realized over the years how stubborn and obsessive I am about little details—having a sign, the right spot, onramps vs. interstates. I've met a lot of people who seem to just stick their thumb out and not think about it. I also know a lot of people who've given up on this essentially uncertain form of travel, and I haven't.

So I'm half-heartedly sticking my thumb out while walking down the interstate and what do you know, against my stubborn obsessive desire to get to the next exit, someone veers out of the thick, fast moving traffic and comes to a stop far up in front of me. I run up and am overjoyed at how easy that was, I'd only been walking for five minutes or so. Maybe my onramp doctrine should be rethought? Who knows. I reach my head in and inquire as to the driver's destination, and discover that he'll take me straight to Manhattan. Hot damn.

Peter is a mathematician from the Czech republic, who has been visiting friends in Canada and is driving to New York for a mathematics conference in a rental car. It's nice to be picked up by someone who is very interesting to talk to and exhibits a passion for his chosen profession, but also someone who doesn't question my method of travel but takes it as a given. I ask about his work and he tries to explain his latest research in algebraic K theory, which mostly goes over my head.

"Have you ever taken calculus?" he asks, as he tries to explain himself. When I say no his brow furrows slightly and he goes on, "this might be tricky…" I ask him about chaos theory and he seems to think that it was mostly a fad of the late eighties. Despite the charismatic portrayal of said theory by Jeff Goldbloom in *Jurassic Park*, sparking excitement in my twelve year old brain, Peter insists it's not all that cutting edge anymore. Don't tell Hakim Bey. I think about how scientific theories get popularized and diluted to the point where the meaning is obscured enough to make good conversation at parties, but not much else. And here I am talking to someone who has immersed his entire life into mathematical theory and he quickly dismisses something I've been intrigued about for years.

We talk about politics and he tells me about Alexander Grothendieck and his anarchist parents. He tells me how influential some of Grothendieck's work has been on himself and others in his field. This curious figure in the history of mathematics surprises me. Peter recounts anecdotes and explains the eccentric approach Grothendieck had to science in general, his commitment to politics, his withdrawal from academia, his disappearance and self imposed isolation.

The beauty of stories—an accidental and contingent sort of knowledge transmission. If I'd waited five minutes I'd never have heard this story. The influential mathematician of our times born to anarchists, who would have thought? Peter asks me about my political beliefs and I try to summarize my own anarchism for him. He's curious and asks thoughtful questions rather than offering disagreements. Before too long we're approaching the city and he wants me to navigate. I do my best at weaving us through New Jersey and finally into the Lincoln Tunnel. He actually seems quite thankful to have me here, and keeps insisting I've been a huge help.

He makes his way to the hotel where he's meeting his mathematician friends before the conference tomorrow. We see a sign for the subway and he lets me out, a quick handshake and we're on our way, our separate paths.

We experience these tiny slivers of other people's lives through brief moments of connection, and from that the imagination runs wild. We create ourselves as the link between these accidental stories, these fractures and incomplete understandings of the world. I walk the streets of Manhattan wanting only to hang on to this fleeting mystery, the story we can tell over and over again without ever really capturing the magic of it. It's easy to measure your own story, to calculate the equations. To live absorbed by these numbers. Even mathematicians can find adventure when summoned from the void. I want to live like this. Beyond measure, beyond calculation. And that might just be what awaits on the horizon, just across the country…

# My Story of Mitch's Accident

Jennifer Robertson
lefthandeddrawing@gmail.com
www.jenniferrobertson.com

## CRITICAL CARE

On Wednesday I was visiting my parents house when Jeremy called. He said he had some bad news, and was I sitting down? He told me that last Friday night, while biking home from the bonfire, Mitch had been hit by a drunk driver. He was currently in the Critical Care unit of Victoria Hospital's Westminister Campus. He had not suffered any brain injury, but had broken several vertibrae and was paralyzed from the neck down. The doctors estimated a 1% chance he would ever walk again.

Its been a really long time since I cried that hard.

growth ~ ... part found with the spore-bearing organs of some ... and mosses
**par·a·ple·gi·a** (par′ə plē′jē ə, -jə) *n.* [ModL. < Gr. *paraplēgiē*, a stroke at one side: see PARA-¹ & -PLEGIA] motor and sensory paralysis of the entire lower half of the body —**par′a·ple′gic** (-plē′jik, -plej′ik) *adj., n.*
**par·a·prax·is** (-prak′sis) *n., pl.* -es (-sēz) [PARA-¹ + PRAXIS] an action in which one's conscious intention is not fully carried out, as in the mislaying of objects, slips of the ... pen, etc.: thought to be generally due to a ... intention: also **par′a·prax′i·a** (-sē ə)

*partite* pact.]
**quad·ri·ple·gi·a** (-plē′jē ə, -jə) *n.* [ModL.: see QUADRI- & -PLEGIA] total paralysis of the body from the neck down —**quad′ri·ple′gic** (-plē′jik, -plej′ik) *adj., n.*
**quad·ri·sect** (kwäd′rə sekt′) *vt.* [< QUADRI- + L. *sectus*, pp. of *secare*, to cut: see SAW] to divide into four equal parts

I didn't know what to do.

There was nothing I could do; Jeremy had said he wouldn't be able to have visitors for at least 2 more weeks.

I was useless all Thursday and Friday thinking about it. My kind-hearted boss let me off work early on Friday afternoon because there wasn't much to do and I was a wreck anyway. My boss has a good friend who fell off a balcony at 21 years old and has been a quadriplegic since then. I got a lot of sympathy and worrisome stories from him.

Human Spinal Column. — *A*, side view; *C*, front view; *c*, seven cervical vertebrae; *d*, twelve dorsal; *l*, five lumbar; *s*, five sacral, fused in a sacrum; *cd*, four caudal or coccygeal, forming a coccyx.

I sat at home worrying until I got up the nerve to call Critical Care and ask how he was doing. The nurse on duty was cold at first, and told me she couldn't release any information about his condition if I wasn't a family member. I pressed her, and she eventually told me that the operation he had undergone that day to install a steel rod in his neck in hopes of stabilizing it had gone well. She said he was fairly stable, awake and alert at times.

I asked her to tell him I'd called for him, I said, "Tell him its Jen, his dance partner." That seemed to catch her sympathy, and she said, "Well, just hold on a minute and let me ask him..." When she came back on the line she said he'd given a big smile when she'd told him I was on the line, and that I could come in and visit him for a few minutes if I wanted.

I was amazed at the complete about-face, but I got on my bike (with helmet and blinking lights and more than a little hesitation) and headed to the hospital.

I met Gord in the waiting room and we went in together. I didn't know what to expect, but I must have been prepared for the worst because I was actually cheered by seeing him.

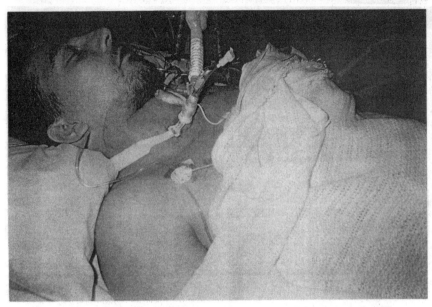

He was lying on his back, bandaged in a lot of places, with a trach and an IV and breathing with an oxygen mask. A suction tube that ran into his mouth was constantly removing spit and phlegm.

I think the thing I was shocked by the most was how swelled he was. It looked like his whole body had inflated by 2 inches all over. His fingers were like sausages, his neck like a meaty college football player. They told me it was a reaction to the large blood transfusion he had received during the operation.

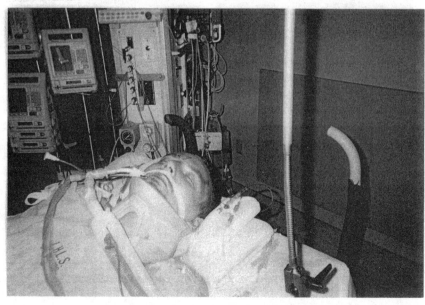

He couldn't talk because of the trach in his throat, but he tried to mouth some words to me. They were nearly impossible to understand because of the tube in his mouth, but it was something about dancing.

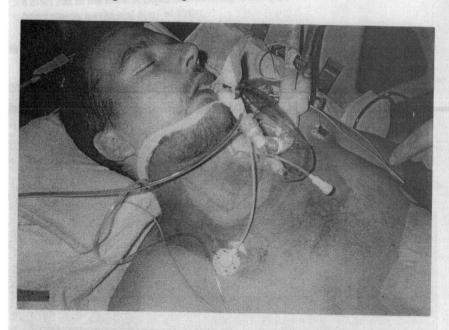

Gord got out a clipboard with a chart of letters and we tried to get Mitch to spell a short message through a system of us scrolling over the alphabet and him blinking when we came to the next letter he wanted to use. It didn't work that well, so eventually we settled for holding his hands and smiling at him.

On March 30th we held the first real Critical Mass ride of the Spring..... and Mitch lead the ride. His new wheelchair can go up to 15 clicks; we had been experimenting in Springbank park earlier in the week, and figured it could handle the speed and the hills pretty well, and the battery barely used one bar of power in 5 hours. The potholes on Dundas street were the biggest problem....hes got some mad shocks on the chair, but its still hard on his neck. It was a pretty spectacular Critical Mass; just six months after his accident, and Mitch was back on wheels with us.

There's still a long road to go on this recovery, but Mitch has come through the first of it with flying colours. We're still waiting for his fingers to regain mobility, but the physiotherapist has told him that it takes between 18 and 24 months for nerve tissue to begin to grow again.... So about a year from now he should be starting to write, play guitar and massage people again. He's also been looking into stem cell procedures currently being researched in the US and China. By the time his body has done as much recovery as it can on its own, there might be other options for treatment. If you ask the doctors... well, they won't say one way or the other what his chances of walking again are. But if you ask Mitch, its only a matter of time, and I expect he's the one that knows best.

# When You Can't Stand Yourself, Go Outside

Shawn Granton
PO Box 14185
Portland, OR 97293

# Sourpuss #1

Robyn Chapman
PO Box 204
White River Junction, VT 05001

I have no idea why my parents chose to live here.

Why anyone would choose to live here, why this stupid town even exists is beyond me.

Nothing ever happens here.

It's like living in a black hole

A black hole inhabited by rednecks and white trash.

# Old Weird America #2

**Rosie White**
**PO Box 6598**
**New York, NY 10150**

THE PEEP SHOW

7.21.06

"When I was sixteen, I visited Times Square before it got cleaned up, when you could put in a quarter for a peep show," Stephan said once. "And for a dollar, the partition slid up, and you could *touch*."

Now, I'm an anonymous peepshow girl. The peep show seems so antiquated, so mildly naughty if you consider all the other vices you could engage in here; I'm surprised people still pay money to see a naked girl behind glass. The anonymous, transactional nature of the setup is what makes it so seedy, and it's also what I find so attractive: I don't have to talk to anyone, or hustle, or be social. I just sit, look at the *Times*, and wait to be chosen.

Walk up to the second floor of Exxxotica Video at any time of the day or night and they'll be there, one or three or six girls, just waiting. They come from all over: Queens, the Bronx, the homeless shelter down the street. They have kids and bills and girlfriends and husbands. They're eighteen, twenty-five, forty years old, black, white, Puerto Rican, Haitian, Cherokee, or a mix of all of these.

We get on the microphone to encourage potential customers to come up: *Gentlemen, don't forget, we have live, nude girls upstairs, waiting to give you a fantasy peep show…"* Sometimes we get bored: *Gentlemen, please don't forget that ten percent of the profits of every peepshow go towards a good cause. That's right, we're helping underprivileged New York children learn how to read.*

The weirdest is working the graveyard shift, usually with one other girl, but sometimes by yourself, listlessly watching the customers on the other two floors of the store on the full-color video monitors. A wayward person will wander up: "Just you tonight?" "Yes." "Can I get a show?" "OK."

Or, perhaps they'll be dissatisfied with their lack of choice: after coming up the stairs, they'll look at me for a few moments, surveying the lone merchandise——*I've got a monopoly on the market tonight!*— then turn around abruptly.

"I was looking for a black girl," they might say. "I was looking for a thicker girl with more flava." "I'm more into blondes… no offense." "Is Green Eyes around tonight?" Or, my favorite: "You got any other girls here?"

"Do you *see* any other girls?" I ask.

"Naw."

"Then there aren't any." Other girls are more abrupt: "The fuck outta here," they'll say.

Girls might sit for six, seven hours and not do a single show, or just do one show: that's thirty bucks. Or, you might be inexplicably popular that night, and make several hundred dollars. That's the excitement and the cruelty of the job: you just never know.

You never know, for example, when something like this might happen: a large, fortyish gentleman comes in with his companion, a middle-aged Hispanic woman dressed conservatively and elaborately made up. He asks Nelly for a show, and asks me if I'll give a show to his lady friend.

Sure, we say, whatever. I figure that they're a couple out to "spice things up" for the night, but when I see him giving the woman two fifty-dollar bills—he is paying me, and also paying *her* to watch *me*—I realize that they barely know each other, and that she must be an escort.

Once we're in the booths, the woman watches me dance patiently, with the serenity of somebody who is being paid by the hour. She keeps her hands clasped formally in front of her, as if she's in school and trying pay attention to an important lesson even though she has no idea what's being said.

In the booth next to me, where Nelly is dancing, the gentleman is shaking cocaine out of a plastic bag onto a clenched first, snorting one, two, three, four, *five* bumps in the span of a minute. I can hear him talking: "OK, hon, thanks a lot. Why don't you get your friend in here?"

That's me. She knocks on my door, and I unlock and open it. "He wants us to switch," she says breathlessly. "Quick!" I go into her booth, and he knocks on the window, putting forty dollars into the money slot. "Thanks," I say; he's given me a ten-dollar tip.

I start to do my show, and he knocks on the window again, this time offering fifty, no, a hundred dollars, shoving the bills through the slot. "Thank you very much," I stammer, and start my show again, figuring that I better do a damned good one. About a minute later, he knocks on the window again: "I have to go!" he says, jittery now. "My friend, she needs to leave! I have to respect her time, OK!" From inside the booth, I can hear them leaving, rushing out, and the frenzy is over as quickly as it began.

Nelly and I, after getting dressed, emerge from our adjoining booths at the same time, both with a handful of bills. Even the security guard got tipped; he still seems a little shellshocked.

"Ok," she says. "What the *hell* was that?"

When I was sixteen, I visited New York and put ten dollars in the machine to see a naked girl in a peep show...

123

# There & Back

Zora Moniz
1636 Fairview St.
Berkeley, CA 94703
tomas.moniz@gmail.com
www.raddadzine.blogspot.com

**Soccer, Compost Toilets, and Vegan Restaurants:**
... zora

Okay, dad was talking about this trip for a while and I didn't think it would actually happen. Clover, my best friend, was talking about getting ipods for Christmas (or Rainbow as my dad calls it) and we would use them on our trip to Canada. The next thing I know we're on the road and in our ugly mini-van with my dad, Tomas, Artnoose, a friend, Clover, and I, Zora. We actually got $100 (halleluiah, halleluiah!!!!!) for our trip and we spent the rest we had (which probably was $85) in Seattle at an Asian mall. Most of it on candies that we have never heard of, and experimentally tried them. Artnoose brought a pirate soccer ball and together we kicked some pirate booty! For dinners we usually had vegan Chinese food (considering most of us are vegetarian or vegan). Over our many days on our trip we experienced many different toilets but

our very favorite one was on Denman Island. When I first heard it was a compost toilet I said "cool." but when I tried it, it wasn't so cool. I was confused "How do you do this!" I thought and finally pushed through this compost confusion. I really enjoyed this adventure and want to say thank you to everyone who let us stay with them.

**How to Use a Compost Toilet:** ... not by zora

Before starting to use the latrine, each chamber is half filled with straw, twigs or dry leaves. These provide the necessary additional carbon to the composting process and along with the faeces will compost down to a fraction of their original volume. Occasionally additional straw may be added through the faeces hole if the contents of the chamber start to become wet or slightly odorous. Squat and defecate in the defecation hole and urinate in the urine funnel. After each use, a spoonful of dry cooking ashes or lime should be sprinkled down the faeces hole which is then closed using a simple cover. Wash hands with soap and water.

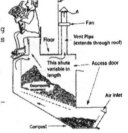

And check out more on the benefits of humanure:

http://www.weblife.org/humanure/

**What I got to do over my spring break:** ... clover

Ok first of all just to let everyone know this trip was one of the funnest I've ever taken. I met so many awesome people and did things I had never done. From playing soccer in various places to consuming very large creampuffs, all the things I will probably remember for a long time if not forever. I can't tell you how many nights we drove, singing along to fergilicious or trying as hard as we could to stump Artnoose. Me and Zora played scrabble so many times

that even though we're not spelling geniuses we're pretty close. Once we went to a house with a composting toilet, I think this was a interesting experience for all of us. We got used to staying in pajamas all day and riding in the car for up to eight hours. When we went to Seattle(which you should definitely go there if you haven't already) me and Zora went a little crazy at an Asian mall, spending $75 each on assortments of Japanese candy and erasers. While Tom and Artnoose read, me and Zora set up the merch table, read, and memorized their readings so that by end of the trip we could recite it back to them. All of this was what made the trip funny and enjoyable, and even if we had to eat at vegan restaurants and all, I had a really cool time.

**10 best things about the trip to Canada (and everything in between)** ... clover

1. I got to meet a bunch of really cool people and I got to spend lots of time with my bestest friend
2. I went to places I had never gone to before like Oregon, Washington, and Canada
3. Me and Zora met lots of adorable babies and friendly kids
4. Me and Zora went to some awesome books stores.
5. I got way better at Scrabble
6. We ate a life time supply of vegan doughnuts

7. Me and Zora went crazy and spent most of our money at a Japanese mall
8. Me and Zora had a chance to eat the largest creampuff we have ever ate (and even though we thought it would never happen we never wanted to eat one again)
9. I finished learning the words to our theme song: "Fergilicious"
10. Me and Zora got to play the Nintendo wii and I almost died of laughter when zora did the Wario dance

# NW Research Journal of John Travolta

**Love Shack Productions**
**Emily J Egbert**
**4127 NE Mallory Ave**
**Portland, OR 97211**
**dietcokeface@yahoo.com**

MYSTERIOUS TATTOO INSPIRED FILM "PULP FICTION"
"I SAW THIS [TATTOO] AND I WROTE THAT [MOVIE]" TARANTINO EXPLAINS.

# Phase 7 #11

Alec Longstreth
5309 Lansdowne Lane
Mercer Island, WA 98040
alec@alec-longstreth.com

NEXT I HAD TO **DISTRIBUTE** THE COMIC, SO PEOPLE COULD READ IT!

HEH HEH... I'LL DO IT **DRUG DEALER** STYLE... THE FIRST ONE'S FREE!

ON MY LUNCH BREAKS I MAILED OUT COPIES TO MY FRIENDS, FAMILY AND ANY COMICS ARTIST THAT I ADMIRED WHO HAD THEIR ADDRESS LISTED IN THEIR COMIC BOOK.

MUNCH MUNCH MUNCH

MUNCH MUNCH

NEXT!

I ALSO SENT A FEW COPIES TO MY FRIENDS IN OTHER CITIES, THUS BEGINNING THE **PHASE 7 STREET TEAM!**

OKAY, I'LL TAKE THESE COPIES OVER TO QUIMBY'S FOR YOU.

THANKS CHARLOTTE!

ALL THAT REMAINED WAS TO DISTRIBUTE PHASE 7 **LOCALLY.**

COMICS

GULP!

DING

HELLO!

H...HI!

IS THERE ANYTHING I CAN HELP YOU WITH?

UM...

W...WELL...SEE, I DREW THIS **COMIC BOOK** AND UH... I WAS WONDERING IF M...MAYBE YOU GUYS WOULD WANT TO C...CARRY IT...?

WELL, LET'S TAKE A LOOK.

OKAY...

HMM! THIS LOOKS PRETTY COOL.

REALLY?

YEAH, WE'LL TAKE... FIVE COPIES.

YOU **WILL**?!

SURE! AND YOU GET FIFTY PERCENT OF THE COVER PRICE, SO THAT'S... SEVEN-FIFTY.

!

CA-CHING!

OH! AND WE'RE PUTTING ON A MINI-COMICS CONVENTION IN BURBANK NEXT WEEK. YOU SHOULD COME!

ALL THE TABLES ARE BOOKED BUT YOU COULD STILL COME AND TRADE COMICS WITH PEOPLE.

COOL, I WILL! **THANKS!**

MY FIRST SALE!!!

MY GIRLFRIEND AND I ARE TRYING TO GET TO THE QUEER HIP HOP SHOW IN BERKELEY. WE ARE CURRENTLY AT "QUEERUPTION," A RADICAL, DIY FESTIVAL FOR QUEERS THAT INCLUDES WORKSHOPS, SQUATTING, DUMPSTERING, KINKY SEX ETC... QUEERUPTION TAKES PLACE EVERY SUMMER AT A DIFFERENT LOCATION, SUCH AS LONDON, BARCELONA....

SO ANYWAYS, WE ARE GETTING OUT OF A WORKSHOP IN SAN FRANCISCO AND ARE TRYING TO HITCH A RIDE ACCROSS THE BRIDGE. WE END UP IN A CAR FULL OF STRANGERS, A GROUP OF PEOPLE WHO SPEAK IN THE LANGUAGE OF THEIR OWN INSIDE JOKE. AS THE 1970'S KEY LIME VOLVO ZOOMS OVER THE BRIDGE, MY GIRLFRIEND AND I ARE TOLD "WE NEED TO STOP OVER AT DADDY'S HOUSE IN OAKLAND FOR A SECOND BEFORE WE HEAD TO BERKELEY. DADDY'S SICK."

WHO IS THIS "DADDY" AND WHY IS "DADDY" SICK?

IN OAKLAND, WE ARE LED TO A ONE STORY, 1970'S HOUSE, THAT HAS THE SAME FEELING AS THE KEY LIME GREEN VOLVO. INSIDE THE CLUTTERED LIVINGROOM THERE IS A BESPECLED GENTLEMAN WITH A HARE KRISHNA HAIR CUT LAYING DOWN ON A SLING. A SHORT

DYKE WITH A BUNCH OF MISSING TEETH COMES UP TO ANNOUNCE TO US THAT "DADDY" IS INDEED SICK, WITH THE FLU. MY GIRLFRIEND AND I FOLLOW A BUNCH OF PEOPLE INTO A CANDLE LIT ROOM. SPRAWLED ON A KING SIZE FUTON IS DADDY, A BIG OL' BALD BUTCH DYKE WITH A CUTE BEARD. DADDY IS COVERED, HEAD TO TOE, IN THICK STEEL PIERCINGS AND TATTOOS. DADDY KINDA LOOKS LIKE A QUEER PUNK BUDDHA STATUE.

"YES, YES... COME." DADDY SAYS, NOW PETTING HEADS. THERE IS A SWARM OF RANDOM QUEER PEOPLE OF ALL SHAPES AND

SIZES ON THE FUTON PETTING AND CUDDLING DADDY. MY GIRLFRIEND AND I ARE MOTIONED TO JOIN AND "HELP MAKE DADDY FEEL BETTER." WE DECLINE.

MY GIRLFRIEND AND I HEAD TO THE KITCHEN, BIDING OUR TIME, WONDERING WHEN WE WILL GET TO BERKELY FOR THE QUEER HIP HOP PARTY. THEN, THE DYKE WITH THE MISSING TEETH COMES UP TO US WITH A GROCERY BAG. SHE PULLS OUT AN ENTIRE CHICKEN FLESH, WITH LEGS. AS A LOVER OF MY FEATHERED FRIENDS AND HARDCORE TOFU LOVER, IMMEDIATELY I FEEL ....UM... LIKE I WANT TO HURL AND STRANGLE THESE PEOPLE.

"DADDY'S REALLY SICK SO I'M GOING TO MAKE CHICKEN NOODLE SOUP TO MAKE DADDY FEEL ALL BETTER." SHE SAYS AS SHE TAKES THE CHICKEN OUT OF THE PLASTIC WRAPPER.

I WONDER WHAT MAKES DADDY SPECIAL? IS IT BECUZ DADDY LOOKS LIKE BUDDHA? I WONDER, ARE THESE MY PEOPLE? DO I HAVE TO BE INTO THIS SHIT TO BE A RADICAL QUEER?

SHE, THE DYKE WITH THE MISSING TEETH, HOVERS OVER A MASSIVE POT WITH BOILING WATER. BEFORE SHE DUMPS THE CHICKEN IN, SHE TAKES TWO FINGERS AND BEGINS TO FUCK THE CHICKEN'S HOLE. SHE IS LAUGHING, HOLLERING, AND HAVING A GRAND 'OL TIME. THEN (AND I KID YOU NOT!) SHE STUFFS HER ENTIRE HAND IN THE CHICKEN'S HOLE. YES, SHE IS NOW FIST FUCKING THE CHICKEN.

"THIS IS TO MAKE SURE DADDY IS ALL BETTER!" SHE SEZ RIGHT BEFORE DUMPING THE CHICKEN INTO THE POT. JUST IN THE NICK OF TIME, A BUNCH OF PEOPLE COME OUT OF DADDY'S ROOM. I SURE HOPE THEY ARE HERE TO SAVE ME! BUT NO! INSTEAD, THEY GRAB MY GIRLFRIEND AND I AND START FORCE-DRAGGING US TO DADDY'S ROOM. "NO! NO! I DON'T WANT TO GO!" I PLEAD. SOON ENOUGH, MY GIRLFRIEND AND I ARE ON THE FLOOR, PULLING AWAY. THEN.... A MIRACLE OCCURS, SOMEBODY KNOCKS ON THE FRONT DOOR. THEY ARE READY TO TAKE US TO THE WEARHOUSE IN BERKELEY FOR THE QUEER HIP HOP SHOW. SEE YA LATER "DADDY."

# Dorothea #1

**Mike Baker**
**PO Box 1174**
**Tallahassee, FL 32302**
**gomek@comcast.net**

## ICE CoLD SoDAS

We had been driving home from my mother's funeral, when we passed a sign for YeeHaw Junction which consists of four buildings and a stoplight. You might have seen a postcard for the Desert Inn. A waitress at the hotel bar told me the place had been a whorehouse in the 30's and for $5.00 they have a tour of the rooms which you'd only know about if you'd been there.

The town also boasted a gas station that was open and an auto parts store that wasn't. There was a fourth building caving in on itself but no one at the bar remembered what it had been.

I bought some cokes and went back outside. My wife and I sat for a while, our car parked on the high end of the north/south axis. I had buried my mom that morning, and for some reason, YeeHaw Junction is where I remembered that I had buried her.

My father, my sister, my brother and I sat in folding plastic party chairs slumped back and exhausted while everyone else stood sweating in the sun. This had been the third service we all attended as my Mother had family all over the place and none seemed inclined to travel.

This time, the actual funeral, we got to bury her or rather two black men dressed like janitor lay in the dirt lowering my mom's ash's tiny urn into the ground by hand. One fella had to poke his head into the hole and then had to dust his hair out afterward.

People threw flowers in over the urn which filled the hole up pretty quick with stems flowing over and out, spilling onto the grass so that when they shoveled on fresh earth, one of the grave diggers had to stomp the dirt down crushing rosebuds and daisies and leaves.

My wife told me, as we sat staring over the flat grass plains around Yeehaw, that when everyone went up to sprinkle a holy water cross over the cardboard box my mom's ashes rested in, my wife spritzed the holy water out in the shape of a smiley face. My Mom would have liked that. The water was in one of those tubes they use in restaurants for mustard, the kind with the squeeze top. She would have liked that too. She had always been a big fan of convenience.

I reckon you might want more out of this story but it just ain't there. We finished our sodas, and with three more hours of driving left until Clearwater, I started the car and we headed north.

# The Rag #2

Marianne
PO Box 10785
Dublin 8, Ireland
ragdublin@riseup.net
www.ragdublin.blogspot.com

## Gendered Revolutions

"Woman, differing from man but not inferior to him, intelligent, industrious and free like him, is declared his equal both in rights and in political and social functions and duties" Michael Bakunin (pretty much all he has to say on the subject)

The Rag received various responses to my article 'Women and Anarchism' in issue #1. One of the reactions I found the most surprising was questioning what difference it makes whether women are involved at all as long as an anarchist revolution happens. I was taken aback at first but after thinking about it, much indifference to feminism within the anarchist movement seems to stem from this idea. The importance of having a gender aware revolution and therefore gender awareness within groups with revolutionary aims is something that gets overlooked or downplayed. Real problems arise in assuming a male-dominated group will have no gender bias in their actions. We only need to look at early feminism to see the problems that arise when a privileged group (ie. rich white women) assumes to represent everyone. If women are not represented their needs will not be met. Revolutions have been affected in this way throughout history and no society has come close to achieving real equality between the sexes, even post-revolution. Neither socialist nor anarchist revolutions have achieved much when it comes to changing the structure of the family and gender relations within the home.

To change this pattern we need to look at how revolutions and social change have affected women's lives. In this article I will look at two revolutions, the Nicaraguan Revolution because, although the society it brought about was not strictly socialist (as there was some private investment a 'mixed economy'), it is relatively recent and is well known for achieving high levels of gender equality. I found it fascinating that gains made by women were lost again so easily after the

Sandinistas left power. The Spanish Civil War, I chose for the obvious reasons that it was an anarchist revolution and the birthplace of Mujeres Libres, an inspirational women's organisation. The real experience of women and women's groups in these revolutions is incredibly valuable to anarchists if we aim to create a truly equal society. I will explore the women's organisations, the ways they tried to change society and barriers they faced.

As most political theory has traditionally been written by men, feminists have found that it can contain a male-bias and the female experience is often overlooked. Those writing about revolution have not paid much attention to the involvement of women in these struggles, or in the part gender plays in the new societies created. It is assumed that with the downfall of capitalism, gender equality comes about naturally. But if we look at real examples, this does not happen. Anarchism calls for all kinds of oppression to be eliminated, yet women's specific oppression has generally been ignored in classical anarchist theory. One of the only anarchist theorists who addressed sexual politics in depth was Pierre-Joseph Proudhon. He wrote that men had a legitimate power and that only illegitimate power should be opposed; that women were only members of society through marriage, through men (Gemie, 1996). His writing greatly influenced anarchist thought in Spain in the 1900s but by the 1930s and the civil war Micheal Bakunin was a much greater influence. In his writing (and similarly in Marxist writing which influenced the Nicaraguan revolution) women were to become free by entering the workforce and joining unions. But poor women have always worked outside the home, have they found freedom through their work? The specificity of women's role in society is ignored. The lack of thought that went into this area of theory reflects on the practice. The work women do in the workplace in reality leaves them with a 'double shift' of paid work and then unpaid work when they get home. This 'double shift', along with low wages and the precarious nature of part-time work are the real problems which need to be addressed. Change for women has happened gradually and rarely through revolution has much been achieved that continued in the long term. So could an anarchist revolution do more harm than good for women? Do we need to wait until this gradual change brings about full equality? Or is it possible for a revolution to bring about a truly equal society?

The work women perform at home and within the family is given little thought in writing about revolutions. When women have gone into paid work, who has taken over the care work, the housework, the family farming? Usually it has been other women, aunts, grandmothers. There's no challenge of gender roles there, no shift in power inequalities. If women have to leave the home and enter the paid workplace in order to become equal, this means they are unfree at home. They are simply chained by housework, care work and family and need to break away. Men may remain as they are; it is women who must change. There is an implication in this way of thinking that it is not just the power inequality between men and women that is the problem, something negative is attached to all aspects of women's lives. Women just need to become, well, more like men. In this way of thinking the home is a prison; the workplace, freedom. Surely this is not the reality. In our homes, our community, children, friends, family, we find our strength. Surely men and women should share and enjoy these things, not escape them.

Revolutionary women's groups
The situations surrounding the Spanish and Nicaraguan revolutions were quite similar in many ways. Both were struggles for a more democratic society. Both countries were relatively poor, deeply catholic and deeply patriarchal. During both revolutions there was an outside force aiming to put down the revolution, Franco's fascist army in the case of Spain and the U.S. backed Contras in the case of Nicaragua. In both, to different degrees, real revolution was taking place. People self-organised within their communities, urban and rural, feeding and educating themselves, working together and struggling to get rid of class hierarchies within society. However, scratching the surface of these societies, we find a level of gender inequality, a real resistance to women's freedom, and a reluctance to change gender structure in society.

In both revolutions I mentioned, women's groups formed which were separate from the main revolutionary movement. AMNLAE were created by, and answered to, the FSLN. Their primary aim was getting women involved in fighting for the revolution (later it became defence of the revolution) and their first loyalty was to the Sandinista movement. This was not recognised by women as a problem because the FSLN were seen as pro-women having brought in laws banning sexist advertising and stating that men must share the housework equally with women. Socialist women were very active in most areas of Nicaraguan society. Women took part in the fighting, first to overthrow Somoza and then to defend the new socialist society. During those first years many gains were made for women and at one point women made up 40% of the militia and 50% of the government. As the war progressed women's needs became secondary even within AMNLAE. In 1984, coming up to an election, while AMNLAE were focused on the war and arguing to have women included in the draft, a national conference was called. The issues women raised there were domestic abuse, contraception, abortion, rape, and machismo (Chinchilla, 1994). The general secretary of AMNLAE stated that

"Problems such as male-female relations, pregnancy, and divorce are complex… It's not that we aren't interested in finding solutions to these problems, no. It's just that we have other priorities"

Leaders of AMNLAE never stood up against the FSLN even when it came to pushing women's needs. They found themselves in charge of 'women's issues'

They sewed knapsacks, raised money, dropped in on the brigadists' parents while their children were away, and set up small libraries…This, after all, was "what women do." (Randall, 1994, 26)

This reinforced the idea of women's roles being different and separate from men's roles. It did little to challenge women's subordination. The issues that were real to women were not tackled in the Nicaraguan revolution and any gains made were easily retracted after the Sandinistas left power. The lack of autonomy of the group was hugely influential in this.

Mujeres Libres formed in 1936 as a stand-alone organisation, however, financially they were quite dependant on the CNT and this became a problem for them. Women began with a support network to discuss difficulties facing women within the CNT but very quickly realised the need for autonomy in their movement. They were afraid the unions could make a decision to disband Mujeres Libres if they had control over it. From their statements and policies we can see that the Mujeres Libres position was much more strongly feminist than that of

AMNLAE. They had long-term goals for the place of women in society and wrote often about the need for men to change their attitudes and behaviour towards women. As a relatively autonomous group they were able to criticise the anarchist movement with greater freedom. They saw that the anarchist society being created in Spain was not equally benefiting women as it was men. Unfortunately the difficulties that came with this relative autonomy included a difficult relationship with the 'wider' anarchist movement. There was a hostility and lack of understanding when it came to the need for autonomy for the women's movement. Mujeres Libres were in the position of having to apologise for their views and were constantly seeking recognition of their status, as well as having to ask for finances. The CNT, never recognising the need for Mujeres Libres to even exist, were unsympathetic to women's needs. While the CNT and other unions. understood the need for women to become part of the workforce and involved in politics, they were blind to the problems of the double shift and childcare provision. Mujeres Libres were often reluctant to challenge the revolutionary movement as they were solid in their anarchist beliefs and many were loyal, active participants in the CNT or other unions. Mujeres Libres also faced difficulties in breaking away from dealing with what are seen as women's issues, childcare etc. Similarly to AMNLAE, these issues included the division of labour in the home and on the family land, domestic violence and sexism within anarchist organisations. Both groups had to stand up to accusations of 'splitting the movement' when they tried to raise these issues.

## Patriarchy in the movements

As well and working in the home women in industrial areas of Spain often worked in the textile industry in factories or from home. In rural areas women worked on the family farm as well as taking care of the children. Women spent most of their time in the home and didn't have much experience of organised politics. They were often paid workers, unpaid workers and carers at home, and had to become politically active on top of that. Mujeres Libres focused on educating and training women, as they believed this would empower them. They tackled women's immediate needs but kept in mind the long term aims of changing women's role and making society more equal. Due in part to their bad relationship with the anarchist unions they had only partial success. Women gained education and confidence but when they tried to become involved in anarchist groups often they were not welcome.

Mujeres Libres faced a struggle against blatant and unapologetic sexism within the anarchist movement. Activists complained that "women were ridiculed, ignored and at worst treated like sex objects" at anarchist events (Nash, 1995, 79). This was a severe setback for the women's movement, struggling to change women's lives and to be equal participants in the anarchist revolution. Nash (ibid) claims that anarchism was, in theory, more sympathetic to women than other groups active in the revolution, socialists and communists. However she notes the "glaring contradictions" between anarchist theory and what actually happened among anarchists in Spain, even before the war. The overall hostility towards Mujeres Libres as an organisation also reflects this sexism. Acklesburg's (1991) *Free Women of Spain* leaves the reader with the impression that there was a deliberate blocking, by anarchist men, of the attempts of women to break free from their subordinate position in society. Mujeres Libres reluctantly organised as a women-only group and intended their separatism to be a temporary strategy. Even so, the male dominated CNT treated them with contempt. The sexism they experienced within the anarchist movement showed them that women's oppression was actively ignored and this made reaching their aims far more difficult for the anarchist women. To begin tackling sexism in society must have seemed far more challenging when faced with this level of sexism within your own organisations.

In the FSLN, sexism was less glaring and worked on a different level. The relations between the women's group and the Socialist movement were less hostile and the inequality more covert. In the militia groups during the revolution women reported feeling a high level of equality with men. But women didn't rise through the ranks of the army in the same way that men did. Once in power the Sandinista government gradually had fewer women and there were never any women on the national executive. War did allow women to be seen as stronger and more able for political activity, but only to the extent that they could be seen as being masculine. Women who were more 'male' were allowed into the male dominated structures and these were usually those who were not feminist or were moderate in their expectations of change for women (Randall, 1994). The unequal nature of relations between women and the wider movements made it incredibly difficult for women to achieve change. As groups and as individuals, women, particularly feminist women, were denied access to power.

## Times of war

In the two revolutions the issue of whether women's needs could be addressed during war came up

In both cases a reason for refusing to address women's needs was that all effort needed to be focused on the revolution or the war. Women in Nicaragua however, gained their most important victories as regards their position in society during the war. By participating fully in all areas of the struggle, including armed combat, the women began to be seen as having a place in society outside of the home. Although this is an example of women needing to take on 'male' roles to gain respect, men in the army also cooked food and washed their clothes, performing roles that were usually seen as 'female'. For men and women, through necessity, gender roles were challenged. Women reported feeling high levels of respect among their comrades. The success in this case implies that it is possible to attempt to address women's needs while participating in struggle. Gender relations are not something which should be left until after the revolution to tackle as the FSLN claimed. The return of women to the home and to their children after the war meant many of these gains were lost. In fact many women were treated very badly on their return from war as they had lived with men, they were seen as being promiscuous. What changed within small groups of men and women living and fighting together was revolutionary but was not made part of the political aims of the Sandinistas and had little effect on Nicaraguan society.

In Spain women were not allowed to take part in armed combat and men and women were separated, with women doing the traditional 'women's work' of nursing, collecting food, and sewing. This separation of the sexes was unnecessary, as we can see from the Nicaraguan example, and related to a failure to question gendered division of labour. The work that women did during the Spanish Civil war was crucial but it did not have the same status as armed struggle and served to affirm women's subordinate role in society rather than challenge it. When there is a war going on the economic situation worsens as resources are diverted to the war effort and this is problematic for both men and women. Usually women have the responsibility for feeding the family and this can be far more difficult in times of crisis. Women's needs and the needs of the people cannot be put to one side. If participation in the war does not have the support of the people, as we can see in Nicaragua, this will harm not only the people of the country but the people's faith in the revolution.

While women left to join the army in Nicaragua it was not men who were taking over some of the women's role as primary carer, but other women. For some it was the grandmother or aunts, for middle and upper class women it was a working class child minder. The class structure was being reinforced by those who sought to challenge it. While individual women were changing their status or becoming empowered, society's view of women was not changing, and men's roles were not changing in the majority of the population. The underlying structure of society must be questioned. Women need to participate in political life, but not if this involves simply passing the burden to older or poorer women, who is then excluded.

If a revolution is to develop a truly feminist agenda and all women are to become equal citizens, issues such as the structure of the family and childcare need to be on the revolutionary agenda alongside and equal to how the workplace will be run. A female perspective, a view of women in revolution adds a new dimension, which if incorporated, could challenge and complete it. A revolutionary theory that included women would have to look at women's subordination within the home and how to 'revolt' with and against those closest to you. Gender roles must be challenged from all sides if men and women are to be truly free. The traditional female roles in revolution and in society must be recognized, respected and shared. If a revolution is to succeed in achieving emancipation for women, it would need to be based on this more balanced perspective of how revolutions should work and what they intend to achieve.

**Matte Resist**
**PO Box 582345**
**Minneapolis, MN 55458**

# SEEDS

I've been gardening for a few years now. About one year into that I ran into a guy at the coop giving out samples of Heirloom tomatoes. I tried a couple and really like the white beauties and this other one that looked sort of unripe and had a dark center. I saved a few seeds and planted them. I've been replanting those same tomatoes for 3 or 4 years now. They're sort of smallish and they don't store for long, or make a very good salsa, but they're great to eat by themselves or in a sandwich or salad. I've taken to calling them 6-pack tomatoes, because they almost always grow in groups of 6, lined up like a 6 back of beer/soda. As you can imagine, they're very prolific! The last couple years I've also been growing yellow pear tomatoes, which are sort of like cherry tomatoes, except yellow and pear shaped. They're sweet and can be eaten plain or in salads. I've also been growing striped stuffers. These grow like bell peppers. They have a thick meaty outside, and all the seeds cling to the middle. So when you cut the top off, they look like a bell pepper. Perfect for stuffing, but I've never actually used them that way. It sort of sounds like I'm writing a catalog her, and that's sort of what I'm trying to do. This guy I correspond with suggested that I do a seed exchange though Resist. I meant to do it last year, but didn't get it done. This year I'm going to do it.

I saved a lot of seeds from the 6-pack and yellow pair, and quite a few from the stuffers. I'd like to trade with folks who have other types. I don't need a lot of seeds, maybe 4-8. Just enough so I can have a couple of plants. If I like them, I can save seeds and plant more the following year. I'm especially interested in good salsa or sauce tomatoes. (accompanying recipes would be good too!) I'd also like some ramp seeds, (it's a sort of wild onion that grows in the Appalachians), chicory (the type you grow for the roots, as opposed to the endive sort), and tomatillos. Oh, and peppers that do well in northern climates. I'm really interested in just about everything. Squash, flowers, or anything that grows well in partial shade (edible or ornamental) would be good.

Aside from tomatoes, I have limited amounts of 3-4 varieties of lettuce, beans (mostly Blue Lake and Kentucky Wonder), Black Beauty Zucchini Squash, some carrots and mint.

As of this year, I also have a bunch of seeds for German Chamomile (a nice looking perennial flower great for filling spaces (and you can use the flower to make tea)) and very limited amount of Echinacea. I also have some new tomatoes: Cosmonaut Volkov, Garden Peach & Green Zebra.

For now I'd like to keep this pretty simple. I've had a crazy year, and I don't want to get too nuts about starting new projects. So for now I'd just like to do an even exchange. You send me some seeds, and I'll send you some of mine. Just let me know what you want.

If you have a lot of seeds and would like to trade with more people, let me know. Better yet, send a list of what you have and what you want. If there's enough interest, I'll compile it all and send it out in zine format this winter and everybody can trade. I'm not going to post any prices, cause that's what I'm trying to avoid. There are PLENTY of seed companies, but I can't afford $2.50+ for a packet of seeds when I might only use 3 or 4. I want a dozen different varieties at least. I could afford a few stamps to trade with people though… and I bet there are lots of other folks in the same boat. Granted, there are some very good seed companies out there, but how cool would it be if we skipped the whole consumer step and just traded with each other?

If you want to save seeds, here's a quick primer on how to do it. I'm actually working on a much more detailed version to be included in the book i'm working on, but that one isn't quite done yet and this is the one i actually wrote to go along with this article (when i wrote it over a year ago)

## HOW TO SAVE SEEDS

Here's a quick primer on saving seeds. With any seed, it's important to let the fruit/vegetable/flower/whatever fully mature. With tomatoes, I usually get my seeds from tomatoes that I've picked and haven't used fast enough. When they get really soft, I toss them in a big jar and shake them vigorously so there's nothing left but tomato mush. Then I add water and let it sit for a few days. The good seeds will settle to the bottom. The bad seeds and pulp will float to the top. I usually shake the mixture every day or two. This further breaks up any large pieces and dislodges the seeds. It also keeps mold from forming. Then you just pour off the pulp. Sometimes if I'm lazy, I'll pour off most of the pulp and add more water and let it sit a few more days until more pulp floats to the top. Then pour off all the water and save the seeds. I usually just stretch a piece of cheesecloth over the top of the jar and pour through that. Then you can shake the seeds off on a paper plate of piece of newspaper. Let them dry thoroughly, and store in labeled envelopes. You can use this same method for other "wet" seeds: squash, melon, cucumbers, etc. "Dry" seeds like pepper seeds can just be spread out on newspaper to dry, and then store in envelopes. I would avoid using plastic (containers, bags) to store seeds. They keep moisture out, which is important, but if you haven't completely dried your seeds, it will also hold the moisture in and cause your seeds to mold. I use the standard #6 size envelope that you can buy for less than a dollar for 100.

When saving bean seeds pick a plant or two to let "go to seed" or just wait until the end of the season and let them all go. Basically, you just let them do their thing. Let the beans turn brown and start to dry, then pull the whole plant up and hang it somewhere for another week or two to dry. Then just split the pods and put the seeds in an envelope. I think peas work the same way. Alternately, you can save the seeds from beans that have gotten too big. It seems there are always a few beans that you miss when you're picking, and they'll get rather huge before you find them. You could eat them, but they're not very good for eating anymore. Just toss them someplace where they can dry out. We have one of those 3 tier hanging wire basket things that you keep fruit or onions or whatever in. In the smallest basket on top I throw stuff that needs to dry out: hot peppers and beans. I just let the beans sit there all winter, and split the pods come spring when I'm planting.

With lettuce, you just let a plant or two bolt. I usually harvest lettuce by cutting off the leaves as I need them for a sandwich or salad. This leaves the plant in tact so it can go to seed. It'll grow a tall spindly flowering stalk in the center. After it flowers, and the flowers close up, it'll get little furry things which are full of tiny seeds. I usually cut off the whole top and stick it in a paper bag. Let it dry for a couple days, then thrash it around and a whole mess of seeds will fall out. Put them in a labeled envelope.

This year I also started saving flower seeds. It's a little hard to explain how to do it. I saved them from German Chamomile and Echinacea. With both of those, the seeds were kind of imbedded in the head of the flower. Once the pedals fall off, you can see that down below them are the seeds. You can usually get them out by rubbing your thumb back and forth across the flower and they'll just pop out (so do it over newspaper or something). As with all seeds, I let them dry for a few days before I put them in a labeled envelope.

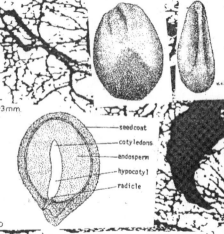

When I say "labeled envelope" I mean, label it with the plant the seeds are from, and what date you put them in the envelope. After a few years of saving seeds, some of the seeds I haven't used are getting old. If I attempted to plant them, I would probably get a pretty poor germination rate, and would be disappointed with the outcome. If I see that the seeds are old, I can either do a germination test first, or plant them more thickly and hope for success. At least I know the seeds are old, and that I'm taking my chances, rather than thinking that the seeds are ones I saved last year and WHY AREN'T THEY GROWING?!

# Peops #3

**Fly**
PO Box 1318 Cooper Stn
NYC, NY 10276
fly@bway.net
www.bway.net/~fly

I GUESS I WAS THE FOUNDER OF AK PRESS - WHEN I WAS 13 I STUMBLED ACROSS PUNK ROCK & ANARCHISM - AT THAT POINT I LIVED IN A SMALL TOWN IN CENTRAL SCOTLAND CALLED STIRLING WHERE I GREW UP - THIS WAS ABOUT 1979 - HOW I CAME TO ANARCHISM I HAVE NO IDEA BUT AT AGE 13 I BOUGHT A CRASS T-SHIRT THAT SAID "ANARCHY PEACE & FREEDOM" - THATS WHY I BOUGHT IT - THEN I HAD TO BUY A CRASS RECORD TO AVOID SOCIAL EMBARRASSMENT - I THINK IT WAS STATIONS OF THE CRASS WHICH I ACTUALLY THOUGHT WAS PRETTY CRAP - I LIKED THE IDEAS & ENERGY BUT NOT THE MUSIC - FROM THERE I LAUNCHED MYSELF INTO THE PUNK UNDERGROUND - THIS WAS PRE-INTERNET SO I WAS A BIG LETTER WRITER & I WAS IN BANDS & AT AN EARLY AGE I STARTED SELLING FANZINES - IN THOSE EARLY DAYS ZINES WERE STILL PRETTY NOVEL - ESPECIALLY IN CENTRAL RURAL SCOTLAND - IN MY EARLY ENTREPRENURAL/PROPAGANDISTIC DAYS I WAS WALKING AROUND WITH A PLASTIC BAG FULL OF FANZINES - THERE WAS A LOT OF POLITICAL IDEALISM & I WOULD WALK UP TO PEOPLE & SAY "DO YOU WANT TO BUY A FANZINE?" - THE TYPICAL RESPONSE WAS "WHATS A FANZINE?" - THE GREAT LEAP FORWARD FOR ME WAS IN 1982 AT A SQUATTED GIG PUT ON BY CRASS & THE APOSTLES I THINK & THEY ALL PLAYED AS WELL AS DIRT & CONFLICT & THE MOB - I WAS WANDERING AROUND WITH MY PLASTIC BAG FULL OF ZINES & THERE WAS

- A TABLE FULL OF POLITICAL LITERATURE RUN BY THESE "OLD" BEARDED DUDES WHO WORKED FOR A POLITICAL BOOK STORE - THEY PUT UP WITH ME & MENTORED ME ON HOW TO PUBLISH & DISTRIBUTE & PUT OUT MORE POLITICAL STUFF - THE BOOK STORE IS CALLED HOUSMANS & ITS STILL THERE IN KINGS CROSS - AK CONTINUED TO GROW & WHEN IT GOT TO A CERTAIN LEVEL - WHEN IT WAS TOO MUCH FOR ME TO HANDLE - IT BECAME A COLLECTIVE WITH ME & A FEW FRIENDS & THEN IT JUST GREW FROM THERE - WWW.AKPRESS.ORG
— EDINBURGH, OAKLAND & PURGITSVILLE WEST VIRGINIA

FLY · 03·23·2K7

I WAS A NEW WAVE TO PUNK GIRL - DURAN DURAN WAS MY FAVORITE BAND - IT WAS THE MID 80's & SKATE PUNK WAS HAPPENING - THERE WAS DEAD KENNEDIES, CIRCLE JERKS, BLACK FLAG - THERE WERE SKATE JAMS & I WAS SORT OF FINDING MY PLACE IN THIS WHOLE SCENE - THE TOWN WAS CALLED STATE COLLEGE PA - HAPPY VALLEY - I WENT TO STATE COLLEGE AREA HIGH SCHOOL - THERE WAS AN AWESOME PUNK SCENE - & THERE WERE COLLEGE KIDS SETTING UP SHOWS AT THE UNIVERSITY BRINGING BANDS LIKE AGNOSTIC FRONT & THE DESCENDANTS & DRI - IT WAS 1987 & I STARTED DOING THE ZINE CUZ NOONE ELSE WAS DOING IT - I WAS READING MRR RELIGIOUSLY SO I KNEW ABOUT ZINES & I WAS A BUDDING PHOTOGRAPHER - I DIDNT WANT TO BE IN A BAND SO I THOUGHT - I'LL DO A ZINE! - AS I WAS CONCIEVING THE IDEA I WENT TO ENGLAND & I SAW A PUB CALLED "SLUG & LETTUCE" & IT WAS SO WEIRD I THOUGHT THATS WHAT I'LL CALL THE ZINE - I WAS 15 - IT WAS COOL DOING THE ZINE - GAVE ME A WAY TO GET SOMETHING OUT - I WENT TO THIS PROGRESSIVE HIGH SCHOOL & I GOT ENGLISH CREDIT FOR A YEAR FOR DOING MY ZINE! I HAD A LOT OF SUPPORT & HELP

- I CAME TO NYC IN '89 & I THOUGHT I WOULDNT BE ABLE TO CONTINUE THE ZINE BECAUSE I DIDNT HAVE THE RESOURCES BUT IT WAS SO MUCH A PART OF ME THAT I COULDNT NOT DO IT - SO I DECIDED TO FOCUS ON THE MOST IMPORTANT ASPECTS — THE CLASSIFIEDS, THE REVIEWS & THE PHOTOGRAPHS - I SAW IT AS A RESOURCE FOR CONTACTS & COMMUNICATION - AT THE TIME I HAD HUNDREDS OF PENPALS - SO I WOULD MAKE AS MANY COPIES AS I COULD OF A ONE PAGE ZINE & GIVE THEM OUT - THEN I GRADUALLY EXPANDED - ISSUE #20 WAS WHEN I STARTED PRODUCING IT AS A TABLOID - SQUAT OR ROT HOOKED ME UP WITH THE PRINTER - ISSUE #83 IS GONNA COME OUT NEXT MONTH & I'M PLANNING MY 20 YR ANNIVERSARY PHOTO BOOK.

FLY. 03/03/2K5

AMAZING PHOTOGRAPHER! & JUST AMAZING IN GENERAL - SLUG & LETTUCE PO BOX 26632 RICHMOND VA 23261-6632

# Battle Come Down

Dave
PO Box 5332
Columbia, SC 29250
battlecomedown@gmail.com

## heavy metal atlantic

Spring semester freshman year, a listless weekend outlook; partly cloudy with a 70% chance that the confines of the Queens campus will bore us out of our fucking minds. An icy winter is over, the weather's improving and Myrtle Beach seems as good a destination as any. So Joe, Patrick and I make plans to travel interstates and state roads out of the Piedmont and onto the South Carolina coast.

Away from urbane, gentrifying Charlotte, to spend a weekend in the thick of that bright neon frontier. I've lived weeks of my life in Tennessee, traveled northbound 95 through Florida, Georgia, Virginia, but this is different, dude. This is Myrtle Beach.

Steal food from the dining hall, because finances dictate a hard choice between gas and purchased food, and I've never liked spending when I don't have to anyway. Walk through the lines of the buffet-style dining hall and shove a loaf of bread into my patch-ridden bookbag, sliding half a dozen apples in alongside, saving room for peanut butter and oranges. I attempt discretion, but the place is full, and invariably, someone notices, an appalled look spreading across their face, as they stare. I stare right back, smiling, but careful not to overfill, as I hold an empty half-gallon milk jug under the spigot of a pink lemonade fountain.

Charlotte's only a few miles removed from South Carolina, a few exits shy of the Palmetto state, but it could be hundreds of miles, for all the differences between the two. Like a disgraced cousin or creepy uncle never visited by relatives down the road, the southern half of the Carolinas lives under the scornful glance of the Old North State, bigger, stronger, haughtier. Sibling rivalry on a statewide scale.

Driving south, roadside firework stands and SC Lottery dealers rule the landscape, dealing in vices that Raleigh won't bother with. "Boiled Peanuts. 99¢!" shows up as often as speed limit signs, while big towns and their peripheral fast food empires give way to small, speed trap burgs and downtown Main streets. In one of these towns, out-of-state tags get us pulled over. Joe's PBA card and mention of a cop relative don't help, but New Jersey origin elicits a sincere and friendly "Oh yeah? I'm from Brooklyn!" and a handshake from the cop, as a $100 citation is issued, reduced to fifty if Joe appears in court a month later.

A couple of hot, hungry hours later, we hit the beach, at dusk. Bright orange radiating off the Atlantic and masses of people on the sidewalks, a parade of chrome rimmed, tricked-out rides blaring booty bass across the strip. We join in, a tiny Red Sephia cranking Dee Snyder's radio show through tinny speakers, heavy on the treble, hair metal and our fists pumping through the air. We yell at bystanders, and turn the volume up if they laugh, louder if they glare. Bike cops ride by, impotent in their helmets and tight shorts.

-Knock it off!

What's the matter, dude? I wanna rock. I *want to* rock.

Down the strip and later that night, someone else does. He walks up to the driver's side window. Lanky and sunburnt red, rockin' a mullet and crusty mustache, tank top and shorts, he speaks through the lowered window. Blurry eyes try to focus, while he lets us know, "I don't care what anybody says. You guys are cool as hell!" Fuck yeah, man. We crank up the volume in respect as we drive off.

Spent the rest of that night walking around, rating souvenir t-shirts by their offensiveness (winner: a drawing of the Capitol Dome flying the Stars and Bars, with the caption: "I Have A Dream…"), taking pictures and making fun of the drunk college kids stumbling

around, red-eyed and stammering, heads and necks heavy with backwards ballcaps and Mardi Gras beads. A cramped night in the Sephia, sleeping suitability having been overlooked by its Korean engineers. A grey sky over a cold Atlantic on this hungover Sunday morning. I swim for a while, and head back to shore. We walk to the car and drive away.

At a gas station stop, I'm browsing music racks for a tape to replace weekend DJs and commercial radio on the long drive. Under *Shadowlife*, I grab a copy of *Brave New World*, Bruce Dickinson's sword-wielding, pyrotechnic return to Iron Maiden. Six bucks well spent, as double bass, impossible solos and nine-minute songs carry us back to Charlotte, a city miles removed in attitude and experience from Myrtle Beach. Both Carolina cities, existing on different ends of that defining spectrum, the survival of one impossible without the other. Without cities like Charlotte or Chapel Hill, the stereotypes that paint the region as a cultural backwater would be harder to combat. And without gaudy tourist beach towns like Myrtle Beach, firework stands and gas station metal, things might be a lot less interesting.

# Caboose #6

**Liz Mason**
**Quimbys Bookstore**
**1854 W North Ave**
**Chicago, IL 60622**
**www.flickr.com/photos/elizabethmason**

Many weeks into my pain, a friend referred me to an acupuncturist/Chinese herbalist. I made an appointment with her, and she told me not to eat a big breakfast that morning but do eat something. I drove out to bumble Illinois to meet with her. Sitting in her office waiting since I got there early, while she finished with her previous client, I noticed cool book titles on her bookshelf, like stuff about raw food eating and herbal remedies. Her various certificates and degrees were on the wall like a college degree in some science-y subject like biology. The fact that she had backgrounds in both traditional science and eastern medicine was comforting to me, because it seemed balanced.

She was pretty, tall and thin, and said, "I'm kind of redoing my customer file. Could you fill this out?" She handed me a sheet of letterhead. There were no questions on it. I wrote down my name, address and phone number.

We spent an hour discussing my symptoms and habits. I told her about my itching/pain. She talked about itching being "wind of the body"—wind I guess because it moves around a lot, and you don't feel like you ever get a handle on it. The thing was, it was sort of hard to explain that it was more than just itching. That it was pain too. She suggested that I had a lot of "dampness," which I took to mean I poo a lot. Then she had me lay down on her table.

The needles were small and looked harmless but the idea of sticking anything in my skin freaked me out. I decided to be brave because at this point, I'd tried so many things that didn't work: pain killers, allergy medicine, meditation—I was open to anything.

I kept my eyes closed the whole time because I was afraid that if I saw the needles in my body, I'd freak out and immediately make her take them out. She would clean each area on my skin with rubbing alcohol on a cotton ball before inserting the needle. The needles were very small, probably even skinnier than a sewing needle. The end of the needle that's not in your skin has a little wooden knob.

At one point she asked me how I was feeling, and I said, "Fine," my voice high and anxious. She responded, "I should have put needles in your ears, that would probably helped you relax; we'll put them in there first next time."

She put needles in the side of my knees but not very far in because I made some scared noise and she said, "We'll come back and put those further in later," which helped alleviate some fear. She put a couple needles somewhere above my eyebrows, and I peeked at them hanging over me for a second, and that actually helped alleviate some of my fear because I saw how flimsy the needles were, and that they were harmless.

After she had gotten needles in various places, she burned some kind of incense-y stuff on a piece of foil resting on my solar plexus area in such a way that it would merely heat me up but not burn me. I think it was supposed to open some chi channel. Then she turned the lights off except for a heat lamp above me, with the needles all over my body. She left me to lay marinating in my chi for twenty minutes.

When she came back I was drowsy. She took out the needles. After the treatment she put these things called ear buds in my ears that operate

141

on reflexology principles. She poked around in my ears with a sharp instrument, and whenever she got to a point where I flinched she adhered a seed (of what kind of plant I have no idea). Anytime I was in pain I was supposed to press the seeds with my fingers. Every week when I came for treatment she would put in new ear buds. I don't know if they did anything, but I spent a lot of time pressing down on them very hard. My husband said he thought they looked gross. I'm sure they did.

She gave me some Chinese herbal pills that were supposed to detox me, which I suppose is code for "shit a lot every morning around 10 AM." Also, she gave me a red clover tea for liver purification. I knew a little about red clover because I've used it in homemade herbal remedies. Once she got me some liquid tonic thing in Chinatown, but I never really knew exactly what it was or what it's supposed to do. I looked up some of the ingredients on the web and found that one of them was some sort of "precursor to a neurotransmitter," which I thought was strange phrasing that I didn't understand, but I figured it was unwise to consume since I was already on all these psychiatric drugs that deal with neurotransmitters. I didn't want to fuck with that. I know that if you're on antidepressants, they tell you not to take St. John's Wart, so I thought this might be a similar situation. I still have the bottle. It looks really cool and secret potion-y, like if I was buying Chinese medicine, this is exactly what I'd want it to look like: big brown weirdly shaped bottle, a picture of some kind of root.

In the car on the way home, the pain was still there, but I wanted to believe that the treatment would help, so I decided to give it a few more tries before I gave up on it. After a number of appointments I told her that the treatment wasn't as effective as just being in her office. When I told her that, she just said, "I'm not doing anything except soothing you; you should try it sometime."

Something that coincided with the acupuncture treatments, and I say coincided because I think they are unrelated, is that my legs started doing these crazy spasmodic jerking motions all the time. What was weird about the spastic jerking motions was that this weird tension would sort of build up in my legs until the muscles would just sort of get full of this tension that move around like a burr inside my legs until my legs uncontrollably jerked out. And if I was sitting with my legs folded in any way it was painful. I think my right leg was worse than my left leg, but they were both pretty fucked up. Does it have anything to do with the acupuncture treatment? Was it the movement of my chi going crazy in my body? Probably not. Is it weird that the restless leg stuff should start right after I'd already started acupuncture? Yes. However, I realize the correlation is not the same as causation. I looked around on the web and didn't find anything that described negative effects of acupuncture related to restless legs, so I decided they were unrelated.

After about four or five treatments I decided it wasn't doing anything for me, so I gave it up. I'm not saying that acupuncture is useless. I'm saying it didn't work for my specific ailment. Maybe it would work on me if I had some other ailment? I just don't know. I do know that it was way expensive, and the drive back into the city on the highway full of construction and bumper to bumper traffic on a Saturday afternoon didn't do much to calm me. It was time for me to let acupuncture be.

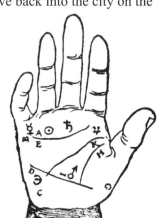

# Laterborn #5

Jason Martin
PO Box 123
Belmmont, CA 94002

Laterborn
No. 5
$2.00

By Jason Martin

## Sausalito

I found out a girl I knew in high school killed herself.

The Mercury News

Obituaries

The obituary didn't say how she did it, just that it happened in Sausalito.

26 years old, of Los Gat
8, 2005 in Sausalito, Cal
ing time with her friends

I had a job interview there the next day, and it was all I could think about.

Sausalito →

EXIT 15 MPH

Everywhere I looked there were yuppies shopping and smiling.

Why would someone come here to die?

# Doris #24

Cindy Crabb
PO Box 29
Athens, OH 45701
www.dorisdorisdoris.com

ohio

 Did you know that on some kinds of turtles you can read their age by the ridges of their shells? Each section of shell has concentric ridges circling in and in and in, and you can put your fingernail gently there, move it slowly, read the lines.

And some turtles, they have a hinge, like a little door they can pull their heads into and close themselves off from the outside world, and then you can only jab at their feet, you can't peck out their head. Not that I wanted to do any pecking.

We were in Ohio. Paul had told me about the age lines. I was holding the turtle, counting, thinking about the years that had marked me. Thinking about this land we were trying to buy and this chapter in my life, Ohio.

We were walking the perimeter, me and Caty and Roger and Paul. Paul owned some land nearby. He was our guide, blazing through the wild roses and the poisonivy, pouring out information - what trees were hardwood, what trees were boundry markers, what plants

 were invasive, what our priorities should be to help the land recover and regain ballance, what we could do to make the wild animals happy, who owned the surrounding hillsides, where pasture land had been, how much the area had been strip-mined, how much was underpreservation now, where we could put in a pond, where we could grow ginseng and goldenseal.

Paul is a New Yorker. He moved to rural Ohio in the 70's, but he's still a New Yorker with the quick and certain way he talks.

He moved to Ohio; 19 years old, long haired freak. He sat down, he told us, he just sat down and watched.

HE WATCHED THE STUNNING RHYTHM AND BEAUTY OF THIS FADING WAY OF LIFE. THE HORSES GETTING HARNESSED UP, THE CLOMP OF HOOVES, THE PLOW BEHIND THEM, THE TURNING OF THE SOIL, THE NOSES SNORTING AND STEAM EXHALING IN THIS FIRST WARM ENOUGH DAY OF SPRING.

Most people didn't want him there. Outsider. City boy. But one man took him under his wing, taught him about horses and anything else he wanted to know.
    The first year was ok. Hard work day and night.

"THIS IS WHAT HAS BEEN LOST IN AMERICA," Paul says "THE KNOWLEDGE OF HOW TO WORK REALLY HARD."

His second year in Ohio was the coldest on record. The horses were freezing, the well was freezing over. He had to wake up three times a night to go break up the ice so their water-source wouldn't become a solid block and leave them waterless. He brought one sick horse in to the house to warm it, but by the end of winter, he'd lost half his team. He stuck with it all, and over the years he won his neighbors grudging respect.

I used to be afraid of rural America. I thought all the guys out there would be macho assholes like the ones who yell at me in grocery store parking lots about how disgusting I am because of my mustache, or the ones who tried to fight me in the bar because I wouldn't say if I was a boy or a girl. I thought rural america was all ignorant assholes out looking for fights

When I moved 3 years ago to the North Carolina country and I didn't even have a car, just had my friends drop me off with all my belongings at the last house on the dead end road in the middle of switchhback roads and mountains, when they pulled away waving, saying "call us when your phone gets turned on," I watched them drive away and I felt overwhelming relief, and home at last, and fear.

The house came with a 30/30 rifle, and
I slept with it loaded next to my bed. I
brought it with me to the bathroom when I
took a shower. I even brought it with me
when I just got up to pee.

I started listening to country music,
because that was the only channel I got
out there, and it wasn't what I expected.
It wasn't "Let's kill all the Iraqi" or even
the old standard "I caught my woman with
another man so I shot her dead.": The songs
were mostly really sweet, about men trying to
feel their feelings and remember what is
important in life, like family and community
and land and helping eachother, and not needing
a bunch of materialistic things. Like: "who
needs a stupid country club, we just take all
our shitty boats down to the swimming hole and
tie them together and kick back and we've got
ourselves our own redneck yaght club." or "I lost

my job so my wife said she'd get one and I could take care
of the kids, which I thought would be vacation, but it is
the hardest thing I have ever done. I don't know how she's
done it all these years," or "My dad taught me to listen to
old people, and he's right, they have a lot of important
things to teachuus," or "I caught my wife with another man,
so I cried," or "you don't really need a lot of money, as
long as you've got a lot of heart," or "that girl is really
smart and well traveled and strong minded, but hasn't let it
turn her in to a snob and that's hot," or "they say you
can't go home again, but they're lieing, because you can and
nothing beats real community."

After listening to the music I stopped being so scared.

I thought I would grow flax, a whole field of it, and
I would spin it in to thread and weave linen, but I was
too shy to ask anyone to plow my field, even though the
neighbors told me to let them know if I ever needed
anything. Living the way I have, I never learned to ask
for help. Or I learned that if I asked, there would be
strings attached. and I learned to be afraid of judgement.
So I just dug a small plot. Jono helped me. We planted
tomatoes, more than I could ever eat. I picked dandilion
greens and red clover and dried them for tea.

I pickled greenbeans. I grew Luffas. Did you
know Luffas are a gourd? not a sea creature!?!
It is true. They grow on a vine like a pumpkin.
You dry them out and peal off all the skin and
squashy stuff and turn it inside out and scrape
out all the
           seeds, and you're left with a soft
intricate skelatin. turn it right side in and
dry it slowly until it's done, and there you
have it, a bathtub skin scrubber. Mine has lasted
so far for 2 years.

politics

Yesterday I was reading a book that was talking about
off-road-vehicles, and the author said - how could the
world ever change when people destroy nature just in the
name of recreation. If people will destroy wnat is
beautiful just because it's fun.

Across the mountian from where I used to live was a group
of people who thought that if you weren't striving to live
like the hunter and gatherers, you didn't really deserve
to live.

I go to the global warming movie, and outside there's a
table of urgent and well meaning ladies selling wholesale
energy conserving lightbulbs, and I think of the amount
of energy I use compared to the gas station down the street
from me that leaves it's millions of lights on full blast
blindingly bright, all night, even when it's closed.

I think of friends who have given up because nothing seems
like enough, or because people let them down and political
projects fell through,  or because they simply don't know
any more what to do.

A lot of people who simply don't know what to do.

# Privilege & Solidarity

Tyrone Boucher
tyronius.samson@gmail.com
www.enoughenough.org

## Money Stories

"Storytelling often represents the most ideological moments; when we tell stories we tell them as if there was *only one way* of telling them, as the 'of course' way of understanding what is happening in the world. These are moments when we are 'least aware that [we] are using a particular framework, and that if [we] used another framework the things we are talking about would have different meaning.'"
-Eduardo Bonilla-Silva, Racism Without Racists

When I was growing up, I never thought of my family as rich. Even when I became involved in donor organizing work, I resisted identifying my background as owning class – I knew I had class privilege, but I thought of myself as "upper-middle class" for a long time. After doing some probing about my family's wealth and doing plenty of reading about class in the U.S., I finally realized that this perception of my family's class status had more to do with dominant ideology around wealth and my own resistance to identifying as "really" rich than with actual reality.

The more I've learned about wealth and class privilege, the more I see my incorrect interpretation of my own class status as symptomatic of a bigger problem. An important first step in taking responsibility for class privilege is to begin looking at our personal stories as part of a larger system. Or actually, multiple intersecting systems that work together: systems of institutionalized oppression like racism and patriarchy, the economic system of capitalism, and systems of ideology that keep all the other systems in place.

I've had anti-capitalist politics since before I became involved in donor organizing and began to look closely at my own class position. The work, energy, and conversation happening in U.S. activist movements around the time of the 1999 WTO protests in Seattle radicalized me about the globalization of neoliberal, corporate, US-led, imperial capitalism. Later I got involved in labor organizing and started thinking more about the history of capitalism in the U.S., and all the ways our economic system has supported and perpetrated various forms of oppression. When I finally did start to examine my personal privilege, I began trying to figure out where I, as a person with inherited wealth, fit into my anti-capitalist analysis.

In the process of thinking about this, I called my dad to ask him some specific questions about our class status as a family and his interpretation of it. I'm trying to create an ongoing dialogue between my dad and me about class and privilege, and part of it focuses on learning more about how, as a first-generation owning-class individual (he grew up upwardly-mobile working class), my dad came to accumulate wealth and power. He's always had a very simplistic story about how he "made it," basically centering on a combination of luck and hard work. Around the time I was born, he started a company that produced some kind of software publishing product; the company ended up taking off and the stock value skyrocketed; hence, new owning-class status for my family.

I respect my dad a lot; he's thoughtful and kind, and doesn't at all fit stereotypes of greedy corporate CEOs. The point isn't to dis my dad and call him out as being oppressive, but to look at our position as wealthy people within a greater structure of capitalism and oppression. If we don't step back and challenge the broader framework that we're situated in, it's easy to play a complicit role in oppressive systems; that's how privilege works. Sociologist Allan Johnson describes this at the "path of least resistance." He writes: "Good people with good intentions make systems happen in ways that produce all kinds of injustice and suffering for people in culturally devalued and excluded groups…If we participate in systems the trouble [of oppression] comes out of, and if those systems exist only though our participation, than this is enough to involve us in the trouble itself."

My dad's story of wealth accumulation – the way he tells it – is straightforward, honest, and true to his experience. It also could have been ripped verbatim from the pages of the Resource Generation book *Classified* (check out the bibliography in the back of this zine); specifically the chapter on money stories, which describes some of the myths and archetypes that go into creating ruling-class ideology. Karen Pittelman, the author of *Classified*, writes,

...the majority of the money stories begin to take on a strange similarity to each other. They focus on one person, often a man, and they center on how his hard work, intelligence, ingenuity, willingness to take risks and temerity lead to eventual financial good fortune. While the details of each story vary, the same plotlines – even the same phrases – occur again and again: "pulled himself up by the bootstraps," "wise investor," "rags to riches," "worked day and night," "never took a handout," and "self-made man."

My dad's story is a lot like this. It can be hard to talk about the oppression that is linked to wealth accumulation for him *personally*, because of course he doesn't see himself as an oppressor. He's a liberal. He sees his wealth as having been acquired basically in a vacuum, without negatively affecting others in any way. He spent his work life in offices and board meetings, not cracking the whip in a factory or overseeing the plantation. He isn't making policy decisions and he doesn't support the Bush administration. He isn't an active participant in outsourcing jobs overseas, privatizing public services, breaking up unions, deregulating trade laws, exploiting immigrants, or most of the other obvious methods by which power is concentrated in the hands of a few.

But his ability to accumulate wealth was influenced by more than just his hard work and blind luck – although both of these played a part. As an entrepreneurial white man, he was well positioned to benefit from capitalism, white supremacy, and patriarchy. He was able to make business connections, leverage influence, wield power in the worlds of business and technology, and be taken seriously to an extent that wouldn't likely be available to a man of color or to any woman, thirty years ago or today.

In the book *You Call This a Democracy?*, Paul Kivel gives a good analysis of how wealthy people in the U.S. benefit from and support oppressive systems, even when we don't directly make the decisions that create and enforce them. He draws a distinction between the owning class (which he defines as the wealthiest 20% of the population) and the "power elite" – a much smaller group within the owning class who are leaders in business, politics, philanthropy, and culture, and who are directly involved in high levels of society-shaping decision making. Though most rich people aren't members of the power elite, we benefit in various ways

from their decisions. Even if we have leftist politics and a scathing critique of neoliberalism, colonialism, global corporate takeover, militarism, and the rest of the U.S. power elite's evil agenda, if we are in a position to benefit from the systems that support this agenda (like capitalism, white supremacy, and patriarchy) we are implicated in it. It's very easy for wealthy people to maintain an individualistic perspective on our lives when the realities of most people in the world are invisible to us. So we end up with stories like those that *Classified* describes – ideological narratives that keep the focus off the owning class and shield us from blame or responsibility for oppression.

It's important to note the way these stories play out not just in our own lives as people with wealth, but in the greater society. As members of a dominant class, wealthy people hold systemic power – which allows us to frame everything from our perspective. This framing takes place not just on a personal level, but in all upper-class-controlled institutions (media, government, philanthropy, etc.). Classist ideology teams up with other forms of oppressive ideology and creeps into nearly all of the institutions that exert power over our lives. Reagan's racist characterization of poor Black women as "welfare queens" created the climate for deeply harmful welfare "reform." Invisibility of poor people (except as criminals) in media and popular culture erases the realities of the majority of U.S. citizens and encourages a blame-the-victim mentality that helps corporations and the government get away with deeply oppressive policies and practices. Philanthropic rhetoric that deems rich people to be the ones best equipped to fund social services allows for increasing erosion of the federal safety net. The myth that racism is over takes the responsibility off the government and private institutions (corporations, universities, foundations) to respond to the movement for reparations.

I think it's crucial to draw connections – between media storytelling and the stories we tell in our families; between the racism of politicians and legislators and the insidious, institutionalized racism that affects us without our even realizing it; between the paternalism of philanthropy and the privilege that we as individuals unconsciously enact; between the oppression by obvious perpetrators like police, military, and sweatshop-owning, union-busting multinational corporations and the oppression underlying our personal family fortunes.

Anti-capitalist social justice movements continually inspire me to challenge myself as a rich person and to challenge other rich people, because they situate us as players in systems that deeply harm the majority of people on the planet. It's crucial to me to incorporate a radical critique of capitalism into both my understanding of my own wealth and privilege and into the donor organizing work I do. The "progressive philanthropy" world tends to take a stance that resists truly challenging capitalism and oppression in order to accommodate more moderate wealthy donors. Much of the landscape of social change philanthropy seems designed to make rich people feel better about ourselves and to channel *some* funds to progressive (or even radical) organizing without actually challenging the roots of inequality.

You don't have to look hard to find clear explanations of how capitalism is inextricably linked to multiple oppressions: racism, through (for example) slavery, imperialist acquisition of land and raw materials, and dividing white and POC workers to keep them from organizing; sexism, through exploiting the labor of women (who are already culturally devalued) and relying on women's unpaid and unrecognized labor; ableism, through laws allowing companies to hire people with disabilities at less than minimum wages; and so on.

We should talk about these things when we talk about having class privilege, because as the beneficiaries of capitalism we are implicated whether we like it or not. For white folks with class privilege, the history that gets erased when we tell our simplistic "pulled-himself-up-by-his-bootstraps" money stories is the (continuing) history of explicit and institutionalized racism in the U.S. Some of us can trace our inherited wealth to slavery or other systems in which white people directly profited off of the stolen labor or land of people of color. Even for those of us with "new" money, previous generations of our families are more than likely to have benefited from racist policies and institutions that helped white people and discriminated against people of color (Homestead Act, G.I. Bill, land grants, New Deal, loans, jobs, contracts, unions…). Throughout U.S. history, people of color have been explicitly prohibited by racist government policy from building assets; and since the most important indicator of wealth is how much money your parents had, cultural myths about a "level playing field" start to look pretty empty.

For class-privileged people to be allies in social justice movements, we have to take responsibility for the bigger picture behind our own wealth. Our personal decisions about money and the stories we tell (to ourselves and others) have reflections and repercussions connected to our place in the larger class system. Challenging these decisions and narratives, and challenging ourselves to look deeper, is a good way to start shifting our participation in oppressive systems.

From *Racism Without Racists: Color-Blind Racism and the Persistence of Racial Inequality in the United States* by Eduardo Bonilla-Silva, p. 75
From *Privilege, Power, and Difference* by Allan G. Johnson, p.86-87
*Classified*, p.67

# Portland Amusement

**Lotus Seed**
pdxamuse@yahoo.com

OAKS PARK was the first Portland amusement park to open May 30, 1905. Interestingly, it is the only one still in existance.

Located in Sellwood, right on the Willamette River, Portlanders have been loving the rides, beach, roller skating, picnics and cool oak trees for over 100 years. Gone are the monkeys, bears and roller skating elephant. The dance pavilion and huge bathing house (who'd want to swim in the Willamette NOW?) have been torn down. However roller skaters can still be delighted as they were when women always wore skirts and men suits. Not only is the rink wooden (very rare these days) it has an old time Wurlizter organ. For old schoolers this is the only place in the WORLD to skate to traditional organ music, which was of course the way it was before records and DJs.

Another fascinating thing about the Oaks rink is that because of frequent flooding of the river, the wooden floor was put on pontoons so it can be detached from its foundation and not get damaged. Ingenious!

So come take a visit to Oaks Park on a summers day for crazy rides, warm beaches (with friendly dogs), cotton candy (see it spun!), and have a roll to a beautiful organ (open all year).

oakspark.com

*Oaks bath house*

*Wurlizter organ on the roller rink circa 1964*

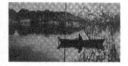

*Oaks flooded, 1948*

*"One or two hundred consecutive hours of skating mean nothing to "dad" Miller, 69 (left) and Miss Lillian Wash 18, the oldest and youngest competitors in the roller-skating marathon at the Imperial skating rink. They reckon their skating in nothing shorter than weeks, and have already outlasted 32 rivals."* March 13, 1929

*Dance marathons were all the rage in 20's and 30's. "They Shoot Horses, Don't They" is a film showing the dark side to these events. These two cuties just look like they are having fun. Check out the hands holding up the sign in the background!*

"Making candy while you wait." Edward Klees does his stuff (most likely taffy) circa 1912.

*Making icecream cones*

*Our handsome hero relaxes*

LOTUS ISLE, which opened June 27, 1930, was the most fantastic amusement park Portland had ever seen, and ever will see. Called "The Million Dollar Pleasure Paradise" and "Wonderland of the Pacific Northwest" it was the biggest park and probably the biggest park failure in the country. Built on Tomahawk Island, on the old Columbia Beach site, it was 128 acres.

The $90,000 Peacock Ballroom, with its 100 foot shimmering gold dome, held 6,600 dancers. The Alpine Rollercoaster was 3/4 mile long. Tusko the 12 ft elephant bought from a Ringling Brother was the park mascot. There was a $40,000 carousel, $15,000 Ferris Wheel, English bowling greens, golf course, mini railroad, rollerskating, zoo of Asian animals, modern bath house holding several thousand people. The whole park was the brainchild of T.H. Eslick. At that point he had been a mover and shaker in the park world for a few decades - responsible for other bigger than life parks around the world such as Luna Park in Australia, and the Santa Monica Pier Ballroom. He dubbed himself the "Pied Piper of Portland" and ads for opening day showed his fondness for rubbing elbows with the public and seeing people's smiles and awed faces. Lotus Isle's buildings were a mix of Middle Eastern and sheer fantasy. Nothing was done cheaply, expense was not spared, and Eslick went over budget

The rest of the story reads like a sensational novel from the era. It was as if there was a curse. Starting off on the wrong foot from the start, it was rumoured the park was built in hopes of Jantzen Beach buying them out. This of course did not happen. At one point Tusko was scared by a low flying stunt plane, got loose and destroyed several buildings. On August 28, 1930 an 11 year old boy fell from the Alpine coaster and drowned. The next day president Edwin Platt committed suicide. March 21 1931 a low flying plane crashed into the artificial Northwest Mountains that were part of the Scenic Railway. Luckily no one was killed. On August 21 1931 the ballroom burned to the ground. It was said you could feel the heat of the burning dance floor in Vancouver WA.

The park managed to stay open through 1932 and assets were sold in bankruptcy. All that is left is a small Lotus Isle park on Hayden Island.

# Galatea's Pants #21

Lauren Eggert-Crowe
1540 Merrill St.
Santa Cruz, CA 95062
lauren@galateaspants.com
www.galateaspants.com

Change the way you see . . . . . *Immigration*

**COMMON SAYING**

**ANOTHER WAY TO SEE IT**

**Immigrants should make a better effort to learn English.**

It isn't that easy to learn an entire language quickly, especially if you have no access to language classes, you're working 50 hours a week, or you don't stay in one place for a very long time. Also, the U.S. has never been a monolingual country, and considering the linguistic diversity of our population, using English to represent American identity excludes millions of people.

**Immigrants should assimilate into American culture.**

What is American culture? Who gets to define that? What would assimilation look like? What is particularly important about assimilation? What is threatening or discomforting about non-assimilation?

**America is a nation of immigrants. We were founded by immigrants.**

Well, no. The political United States were shaped by colonizers, settlers, missionaries, railroad barons, gold miners, traders, Chinese, Jewish, Italian, Polish, Irish, Mexican and Greek immigrants, natives, and slaves. Some of these people had enormous power in shaping the political borders of the nation. Others were colonized or used as tools for the Anglo's accrual of power. To say that *America is a nation of immigrants* erases the history of peoples like Blacks and American Indians. It also erases the violent history of the United States' birth.

**Immigrants make a choice to come to the U.S.**

The word 'choice' gets complicated when you only have *one*. Many people cross the border because they've run out of viable options in their home countries. Their town's only factory may have just shut down. They may experience violence under a military dictatorship. Sometimes the decision means the difference between starvation and survival.

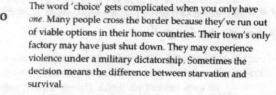

**Immigrants come here for a better life, and should be grateful for everything they get in the U.S.**

Many immigrants do come here to improve their living situation, but they also meet much adversity. If someone makes it across the border (even legally), they still face poverty, housing discrimination, barriers to education and healthcare, ICE raids, arrest and detention, long prison sentences, harassment from their employers, police violence and racial profiling, the ever-present threat of unemployment, intimidation if they try to unionize, and of course, RACISM.

**Mexico needs to clean up its economy to keep people from coming here.**

The economy is certainly a huge factor in immigration. But the blame cannot be solely placed on Mexico. One of the biggest events that has affected immigration since 1994 is NAFTA (the North American Free Trade Agreement), which was the Clinton administration's darling. Since NAFTA's loosening of trade barriers, Mexico has seen skyrocketing food costs, plummeting wages, the loss of thousands of family farms, and the displacement of approximately 1.5 million of its citizens.

**A guest worker program is a good compromise.**

The word "guest" implies there's a gracious "host" on the other side of that arrangement. In fact, guest worker programs afford very little protection for immigrants, who still aren't granted citizens' rights, and they leave employers much room for exploitative tactics like deportation threats and harassment. The 1960s Bracero program was a perfect example of this. Guest worker programs basically create a controllable mobile labor supply with fewer rights than citizens.

**Immigrants bring crime to the U.S.**

Between 1994 and 2005, the immigrant population in the U.S. more than doubled, while the violent crime rate fell 34.2% and the property crime rate fell 26.4%. This is a problematic way to judge criminality because it assumes that the U.S. definitions of crime and punishment are just. But basically, the claim that immigrants are criminals is not informed by an observed rise in crime, but by prejudices about Latinos and other immigrants of color.

**We need secure borders to combat terrorism.**

People who come to the U.S. are workers, children, families, and refugees, not terrorists.

GREE~ BORDERLAND~

*When too much light falls on everything
a special terror results.*

– Annie Dillard

In summer the sky goes flat and rapacious
Thirsty doves hurl themselves through it
and mountains rise up against the light's authority
but they can hide nothing. Visiting
rivers and relatives never stay very long.

What are we possessed by? Love
of a place? Fear of a place? Devils?
As our fair flesh burns we remain
where those before us have bowed to the light
and created monuments to the transcendence
of suffering, but we have no gift for suffering.

That is for the permanent poor who cross
the desert on foot to work or die, who offer us
their hands for our labor that we might be
free to find redemption or pleasure,
who forgive us our lives, our complicity.
Their bodies are candles burning for us
so we will not stumble on our pathway to God.

– Richard Shelton

© CURT TEICH & CO., INC.

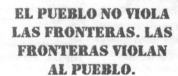

**PEOPLE DON'T
VIOLATE BORDERS.
BORDERS VIOLATE
PEOPLE.**

**EL PUEBLO NO VIOLA
LAS FRONTERAS. LAS
FRONTERAS VIOLAN
AL PUEBLO.**

# An Observance of Hermits

ckbertck@hotmail.com

## 2. Dog Spray

For gear I have marking paint and dog spray. Both are endlessly falling out of my blaze-orange vest and making me look like a goof. I also have a compass, which I use to write directions for tree trimmers who don't carry compasses. I don't trim the trees myself. I identify and name hazardous trees and prescribe the cuts that are needed on them. I should also carry a diameter tape, so I don't screw up the diameters of trees, and a view-finder for determining heights. Both of these are too burdensome so I guess with about a 85% success rate. This is an ongoing issue in my reviews. The reviews consist of me driving around with a boss while he shows me all of the things that I do wrong. Then, I go "yep, that's wrong" and we move on. Often the tree's distance is a matter of opinion and it's rather difficult to tell if a tree is six feet or five feet from the line. Various supervisors are constantly contradicting each other and telling me conflicting tasks.

I almost used my dog spray once. A foaming bloody faced German Sheppard sprinted toward me. I took a step back and braced myself, arm outstretched with the safety turned to "on" for my defensive spray. I was studying the hound's habits. Was this going to be a cowardly charge in an effort to remove me from its territory? No it wasn't. The dog lunged for my throat but luckily the owner was not far behind and he grabbed it. He was pissed, like the dog, mumbling, "I gotta get wet for a goddamn dog" (it was raining, oh, and the dog wasn't foaming, or bloody, or a German Sheppard, it was a Labradoodle [just joking again, it was a German Sheppard]). The man was shaking his head at my unknown blunder. I needed to talk to him about his trees, because I was going to cut them, but he waved his hand dismissing me then disappeared into his house still ranting. He will see it when it happens. I constantly tell myself that people who intentionally try to make me unhappy probably aren't happy, but I'm happy, and I always try to shake it off. Often both of these ideas are false.

I couldn't ask for better surroundings to work in.

Humboldt County is strikingly beautiful. A large percentage of my time I'm enjoying ocean, mountain, or river views while working. Many of the natural areas are relatively fresh and healthy. These are views people send around the country on postcards and are in magazines. This is an area of many hugely contentious environmental concerns, and with good reason. Most of the county is very rural. Often huge areas are undeveloped. Many people live with a lack of nearby neighbors.

This wasn't the only time I pulled my dog spray at a goose-bump raising sound. I may have been speaking with unbelievable hyperbole in the story above (with the dog) but trust me, the following story was real. It sounded like Zeus yelling for his life. I was in the middle of a foggy, winding backwoods road and I couldn't see the source of the sound. I was maybe 100 feet from my truck, so with my pepper spray ready for use I slowly backed toward my truck. I heard the sound repeatedly and peered through the big leaf maples and Doug fir trees on the edges of the road. The roar was getting closer. It kind of sounded like when Sloth in "The Goonies" is locked in the basement but much more meat and powerful. I got to my truck and opened the door. stood in this spot sipping a soda waiting for the beast to show itself.

I heard the sound again; it was close to the only nearby house. It was early in the morning and I thought for sure the sound must be waking everyone. Why aren't the two people living near here running from their houses, armed as best as possible? Then I saw it. It was an enormous black bull and it looked at me. It was not the usual Hereford or Longhorn even, it was something else. Its muscle definition and the lack of empathy in its eyes were alarming to say the least. It continued to walk at me and scream like a tyrannosaurus. I stood my ground I figured I could seek refuge in my truck if needed. I ha hiked away from my truck in many pastures with bulls in them. The bulls were often separated from the cows and calves. This bull was different and it walked within four feet of me, by this time I was sitting in my truck, with the door closed but the window down. It stopped to ge a better look at me with a moment of silence then he screamed in my face and walked slowly and deliberately away. It had the most enormous balls I had ever seen and walked down the middle of the road, still screaming. I imagined a car appearing from around the corner and colliding with the animal without any sort of compromise from the bull, just the car crumbling against it.

I wanted to work in a scientific field. This was not what I anticipated as I studied the scientific names of hundreds of plants or learned the feeding dynamics of Montana's wolves and grizzlies while in school.

### 3. Orientation

At this point I have been working the job for nearly four months but I'm sent to orientation or training anyway. This is five hours away from my apartment. I drove the work truck, which oddly I'm growing attached to, as we spend so much time together. It has a squealing belt and fishtails at every bump. This often sends my heart racing as I hear my wheels squeal and I head into the opposite lane at 60 miles per hour. Mt truck is a ten year old white Ford Ranger pickup but has an off-road package which means the suspension is not engineered for high speed road travel. It has a four cylinder engine and is stick shift.

The previous user of the truck spewed his dip spit directly on the ground. He also patrolled with his dog, which I would do too, if I had a dog. I already have an odd habit of talking to the dogs I meet while on the job, "shit, you think that tree will hit the lines within a year, what kind of oak is this anyway?" The dogs stare with their heads half cocked, wondering why I'm standing somewhere no one else has been since we checked the lines last year. Guessing by the smell the previous owner smoked in the truck and must have perspired profusely. The center console, which was broken and endlessly popping open, was shiny with grime of unknown origins. I have two file boxes full of bureaucratic papers of ever esoteric sort. These pretty much hog shotgun at all times and are rarely opened. I also have hordes of soda and fruit and Clif bars as well as assorted personal field guides and binoculars.

But as of now I'm in a hotel, pondering the three days of exceptionally redundant lectures ahead of me. There is always a person asking way too many questions. Then Subway for lunch, again. I thought the suburb I grew up in New York was gigantic and sprawling but here, outside of Sacramento, the suburbs are rambling for eight years. I decided to go for a walk and found nothing but numerous beauty and tanning shops, weird Asian eateries, and other bizarre food places like Jamba Juice. This may not sound peculiar to some readers but in Humboldt County we are a bit in the cut and this keeps us from what I consider a horrible tyranny of mundane chain food places. Every block in this suburb is huge, plaza size, and every road I cross is at least four lanes. I'm very scared to traverse the roads as people honk and I feel like I'm in the game Frogger. I try to play it off cool with the half-run half-jog type deal to the other side. Acting like I'm jogging for my own convenience, maybe to help out the drivers but certainly not out of necessity and most defiantly not because they want me to. But really I fear for my life and am not used to this. I can't wait to be back in the mountains.

I sit on my hotel bed and look around. This seemed to me like it should be something pretty fun but it was really boring. My thoughts began to drift. I was afraid that I had already begun to work my life away. My father had worked the same job since he was 18, everyday, all day. I thought about this and how much my own father means to me and how odd father and son dynamics are.

I was thankful to my father for making me fix my own truck when I was younger. I also had to, much to my own protest, install a bathroom, build a deck, reroof the house, run my own cable and telephone line into my bedroom, even though I had the money to pay someone else to do it. I'm glad to now know these things. People like my father learn a trade without going to school. This was hardly seen as noble but while I was at school I met students who couldn't fix a bike brake, change a taillight in their car, or fill a nail hole in order to retain their security deposit. I thought about how easily my dad could have done both of the jobs that I had had since I finished school and how he would have never been hired because he didn't spend year after year in a classroom. I would never tell him this.

# Bowling Stars of 1989

Chris Pernula
chrispernula@yahoo.com

# Hannah's Pink Pajamas

Hannah's Pink Pajamas
Bellevue, OH
rebelgirl89@hotmail.com
www.myspace.com/dirtyjuly

## Tommy

In October 2006, I lost my beloved cat of 5 years, Tommy. I found Tommy at work in 2001. He was a stray left behind by his previous owners. He was so lovable and so small. He had this big bushy tail that was the same size as his body. He loved me up until I finally decided to take him home. *It's not that I didn't want to take him home, it was that my apartment wasn't exactly one that allowed pets.* I waited a month until I told my landlord that I had this kitten. I wasn't sure what to expect, but luckily she was OK with me having a cat since (in her words) I was such a clean person.

For the longest time it was just me and Tommy. He was pretty much afraid of anybody else that entered the apartment. Soon after we found him we were informed by a girl that used to have the cat that he was abused. They used to tie him down so he couldn't move because he would scratch them. Well, duh! He was a kitten and that is what kittens do. I don't know what else happened to him but I could tell that he didn't trust just anybody and I felt special to know that he trusted me.

Tommy and I lived just the two of us until 2004. That's when Nate moved in. Nate had a cat of his own named Hookah but Tommy wasn't having that cat moving in with us. Not in *his* house. So in July 2004 we all moved into a new apartment. But, before Tommy could move in, Hookah got to move in first. It only took Tommy a few hours to adjust to the new place, he seemed to like it just fine. He even liked his new roommate which definitely surprised all of us.

Tommy and Hookah were like best friends. Always together. Sleeping side by side. Sure, they'd have their fights too, but they were still so cute together. In March 2005 a new addition came to the family. A baby. The cats didn't pay much attention to her. Not a first. Once the baby was able to move on her own did the cats not like her. Tommy was scared of Hanna. Every time she tried to touch him, he'd take off running! Hookah on the other hand, let her do what she wanted. He's pretty easy going that way. But you could tell he didn't really enjoy it!

In July 2006 we moved yet again. This time we moved into a HUGE downstairs apartment. The cats had plenty of space to run around in. And plenty of new places to sleep at!

Shortly after we moved in, we noticed the kitchen sink leaked. Nate checked it out and discovered the hose for the sprayer would leak every time you turned on the water. Nate called the landlord to tell her what was wrong. She said she would see if the island (yes, we had an island, something I always wanted!) was covered by their insurance and would get back to us about fixing it. So in the meantime Nate fixed it the best he could until the landlord came over to actually repair it. This was early August 2006. We waited and waited and she never got back to us about the island / sink problem.

One Saturday in October I went to work. I was only working a half day so I came home around 12:30. When I got home, I noticed I couldn't find Tommy anywhere. I looked all over the house, but still no cat. I got in the shower and while I was in there, Nate called for me. He found Tommy.

Tommy was in the cupboard in the island on the opposite side of the sink. Nate tried to shoe him out of there and he wouldn't move. Well, it turned out he couldn't move. Tommy just rolled over out the door and onto the floor. He was paralyzed. All he could do was meow, move his head and move his tail. Nate called the vet. No answer. He called back to their emergency pager number and left a message. We waited and waited for them to return our call. Nate called 3 more times and left three more messages. Still nothing.

I noticed that Tommy had something black on his paws and on his face. He smelled bad too. It was mold. He was trying to

wash the mold off his paws and got it in his mouth / all over his face. I put him in the bathtub and turned the water on to see if I could wash it off him. The water just scared him and he tried to get out of the tub but he just couldn't move. His muscles were damaged. I couldn't stand to see him like that and hurried him out of the tub and layed him on a blanket.

I kept him in the bathrooom for a while. Tried to give him water. Nothing. I kept thinking if he had fresh air and had something to eat or drink he would get better.

I moved him into the living room. Where he layed all night long. I went to bed and Nate and his friends did their best to comfort Tommy. They talked to him, took him outside. Did whatever they could. He seemed to improve a little, but then just got worse.

he couldn't move his tail anymore or his head. His moews became cries. All he was doing was suffering.

The next morning I got Hanna up and she went to church with my mom. I stayed with Tommy on the floor. His breathing was getting worse. It was 12:15pm Sunday. My mom came to drop Hanna off. At the same time I watched Tommy take his last breath. At around 4:30pm did the vet finally decide to call back. Well it was a little too late then.

After this happened things turned into hell at the house. We, along with the upstairs neighbors got into a huge fight with the landlord. The landlord new months ago about our problem and failed to do anything about it. If that mold killed my 14 pound cat within 24 hours what could it have done to my daughter that was

1 1/2 at the time? It took the death of my cat for the landlord to finally come over and fix every little problem in both apartments. I just wish I would have known how bad that was under the counter in that cupboard. I just wish I could have saved my cat. I still miss that little furball. I don't know if I will ever stop.

Tommy
November 2001 - October 2006

# Baby Girl #8

**Lindsey Morrison**
heartofkudzu@gmail.com

**November 4, 2005**

Last night my mom came home from her doctor's appointment and we ended up talking, both of us exhausted, in the living room about death and degeneration and other fun things...her left knee has been bothering her lately, to the point where she can't really bear much weight on it and it can buckle without any notice at all. The doctors did x-rays and MRIs...the bone is covered with cancer lesions, and she has a lump that is most likely a tumor. The doctor, Dr. Longnecker, told her that if she were to have another nuclear bone scan that her bones would "light up all over" because the cancer is everywhere. I guess on some level I *knew* this, but to actually hear my mom say, "It's in my ribs, in my back, in my shoulder, in my knees," made it *real* in a way that I've been able to avoid in my head.

She said, "I've never really thought about not being able to walk. I guess I always pictured the pain getting to an unbearable point, or being so tired all the time that I couldn't do anything." She didn't spell it out, but the unspoken sentence was, "and once it gets to that point, then I'll kill myself." She probably wouldn't say "kill myself," as it sounds kind of crude, so perhaps some sort of euphemism would be appropriate. But I know she would loathe being immobile and being even more dependent on others, so I don't know what would happen if this knee gets any worse. Her doctors are going to get together to decide whether radiating the knee would help, and I know she would dread daily radiation. she did it before, after the mastectomy back when I had just turned 14...I don't know how she did it, but she had 45 (I think) days of daily radiation, and on the last day she finished radiation

and drove 10 hours straight to Virginia to spend time with my Aunt Pat in Arlington.

She was telling me about her dad and grandmother (granddaddy and great-grandmother to me), how they both died in the best way possible. "My dad was terrified of dying like his mother. She was blind from the diabetes and couldn't walk. She had dementia and was in a home, and sometimes when you came to visit she would know who you were...the whole time, she would be begging for you to kill her, to put her out of her misery. Daddy didn't want to be like that, so I remember sitting out on the back porch with him trying to think of different scenarios. 'Just take me out behind the little house and shoot me,' he'd say, but I'd say, 'You don't want me to go to prison for the rest of my life!' We spent hours out there talking about different ways I could help him—Shearer humor can be very dark, and not many people understand it—but we finally decided that I'd take him fishing, and he'd 'accidentally' fall off the back of the boat. But in the end, he died in his sleep. Momma told me he woke up in the middle of the night and she went to the bathroom across the hall to wet a washcloth for him. When she got back in the room, he was dead. No noise or anything. And your great-grandmother was 94 before she died! Her body wore out, but her mind was still sharp as a tack so she could enjoy her life and read books and see her family. One afternoon after lunch, she lay down for a nap—all dressed up and looking good—and never woke up." I said, "Put me on that list!"

She said, "Shearer women live a long, long time, against all odds. Look at your Aunt Blanche! She was supposed to be dead 60 years ago, after a brain aneurysm, but she lived on into her 80s. She's written up in the AMA somewhere, because they

Mom and Granddaddy when she was about 22, around 1970.

never expected her to live that long. And look how long I've hung on, still fighting."

I allow myself to get caught up in an idealistic future—I think about her living until Katherine graduates high school, and then at some point after that she'll choose when to leave and it will go peacefully. That seems like the best case scenario, even though it still means she wouldn't be around to see me graduate with a higher degree or have a baby (or possibly even be here to see me get married). I don't really like to think about the potential that she could start getting sicker very quickly, even though I know on some level that it's very likely. It astounds me how she can be so positive, at least on the surface to me and

Katherine, because she came in my room last night to tell me, "I'm so lucky and I have so much to live for. Everything is going really well in my life, and I have nothing to complain about." I cannot even imagine how I would be if the roles were reversed. I'd probably be dead by now.

Jesse encouraged me to talk about it last night on the phone, but I know that he doesn't want to hear about it. Not in a derogatory way, but in a "does anyone ever really *want* to hear depressing news?" way, which is understandable but still makes me feel guilty for talking. I said, "I'm going to get off the phone, you don't need to hear this," and he said, "But I'm your boyfriend. I'll listen if you want to talk." What I really needed was physical reassurance, maybe a good hold-me-while-I-cry session, but that wasn't possible. Writing about it would have been good, but I just wasn't up to it last night. (Hence, writing about it now. I know that even though it's hard to write about, I'll want this recorded for future reading.) I kept telling him to get off the phone and play poker with his friends, responding to his queries of "are you going to be okay?" with "I'll be as okay as I always am," which is a vague and frustrating answer that probably means, "no, I'm not going to be okay, but I'll get over it like I always do and feel better tomorrow, even though I know I'm not dealing with all of this as well as I'd like."

# My Friends and Their Tall Bikes

**Kelly Peach**
**PO Box 7368**
**Santa Cruz, CA 95061**

## DEAD BUNNY'S TALL BIKE
### ( w/ BURN BARREL )
### TRAILER

seen on many midnight mystery and DROPOUT rides; this guy's always doing his best to keep his friends warm on cold late night rides. FOR WHICH he deserves a lot of love...

just **NO** hugs, seriously.

---

well... used to be chop's tall bike. this bicycle reminds us that even tall bikes get stolen. reinforcing the fact that bike thieves are indeed big ol' assholes. check out all the sweet bling though!

## CHOPS' TALL BIKE

gabe's bikes all seem to follow the same 'RAD AMERICA' theme. this one is no exception. the rack on front is really intense & i often imagine it coming to life & popping my tubes w/ it's scary pokey angles. gabe's awesome b/c he wears totally ridiculous/hilarious outfits all the time.

## GABE'S TALL BIKE

165

# Loserdom #16

Anto & Eugene Loserdom
loserdomzine@gmail.com
www.loserdomzine.com
(email for current postal address)

## CYCLING TO THE HOGE VELUWE

In December 2006 my friend Aoife and I visited the Hoge Veluwe Park. Firstly we cycled to the bus station. After we found the bus stop, Aoife sat down with a cigarette while I hit the road to cycle there on my racer. The cycle lane joined a road and I pedaled up a small hill. I clicked into my hardest gear and booted it down the hill going underneath a building that bridged the road. Soon I was out of town as forest appeared on either side of the road. A cycle lane sign said my destination was 10.5km so I continued on as the cycle lane became the width of a small road. A dense forest to my right, I met other cyclists and then hit an open countryside and arrived at Otterlo. The bus arrived ten minutes later after taking a longer route.

After a brief coffee, Aoife and I walked to the park, paying the entrance fee. Past the gate a path on the left led to the famous witte fietsen - the white bikes that are free to use. As I had my racer I didn't need one. Aoife went

over and picked one of the many. She raised the saddle and put her bag on the back carrier and we took off!

The path led us
through a wood
and then a
clearing appeared.
The first wide
open landscape
of the day

greeted us we went deeper into the park, the paved cycle
lane stretching straight into the distance with tall trees lining
it until we reached a wide open plain
that the path did not dare to cross. we
cycled along the divide between a forest

and this new plain until the path twisted and turned into
the grasslands the cycle lane rising and falling in tiny hills
while we looked into the long yellow grassland. we covered

several kms
of this and
became silent
following the
signs for a
café. we left
this landscape and entered another. Outside the café we ate
our sandwiches and then went in for a hot chocolate. We
got back on the bikes and
took a different route to
Otterlo. First by a forest, then a
moorland and then by dunes.
I pedaled softly and tried to
record as many images as
possible, trying to see the

colours of the landscapes as we cycled through them. Fearing the darkening return-journey, I cycled on ahead while Aoife went for the bus. I pedaled by the open country-side and then the forest, nodding to the other cyclists I waited at the bus stop until Aoife arrived and then we cycled home. It was very nice to visit the Hoge Veluwe in the winter. I especially enjoyed being able to cycle the whole way and also because 2 years before I had some dreams and plans to come live and work in this place, I had looked at the map of the area and saw the nature park. I imagined visiting it and cycling all the way. In the end my plan didn't work out and I was very disappointed but I still had and have the same dreams and I was very happy to have the chance to realise a little dream like that

# dad

**Timothy Colman**
timot@riseup.net
http://tttimothy.blogspot.com

(january 3)

Regret.

i try not to have regrets when it comes to
my dad; i try to be easy on myself. what i
struggle with is mostly the year he was sick,
and i try to look at myself, at 19 18 & 19,
struggling to figure things out and deal
with this other hard stuff, finally, years-
accumulated, struggling to pass my classes,
and i try to xxx say,
        "death and disease are really
        hard. it's really fucking
        difficult to be present."

but i do regret it, the denial, that i
couldn't let myself believe that he was
dying. i wish i'd been able to hold
within me the possibility of death; i
wish i'd told him xxx all the things
that were important to tell him, spent
all the time with him that i could,
asked him all thequestions i wanted to
ask.

"tell about what you believe caused the death."

(january 10)

In 2004, I lived in South Africa for five months. February to
July, I lived in Cape Town, and during this time I took a
graduate course in Oral History at the University of Cape Town.
I talked my way into this course, even though as an undergrad I
wasn't really allowed to take it. The main bulk of work for it
was doing an oral history project, start to finish. Mine was on
"gays and lesbians" active in the struggle against apartheid,
doing life story interviews to explore the relationship between
their politics, their gender/sexuality, their role in the struggle.

Anyway, this is a story about one of the people I interviewed for
the project. A white woman named Sheila, the oldest of the four
people I interviewed, she was very active in NUSAS and the

Communist Party and then went on become active in an anti-apartheid GL(B?) group whose most concrete achievement was getting "sexual orientation" written in as a protected against discrimination in the new Constitution.

she was the most reluctant of the people i interviewed. she'd been interviewed before... she wasn't sure she wanted to be again. she said things that made sense, like that 'as a woman, as a feminist, she didn't like uni-directional exchange of energy, and if i was going to interview her, i'd have to give something back.

she said it assuming i wouldn't be interested but i called her back + said i'd love to do that, and offered a few things i could exchange.

She was not impressed by my suggestions but I think she was impressed that I engaged, and so she told me I could help her in her garden, and I could interview her. An hour of interview for an hour of gardening.

The interview was good. The sound is not so great because we did it in her garden, and she was gardening while she talked, and there were loud dogs nearby. But she really took to it, opened up to me about a lot of her life, we developed a surprising intimacy. When we were done, she thanked me, and said that she actually really liked it, much more than interviews she'd done in the past.

Why all this? Why this story? Well, she was born a few years before Dad, and attended the University of the Witwatersrand, and was active in NUSAS... I noted these things during the interview, and when the tape had run out, I asked her if she'd known him. And she had.

Suddenly I wanted to pump her for information, to ask her lots of questions, but I refrained; she probably didn't know him that well, and it was so very many years ago. But I was standing in this garden, in back of a house in Obs, with a woman I barely knew, and I felt a stronger connection to Dad than I had in quite some time.

Of course, she asked how he was, and I had to say the stumbled-over words, "he died last year." She bluntly asked of what, and I said, cancer, and she asked how old, and I said, 57. and she said, "These Jewish men." (She was raised Orthodox.) "Especially these doctors. They work too hard, and then they end up with cancer."

I remember feeling kind of blind-sided.

January 31, 2007

Last day of this and it's two o'clock in the morning, I'm
sick and coming down from a long day. The last day of
this and it doesn't feel done. I wrote on twenty-seven days,

missed four. There were a few days when i wrote two or
three times. I wrote nine sonnets; I had two phone
conversations with my mom where I asked her questions
and took notes on her answers. The first time, it was 10pm
on a Sunday night, and I was sitting out in the cold on the
little stoop at the bottom of the steps to the bike shop,
frantically writing on a tiny pad of paper; the second, I was
typing onto a computer as she was talking and keep trying
to get it all down verbatim, like really really verbatim, with
my transcribing skills, except it was ridiculous cause you
can't do that live, and it was making me wish I could record
her and write it down later.

Oh. I don't know. What words do I have on this sick late night.

I'm not really good at losing people. Try as I might to fight the
death panic, it does seem to kick in, and I can't see ground in front of
my feet, just the tumble.

Four years since I lost you, since I first felt the ground fall from
under me. The fallout comes easier now; sometimes death's right
around the corner. This fall I couldn't stop imagining my accidental
death, bike accident visions while biking, enough to make me
shudder. But now it's February, and I'm so grateful to be here.

LOVE,
TIMOTHY

171

# Bipedal, By Pedal

Joe Biel
222 S Rogers St.
Bloomington, IN 47404
ragsinyourstabwounds@gmail.com

**Critical Mass** is a public event on the last Friday of every month celebrated around the world. Bicyclists and also skateboarders, roller bladers, roller skaters, pedestrians, and other self-propelled commuters take to the streets in a group. Critical Mass events have no official leader. Participants meet at a set location and time and travel as a group through city streets.

My first experience with Critical Mass was reading about it in 1995. It seemed like an incredible concept; dozens or hundreds of cyclists congregating together to celebrate bicycles, remembering they aren't alone in cycle commuting, questioning the dominate car culture and city planning that infects most of our cities, and to protect each other from being hit by cars - through being mutually supportive and more visible as a group.

The cycle commuting population and the cycle curious meet up in a common, understood location at 5:30 on the last Friday of each month. In Portland we meet up in the north side of the Park blocks near the big elephant (downtown at Burnside/Park St.). Other cities have their own location based on the ease of accessibility and some kind of central location generally. In Berkeley they meet on the second Friday of each month as to not conflict with the ride in San Francisco on the last Friday.

After everyone has

assembled we gather together and s[...] riding our bikes in one or two group[...] Some cities have an understood rout[...] at the beginning of the ride. Others [...] choose not to and decide the route [...] they go. The ride will arrive at an intersection and the people at the f[...] will determine which way to go or people with a strong opinion will sh[...] out which way they would like to tu[...] Sometimes if there is a special cycli[...] related event going on in town that night the ride will be directed to it.

If there is no destination then the ride ends when a majority of the rider[...] lose interest or have somewhere else t[...] be. Sometimes rides can last as long a[...] hours and can snake around the entire city!

I first saw the event take shape i[...] Cleveland around 1997. It wasn't qu[...] the mythical story I had been readin[...] or hearing about. The first ride I participated in was with 6 other ride[...] With such a small group we weren't terribly visible or dominating the streets. In fact, due to the landscape and city planning of Cleveland - most people actually had to DRIVE to the Critical M[...] ride. While everyone had a good attitude and was well intentioned there were a few problems. Critical Mass wasn't exactly creating an alternative to car culture when most of the people involved were participating in it.

Critical Mass is self-organized, non-commercial and n[...] competitive. The rides operate with diffused and informal decision-making – without leaders. Most are unofficial; ignorin[...] permits and official sanction from municipal authorities. Usuall[...] only the meeting place(s), date and time are fixed. Destination[...] are rarely even pre-planned. In some cities, the route, finishing point, or attractions along the way may be planned ahead so t[...] route can be established with riders (and occasionally - police) beforehand.

Participants have differing purposes – celebrating comfort in a group of cyclists, demonstrating the advantages o[...] cycling in a city, bringing attention to issues of facilities and safety, enjoying car-free social time on city streets, confronting police[...] motorists, or dominant culture, and a great variety of other purposes, many unstated. Most people just come for fun with n[...] intended protest or political agenda.

Critical Mass rides are frequently perceived as protest activities. A 2006 *New Yorker* magazine article described Critical Mass's activity as "monthly political-protest rides", and characterized Critical Mass as a part of a larger social movement. A British website, which advertises and publishes photographs of the London Critical Mass

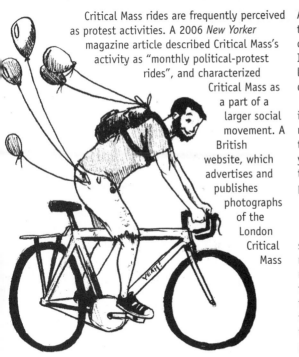

ents, describes this as "the monthly protest by cyclists claiming the streets". However, Critical Mass participants have insisted that these events should be viewed as "elebrations" and spontaneous gatherings, and not as otests or organized demonstrations. This is because people ome to Critical Mass with so many varying agendas or no genda at all. This stance also allows Critical Mass to argue a gal position that its events can occur without advance otification of local police.

Some people involved in Critical Mass are id cyclists as a way to protest the United States' igantic dependence on oil for automobiles. We see cling as a way to reduce this dependence while mmuting within our cities and towns. Granted, in ortland it's a bit easier to use this as a true lternative and never step into an automobile than many other places but nonetheless it is possible elsewhere.

Another problem with the rides in Cleveland at that time was that it was organized by the punks and so most of the true cycle commuters from the city weren't even aware of the rides. It was a cultural ghetto and as a result died out over time from lack of continued interest. I hear that new people have taken it on though and it's now stronger than ever.

Critical Mass rides vary greatly in many respects, including frequency and number of participants. For example, many small cities have monthly Critical Mass rides with fewer than twenty riders, Budapest cyclists hold only two rides each year on Car Free Day (September 22) and Earth Day that attract tens of thousands of riders. The April 22, 2007 Budapest ride participation was generally estimated around 50,000 riders.

### Yeah, but how does it work?

I imagine that Critical Mass tactics were built and refined slowly over the first few years in San Francisco. In addition to riding in big groups and being clustered together, Critical Mass moves relatively slow. This occasionally causes accidents within the ride as one rider may not notice that the person in front of them is stopping or moving at a much slower rate. The reason that the ride moves so slowly is to keep everyone together. When there are more than a dozen riders (let alone a group of 500+) it gets increasingly difficult to keep everyone together due to traffic control signals and other traffic. By moving slowly it allows the riders to catch up if they get stopped or stuck. It also allows people to easily move from the back to the front of even the largest ride with relative ease. Think of Critical Mass as a density. It works by forming a mass of bicyclists so dense and tight that it simply displaces cars. Anytime the ride begins to spread too thin, with areas large enough for a car to drive into, you have a potential trouble spot developing.

The purpose of Critical Mass is not formalized beyond meeting and carrying out the event, creating a public space where automobiles are displaced to make room for alternatives. One commonly used slogan is *We Are Traffic*. All participants, being equal in leadership, are thought to have equivalent claim to their own intentions and the purpose of the ride. Critical Mass grew alongside and probably in conjunction with the environmental movement, which cites private automobile use as catastrophic to the global and local environment, in physical and social terms. Many do not ride in opposition to anything: they simply enjoy an opportunity to cycle socially and in safety, or in a boisterous and celebratory crowd.

# The Book Bindery

Sarah Royal
Portland, OR
sarah.royal@gmail.com

Hello, neighbor!

Have you ever

wondered how a book

is made?

Or rather, have you

ever wondered what

the people who

make books

are like?

Well I once did, on both fronts, and now I finally have some answers.

I moved to Chicago from New York City fresh out of college, but decided to avoid finding a job that used me to my fullest potential. Instead I took the "go for whatever job takes you" route & applied to all sorts of strange & interesting-sounding jobs, one of which was at a bookbindery. I was picturing this Gutenberg-esque warehouse where everyone was setting type, turning hand cranks, holding sewing needles, & being wonderfully old-fashioned.

Luckily, I was hired within a day of applying, after sauntering off to a grungy industrial part of town in my brown dress pants & clicky heels. Later I changed out of my pinstripes back into my usual dirty jeans & sweatshirt jacket, & thanked heaven I had a fake job where that could be my daily uniform.

They took me on a tour of the bindery on my first day, & I felt like I was in an episode of Mr. Roger's Neighborhood. Everyone &

everything had a little station of their own in the great big factory, & they made me feel like a kid on a tour. "This is John — he arranges the tiny metal letters in a tray to spell things! And this is Scott — he pulls a big lever to stamp the letters in gold on the cover!!" My antiquated dreams really hadn't been that far off.

It turned out the whole experience was more fun-filled & fucked-up than I could have possibly imagined. My tenure in Chicago was intertwined with the bookbindery, & in the spirit of Fred Rogers (1928-2003), I've decided to preserve all the stories I have — everything from its façade of mind-numbing normalcy to the layers of ridiculous mayhem underneath.

**Art Bookbinders** of America
Chicago, Illinois 60612-1440

**Sarah Royal**
unseasonably cold bbq
planner, cookie and bagel
bite expert, Monty Python
philosophy student

Three Generations of Quality,
Dependability & Personal Care

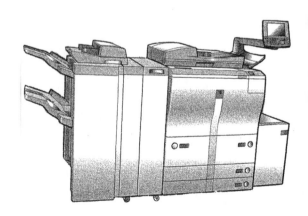

# THE DAILY GRIND, OR
# THE ART OF BOOKBINDING

I was assigned to the copy area of Art Bookbinders, where we print the pages of the books. Books are exciting. Books are what led me to apply to this position in the first place. These books we make... are not books. Don't be fooled by the name, either, they have nothing to do with art. They're compendiums of company mergers and deal closures. Boring law stuff. Dollars and nonsense. It's all garbage that rich people spend their days arranging. Reading the ridiculous year-end bonus amounts some CEOs receive or laughing at the company Morrison-Forrester's innocent "MoFo" abbreviation was about as exciting as it got.

I made the job legit right away by bitching about it. "My brain isn't stimulated enough." Well, no shit, you fucker, it's 10 bucks an hour to make copies. It's a glorified Kinkos, except without the homeless interaction or cash register. I stood over the copiers and nearly passed out in the heat and ozone they emitted, as the copy light scanned across my face, a la Fight Club. "This is your life, and it's ending one minute at a time." The fact that I could see those minutes clicking by on the printer counter made that hit home pretty hard.

I had to climb out of this repetitive rut, but before I realized how entertaining my co-workers were, I slowly learned how to entertain myself. I wore sweaty little rubber caps on my fingertips to count sheets of paper, and I cracked myself up at least three times a day by quoting Strangers With Candy lines, like "When's quittin' time, chief?", as I pushed the big green circle to print the next set. I roamed around the shop and perused the heavy-duty machinery and equipment that resembled medieval torture devices.

If something is shit, you'll probably have some good stories under your belt from what you went through, and hopefully that possibility can be enough to help you through it. "How's tranny bookbinding?" said my friend Kate, who loves stories more than most things. "Not bad," said I, "It's quite a story to tell, I'll tell you that."

# Papercutter #6

**Greig Means, editor**
**PO Box 12409**
**Portland, OR 97212**
**info@tugboatpress.com**

**Drawn by Ken Dahl**

WE CAN NEVER REALLY **ESCAPE** CIVILIZATION. ONLY **EXPORT** IT MORE DEEPLY INTO THE FIELD.

WHICH IS **UNFORTUNATE**, BECAUSE MY "HOME" WAS A SUBURBAN NIGHTMARE — A PURGATORY OF TEPID COMPLACENCE AND PRIVILEGE — AN UTTERLY STERILE, SOMNAMBULANT **PRISON** THAT WELL-MEANING WASPs SUCH AS MY PARENTS HAD WORKED ALL THEIR LIVES TO LOCK THEMSELVES INSIDE.

IT WAS A PREFABRICATED BUBBLE OF CARCINOGENS... A SAND CASTLE BUILT ON A MOUNTAIN OF HUMAN SKULLS... IT WAS, IN SHORT, THE **DOMINANT CULTURE**, AND I SUPPOSE I WAS LUCKY TO BE PART OF IT.

AND SO I'VE BEEN **TRAPPED**, IT SEEMS, BY A CULTURE AND IDENTITY THAT I CAN NEITHER ESCAPE NOR **EMBRACE**.

I COULD NEVER EMBRACE IT BECAUSE IT IS AT ITS MOST FUNDAMENTAL LEVEL A PATHOLOGY, A TRAGEDY, AND AN INJUSTICE TO A WORLD OF SLAVES TOILING TO FEED ITS APPETITES...

# Abort #19

Jonathan Spies, editor
jms390@nyu.edu
45 E 7th St. #106
New York, NY 10022

***

# Kristin

In middle school Kristin and I had the same band class. She showed up to school one day with really short hair as if she took a razor to her head without thinking. It was the first time I felt something down there. The kind of feeling you get when you're in the backseat of a turbulent bus or sitting on top of an old washing machine spinning clothes too fast. Something that only words could describe later in my life. She was quiet and hung out with kids that didn't want to hang out with me because I tried too hard to get good grades. They smoked in the bathroom and got together on weekends.

We started talking because we had to. My band teacher asked if I would help teach her the B flat scale, the easiest scale. She had a hard time because she could barely blow enough air into the instrument to make a sound. Sitting next to her in the instrument closet, young and unknowing, I asked her to watch a movie with me one Friday night.

"Sure," she shrugged.

"Okay," I said.

This was before netflix and indie video stores with DVDs. My only choice for a movie to impress her with had to be supplied by my parent's less than adequate video collection. I had two choices; *The Onion Field* and *A Clockwork Orange*. I knew nothing about either of those films so I chose the better title; *A Clockwork Orange*. The cover to the movie had been lost so there was no way I could read the movie's description. This was before the time of quick internet Google searches and wikipedia. I really wanted to impress her so I snuck into my older sister's bedroom and went underneath her mattress to find the pot she hid. I slid the crumpled smallish plastic bag full of green stems and seeds into the bottom of my shoe. On my way out I also stole her tape cassette soundtrack to *Pretty in Pink*. I really liked that song.

I left to go to Kristin's house with pot and *A Clockwork Orange* really hoping to make an impression. This was the first time I ever felt what the other girls talked about. I wanted my breath to smell perfect and my hair to appear cool. I was tired of looking like Winnie Cooper so I pulled my bangs back with a purple clip and tied my hair into a bun giving the illusion that I might not really have any hair at all.

My mom dropped me off and I waited until her car pulled out of the driveway to ring the doorbell. Kristin and I were finally alone together in her basement. She offered me a bowl of chips.

"Want some?"

"No thanks."

"No thanks."

I pulled the bag of weed from out of my shoe.

"Want some?"

"Do you have anything to smoke it with?"

I didn't know I needed something to smoke it with. I didn't think that far in advance.

"Well, we can use an empty soda can." She impressively designed a bowl out of coca cola. My heart was beating so fast. She took the bag and emptied its contents onto the coffee table. I thought I would burst from nerves and excitement. I wanted to put my hand on her knee but I was too nervous. She ran her hands through the green pile on the table and looked at me disappointed.

"These are all stems and seeds."

"What?"

"Sabrina, you can't smoke the stems and seeds."

"Ummmmm, yeah, sorry about that." I really didn't know.

"Listen, let's just watch the movie. What movie did you bring?" She picked up the cassette reading the title in confusion, "A clock work orange."

"Yeah, it came out last year. Remember?" I completely lied because I needed to redeem myself.

"Well, what's it about?'

"You'll see. It's about this guy. I think you'll really like it."

We sat next to each other in silence. I could feel my chest do that thing when you think you are breathing too much and too loud because you have a crush on the person sitting right next to you. My oxygen intake was too much and too frequent because I really wanted to touch her. Then, I started to do that thing where you yawn too much and you itch your leg too much. The movie started.

Twenty minutes into the movie she asked me to leave. She looked at me sincerely, "Listen, I wanna be your friend but I just don't like this movie. It makes me a little uncomfortable."

Fine, I looked at her saying the only words that could come out of my mouth, "Yeah, well I think your haircut sucks. And, no offense you probably wouldn't understand the movie anyway." I walked home that night crying into my sleeve so my face wouldn't be a mess when I got home. Two days later after much thought, at age thirteen, I decided I would never love again. Love is a horseshoe because you begin and end in the same place anyway.

\*\*\*

I KNOW. IT'S DEPRESSING...

# You

available through Microcosm and Sticky, P.O.Box 310, Flinders Lane, Melbourne, Victoria 8009, Australia, stickyshop@gmail.com, www.stickyinstitute.com

dear you,

my dad's having an affair.

It's this woman at his work. Her last name is jolenski. In fact, that's how he refers to her: jolenski. In my dad's lengthy career as an auto salesman, he's had only a smattering of friends, most of them women. He's never referred to them by their first names, only their surnames, as if this somehow makes them less real, or at least renders his betrayal less potent.

Over the last six months her name has come up with increasing frequency--what we know of her name. It started out simply with, "jolenski, what a funny name," and "That jolenski has one cute dog...she buys it clothes!" But soon it snowballed into a gross display of total indifference. jolenski said he should get an iphone, a $500 investment, and so he did. Now he uses the picture-phone to show my mother photographs of jolenski after work. jolenski thought my dad should get his mole lasered off. She even made his appointment for him. Dad has also started using self-tanner rendering his skin an abrasive and truly hideous orange color. And he's begun wearing new clothes. "jolenski bought these for me. She's my personal shopper." He says he can't wait to see pictures of jolenski's sister's baby. He'll be home late; he has to drive jolenski to the airport. He doesn't understand why my mother's jealous. And on and on.

He hasn't touched my mother in 24 years.

I thought it could never be as bad as it used to be. Dad would stay out late, never come home, and sleep on the couch when he did. He'd threaten to hurt my mother, menace us with knives, and scream at us. Stereotypical troubled family stuff.

My mother stayed with him despite all of this. I moved out at 17, 7 years ago, to escape that life, but mom was convinced that she couldn't survive economically alone. Dad gambled and drank, lost several jobs as well as every cent they had, and now they live with his mother. And although he never hits her anymore, this new psychological form of abuse seems so much more powerful than what preceded it.

I've spent all evening on the internet, searching for clues to his life, and this mistress's life. I've combed through his work webpage, and ransacked the myspaces of his employees. All I can find are profiles of employees from the detailing department, full of pictures from the beach, and sparkly animated graphics that say, "wat up bitches?!" That and I found the phone number for his boss. (Incidentally, this boss is new. He replaced the previous boss whose kids found their dad's mistress on his myspace top friends, alerted their mother, and the rest as they say, is history. How else do you think I got the idea?) So I could call his boss and ask him to put a stop to it. He's already stopped them from going on a work trip together because it "looked bad."

But what I really want is to call this woman, and say...what?..what could I say? In my weaker moments, I fantasize about leaving flaming poop on her doorstep, or even better, getting her fired. It's not about punishing jolenski for adultery and making her wear a big red A, as much as it's about highlighting her lapse in judgment. In case you haven't noticed, my dad's a real loser.

And maybe in my current obsessive-ness, I'm following in his footsteps. I'll definitely be clearing the cache on the laptop before bed to save myself from a seeming genetic loserdom.

One last thing: my dad's a shitty liar. He still sneaks out to smoke as if no one has noticed he's been doing it for 20 years. He also invented a prestigious training school that he was being sent to for great salesmen, but of course it turned out to be a front for a vacation with "you know who." The one comfort is that he's the type of man who'd never leave my mother completely, but as with the cigarettes, would secretly maintain his habit forever— for him, preserving the illusion is enough. Is that a comfort to my mother? Is that enough?

I'm really not sure.

yours,
-s.

# Cramhole #1

**Billups Allen and Amy Shapiro**
Tucson, AZ
cramholethecomic@hotmail.com
www.billupsallen.com

# August in Harveyville

Chantel C Guidry
PO Box 1483
Lawrence, KS 66044
chantelcherie@yahoo.com

## About the Harveyville Project

text from http://www.harveyvilleproject.com/residency.html and
http://www.harveyvilleproject.com/

The Harveyville Project is a creative residence, retreat, and
workshop getaway, surrounded by the distance and alarming
beauty of Eastern Kansas. Enjoy the solid, reassuring
institutional architecture of the early 20th century amidst
fresh air, breathtaking stars and moonlight, rolling hills,
weather you can watch from miles away, and quiet you can
actually hear.

From Harveyville, it is only 50 minutes to Lawrence, 35 to
Topeka, and less than two hours to Kansas City.

Housed in two mid-century school buildings on nine acres on
the edge of a tiny rural town, the Harveyville Project offers a
quiet, secluded, distraction-free environment to jumpstart
creative work. All rooms are outfitted with a bed (linens are
provided), table or desk, and cupboards or shelves for
storage. The high school has wireless internet access.

Utilities and a family-style dinner are included in the price of
residency, along with the use of common facilities.

For more information about the Harveyville Project

Call: (785) 589-2714
Write:  13946 Harveyville Rd - Harveyville KS 66431
or Email: info@harveyvilleproject.com

Photo by Chantel C. Guidry

## My Arrival in Harveyville
Wednesday, August 1, 2007

I arrived at the Harveyville Project in Harveyville, Kansas this
afternoon. Nikol (one of the project organizers) gave me and
Tony the grand tour and then left us to carry in my stuff.

This place is amazing! It's huge and full of wonderful and
mysterious things. It reminds me of one of those movies
where the main characters find an abandoned building that
looks like the people who inhabited it just stepped out for a
moment but were prevented from ever returning. Well, there
are no desks lined up in what used to be classrooms, but
there's enough old stuff still around to make things a little
weird.

My room is the old science classroom, on the first floor of the
building, all the way at the South end of the hall. Since this
was the science room, there is a sink. The room is bigger
than my entire first apartment in Lawrence (an efficiency on
Tennessee Street). I have a queen size bed, a sofa, a
smallish desk, and a school chair (the more modern plastic
molded kind, not the old-school wooden kind). My bicycle
is also in here, and I still have plenty of room to frolic and
dance about. The room has two ceiling fans, and four large
windows, which is good because there is no air conditioning
in the building. I was given 100% cotton sheets to put on my
bed and a down comforter to cover up with if I should get
cold (ha!) at night.

I am right next door to the old elementary school, which is
now also part of this arts complex. If the screens came off
my window and I had a rock, I could hit the wall of the
elementary school. Tony and I explored that building before
he left and found some coat hooks still labeled with the
names of students. More of that eerie, folks-just-stepped-
out-and-never-returned feeling.

I went to the Harveyville Project on a work-exchange
residency, which means I gave 20 hours a week of my labor
and didn't have to pay money to stay. Most of the work was
cleaning and setting up in preparation for the yarn school.
The following are some of the chores I did:

Collect, wash, dry, fold, and put away towels and linens

Collect recycling

Collect and empty trash

Clean kitchen after dinner: Load & unload dishwasher, put
away dishes, hand wash some dishes, wipe counters, sweep
(After the chef arrived, I was relieved of these duties.)

The old Harveyville Rural High School Building at night
Photo by Ailecia Ruscin

## My Favorite Book

Around 1977 some boys tell us girls that someone has
written the bad word "fuck" on their restroom wall. I tell them
I know all the bad words and "fuck" is not one. Kristi
Montoucet says "fuck" *is* a bad word; she knows because
her mom calls her dad that word all the time.

Around 2000 a stranger at the bus stop tells me he likes my
hairy legs.

Around 1995 I am fired from my job selling t-shirts to drunk
tourists on Bourbon Street. I am accused of being
aggressive and having a bad attitude. I squeal on the shop
owners for never paying overtime. A few moths later, I get a
check for $300 in back pay.

Around 1983 I tell Mom that *The Outsiders* is my favorite
book. She tells me it is *not* my favorite book. We have a
huge fight because I insist that she can't decide what is or
isn't my favorite book.

Around 1974 my family moves. The guy hauling our mobile
home takes a wrong turn. Dad demands to know if he is
going to Topeka, Kansas. I confidently say that there's no
such place as Topeka, Kansas. I maintain my position even
after being shown a map I can't read.

Around 1989 my boyfriend and I have clandestine
intercourse on the bus returning from our senior trip to
Disneyworld. I find the act exciting but not physically
satisfying.

Around 2003 I travel to Miami to protest the FTAA. I come
unglued at the convergence center when two young women
tell me they are there to help but refuse to clean restrooms,
proclaiming, "we're artists." Later, I clash with riot cops and
spend three boring days in jail.

# Nuns I've Known

**Nuns I've Known**
**c/o Katie**
**POB 284**
**Jenkintown, PA 19046**
**katie@thelalatheory.com**

### Sister Mary.

Sister Mary was my fifth grade teacher. She's the only one, for some reason, who in the compiling of this zine I thought to myself, I wonder if she's still alive. Sister Mary was honestly evil. Sitting in her class was all about silence. In my memory it wasn't just that no one ever talked; it was as if no one even moved. At recess every midmorning we were allowed to get up for a bathroom break, and the girls and boys would just wordlessly line up single-file, go to the little bathrooms at opposite ends of the hall, and come back, scuffing the floor with our shoes softly. One time Erin O'Connell asked to use the bathroom during a class and Sister said no. A few minutes later Erin raised her hand and asked again, and this time her face was red and she was fidgeting nervously in her seat. She said it was an emergency, but Sister still told her to stay in her seat until lunchtime. A few minutes after that I noticed that the floor beside Erin's desk was blossoming into a large yellow puddle. Poor Erin. Then Sister let her leave the room, and without a word Sister set about fetching a mop and pushing it up and down the aisle. Sometimes I think that if I only had a week to live I would spend it sitting in one of those little desks in one of those deadly little classrooms, watching the fucking clock tick backward. Honestly, it would feel like an eternity. You can't fear death when fifth grade will protect you from it by going on forever.

### Sister Josephine.

Sister Josephine was the principal of our grammar school before she had to leave and was replaced by a forceful, unpleasant battle-ax of a "lay" teacher named Mrs. Kerrigan. All the nuns who lived in the convent at our school left that year. They were sent to different parishes all around the country because there just weren't, and aren't, enough of them to go around anymore. They were replaced by regular teachers, people who weren't nuns or priests—lay teachers. The laity. Anyway, Sister was built like Nell Carter, almost as wide as she was tall, and she had a happy enough disposition, I guess. I don't remember a lot about her, I suppose because she wasn't a teacher so I didn't spend all day every day staring at her. Every morning she made the announcements over the PA system before class started. One of the teachers was named Mrs. Hungerford, and she had a son in the school, Gregory. He was a cute little kid with freckles but he was younger than me so I never really knew him. I think he was younger than my sister, too. Anyway, one morning Sister Josephine meant to call him to the office over the PA, but she said "Gregorford Hungary" instead, and then she stumbled for several seconds as she tried to recover and correct herself. It was one of those classic Catholic school moments where something amazingly funny has happened but you know you'll get killed if you crack a smile so you stifle it, but it still gives you a nice little glow for the rest of the day. Ahhh, Gregorford Hungary. My sister and I still call each other that sometimes and laugh about it all over again.

### Sister Germaine.

Yes, that was her name. No one even bothered making Tito jokes or whatever; we were too busy planning our escape routes. Sister Germaine hated me. I have no idea why. She was the music leader of my all-girls high school—she taught classes on choral music, organized the horrible shouty musicals the drama club put on every year, and was the conductor for ensemble. It would be impossible for me to express to you in mere words how much I hated ensemble. Every week we met 45 minutes before first period and sat in the band pit and tried to get through a limp rendition of some classical piece while Sister Germaine—who had bangs and round glasses—tried to humiliate us with her perplexing, mostly silent rage. It was really only me who she went after, though. Story of my life. I was a good kid, I worked hard in school and got really good grades, and I was relatively well-adjusted, or at least polite. I had an attitude problem, or something, though, that these people could always sense. Something about me brought out the beast in her. Is it terrible to admit that I wished something horrible would happen to her? A couple of times she hugged me, crushingly, to her very thin and hard body. It felt like she was made of wood.

Sister Germaine was either vicious and relentless with a girl, or she was her best friend. Her best friends were the strange girls who were in the Christian Service Corps, a volunteer organization that Sister ran, and hung out with her every spare minute they got, like during their lunch hour. Uugggh, it was such a creepy set-up. They were all in love with each other and hugged all the time, but meanwhile as soon as Sister got me alone, like when I had to perform a song for her on my stupid flute as a graded assignment, she managed to almost reduce me to tears by accusing me of doing the wrong thing when I hadn't, confusing and upsetting me, then getting angry at me as though I'd been the one who made the mistake. I refused to cry in front of her but a few times a couple of tears escaped and plopped down onto my sheet music. Her anger was as scary as my dad's: confusing, silent except for a few carefully chosen rage-fueled insults, and totally focused on me, like two bearing-down headlights. God, just writing this brings it all back, how bad she used to make me feel. She should never have been allowed to work with kids. Does anyone want to go and deface my old high school with me?

The Juniper #9: the meager words of a gentleman farmer
winter 2007/2008 • free or swap by mail

# The Juniper #9

Daniel Murphy
PO Box 3154
Moscow, ID 83843
juniperjournal@hotmail.com
juniperbug.blogspot.com

## Why We Farm: A Primer

What would happen if an ant veered off its path? Or if a brick was pulled loose from the wall? Or if a gear was pried out of the machine? Hopefully it would lead to something positive. Progressive. A welcome change. Something groundbreaking.

When we broke ground out on the farm, we weren't certain if our production plans were keeping up with progression or overshooting it. Is fresh, organic produce really in this high of demand? Will we be able to get rid of all this stuff, or will it rot in the field and only prove to make us look like fools for believing anyone would be interested enough to buy it? Mostly, we didn't care. We just wanted to grow stuff…organically (certified, officially, as of this year). Oftentimes we fly by the seat of our pants. We throw seeds in the ground and see what happens. Things are mostly planned out, but we still do some things on the fly (as everyone should sometimes). The future looks brighter with a little chaos thrown into the mix.

There are giants in this world that appear unconquerable: The onslaught of agri-business. The threat of global warming. A third world war looming. An energy crisis at hand. The future of the earth hanging in the balance. These are things that one person acting alone can't fix. It's questionable even if any of these things can actually be fixed by large groups of people acting simultaneously. But there is one thing that's certain; each individual can work towards achieving sustainability and self-sufficiency in their own life and in their own

way. And together conscientious individuals like this, when holding the reins, help to create a social sea change. The planet as a whole may currently appear to be on a shaky path, but not everyone has to go dropping off the edge of the cliff. Ants can blaze new trails. Bricks can be used to build new walls. Gears can be adapted for new machines. If the tried and true isn't working for everyone, that is if social and environmental injustices persist among traditional and conventional systems, then new movements must be forged in order to change that.

Local, organic farming is part of this new movement. Community supported agriculture is key in this process. We may not be visionaries or innovators, but we **are** part of a bigger solution. We are forward thinkers with trust enough in the soil to believe that the things we plant will grow, and faith enough in the future to believe that like-minded people like you will accept our offerings with open arms and continue to support the cause. This is why we farm.

## Why We Farm: A Rant

Some people are convinced that wealth will trickle down; that when the proverbial rich man's pockets overflow, the poor will have more than just breadcrumbs to eat. Others are certain that a global market is the answer: once all the barriers to free trade are removed, poverty-stricken countries will rise up and finally enjoy the same fruits relished by the industrial world. There are also those who claim that genetic engineering and the continued use of petro-chemicals will solve world hunger. Sure, these ideas may sound utopian, but consider their source. How can money-grubbing stuffed shirts even fathom what life for the impoverished is like? Any hair-brained schemes thought up by the mighty and enthroned could never truly be engineered to benefit anyone but themselves. The poor will still eat crumbs; they may be slightly bigger crumbs from time to time, but they will still be crumbs. The problem of world-hunger will also remain unsolved under these lines of thinking. The planet is lopsided, and the opulent aren't planning on backing down any time soon.

So, what does any of this have to do with organic farming? To me it's obvious. We live in a world of disconnect and excess. Not only are we consuming too much too fast, but we rarely even know where what we consume comes from. We are blind to that concept because as a culture we have allowed ourselves to slip slowly away from reality and connectedness. We have tunnel-visioned ourselves by deciding that the only real important thing is that we have our stuff and lots of it regardless of the cost and with little thought about where it came from or what it took to get to us. Our greatest goal is to hoard our wealth and then revel in it. Community, localness, safety/security, sustainability, wildness and more have all suffered greatly in the wake of collective self-centered global pursuits.

I believe in small, independent, sustainable, local, organic farming because it makes more sense to me. But also because it is one big step in a series of large steps that I feel we need to take in order to free ourselves from our power-hungry addictions & habitual over-consumption. We stand on shaky ground these days and calamities may be looming; localness and sustainability are keys to gaining back our independence and solving problems of security and eco-devastation. Plus, digging in the soil and playing with plants (that are chemical-free) just feels better. Sweeping generalizations and doom saying aside, being out on the farm just makes me feel more alive.

art by eric drooker: www.drooker.com

# Show Me the Money #25

Tony Hunnicut
PO Box 48161
Coon Rapids, MN 55448

## A CURRENCY IN DECLINE.

The dollar has been depreciating against the euro since December 2006. Experts have been predicting for some time that the dollar would eventually go into a nose-dive, and now that time seems to have come. The US currency has lost 50% of its value against the euro, 40% of its value against the Canadian dollar and about 22% of its value overall worldwide. Yet Ben Bernanke, chairman of the US Federal Reserve, has done nothing but look on as the dollar plunges.

A sea change appears to be taking place on the international financial markets. For years, global capital flowed in only one direction, with $2 billion going into the United States every day. Investors viewed the world's largest economy not only as a bastion of stability, but also as a place that promised the best deals, the most lucrative returns and the highest growth rates.

And Americans welcomed foreign investment. For them, it was almost a tradition to save very little and spend more than they earned -- thus achieving affluence on credit. Foreigners financed America's obsessive consumer spending, which spurred worldwide economic growth for years.

Because the US government was unable to fall back on the savings of its citizens, it too was forced to finance its budget deficit with foreign capital. Both consumer spending and the federal deficit kept the dollar high, because the rest of the world was practically scrambling to invest in the United States. This seems to have come to an end.

## INVESTORS PULLING OUT

Investors worldwide are starting to pull their money out of the US. They have realized that a people and a country cannot live beyond their means in the long term. The US dollar's exchange rate is starting to crumble as a result of this withdrawal.

The depreciation is causing growing concern about what will happen to the global economy if the United States loses its role as an engine of growth.

There are two principal causes behind the most recent development. Both have to do with the fact that Europe is becoming more attractive for international investors compared to the US. On the one hand, interest rates in Europe and the US are moving in opposite directions. The ECB plans to continue to raise its key rates in 2007, whereas interest rates appear to have peaked in the US. This means that financial investments denominated in euros are yielding higher interest rates and are in greater demand internationally, which in turn leads to a rise in the euro.

The prospects for growth are also shifting. The US economy is cooling off. The US government recently lowered its 3.3% growth forecast for 2007. First quarter 2007 growth has been 1.5%. If Americans consume less as a result of a decline in foreign capital investment, the US could even face a prolonged period of slowed growth. Ex-Federal Reserve Chairman Alan Greenspan remarked in April 2007 that he forecasted a

33% chance of a recession this year. In other words, it's going to be a bad year for anybody that works and pays bills. Don't get sick, don't let the car break down if you live any distance from work, buy a bike for back-up, maybe get a roommate.

# The Ever-Longer Billionaire Parade

At least 946 billionaires now walk the Earth, 21% more than last year. These lords of avarice and greed now sport fortunes worth a combined $3.5 trillion, over 35% more wealth than the world's billionaires held last year -- and nearly double the $1.9 trillion in net worth the world's billionaires held in 2004. The 946 world billionaires, together, make up less than one-millionth of 1% of the world's adult population. Yet they own nearly 3% of the world's household wealth.

The wealth figures carry some geographical surprises. The United States still leads the world in billionaires, with 44% of the global total. But India now boasts 36 billionaires, 12 more than Japan. Germany still hosts 55 billionaires followed by Russia with 53 billionaires.

Eight American billionaires owe their fortunes to the Wal-Mart retail empire. On the overall list, nine billionaires have built their fortunes selling luxury goods to other rich people.

# *Why do so many Die Young?*

Decent societies don't let young children die. Unequal societies do. Research in the Journal of Public Health show that children under five in rich countries whose wealth in a distributed in a relatively equal fashion die half as often -- and less -- as young children in rich countries that allow the rich grab as much wealth as they can.

The four analysts behind the research, all from Scotland's University of Dundee, compared 21 nations that sport similar levels of gross income per capita, from the United States and Japan to Finland and Australia.

Their data reveal, a very strong association between income inequality and under-five child mortality.

The analysts measured inequality by contrasting, within each rich nation, the share of national income going to the top 20% of households to the share going to the bottom 40%. The United States, the data show, has the widest gap between top and bottom and the highest child death rate. Eight children, per thousand live births, die before age five in the United States.

In Japan, the most equal nation in the study, only 4.25 children per thousand die before five. In Sweden, a nation almost as equal as Japan, only 3.25 children per thousand die before five.

Poor human nature, what horrible crimes have been committed in thy name! Every fool, from king to policeman, from the flatheaded parson to the visionless dabbler in science, presumes to speak authoritatively of human nature. The greater the mental charlatan, the more definite his insistence on the wickedness and weaknesses of human nature.

--- *Emma Goldman, "What is Anarchy?"*

20

# Duplex Planet #178

David Greenberger
PO Box 1230
Saratoga Springs, NY 12866
info@duplexplanet.com

ELEANOR: My philosophy is: I have great compassion for the male because he is born into a role that he did not choose. He is born to procreate, and it has nothing to do with the intellect, it's just the urge that comes that has to be satiated and it has just its own purpose. And sometimes that gets in the way of relationships. That's why men cheat, but they really want to have the young mother and the lover at home and they would still want to go out and cheat. This is not of the intellect, it's of the urge. They're like the lion that will sit in the sun after the deed is done and just lounge, if they could. The female gets together for curiosity and love. The male gets together because of the urge and a home - a young mother. Because after all, you were born of woman - that's a hard thing to get over. And there you are and you have no say on how your role is - your role is already proscribed for you. I don't think that guys realize that they should forgive themselves. They always feel guilty, but that's a natural role. You know what I'm saying? It's just natural. They always feel guilty that they're guilty, but if you saw six people that appealed to you, your intellect would not stand in the way. You could submerge it, and a lot of people have the ability to do that, but naturally your urge is to do the thing and go. A lot of marriages today have an open window so to speak, you do your thing and I'll do my thing, and if it works, it's a neurotic need for both of them and it works. I have friends that do that. That is not now, but I've had friends who had an open marriage and they're fine with it. I have friends that have gone into swingers clubs because they're fine with it. I, my personal self, feel that if you can't figure out, you don't have many lifetimes, you have just one lifetime to do it, and I guess I did it the hard way so to speak. I think my husband has cheated but he's been very kind about it - I never knew it, I never looked for it David, because I knew that it's a compelling thing, and boredom sometimes comes into the picture. So you have to take all that into consideration and give the other guy leeway in a sense. Family and being together and home is one thing. Sex is just by itself, it isn't the whole thing. I mean, you go to bed, but look at how many more hours you have to life, what do you do with those?

DBG: That's why there's rewards that you find in moving on from the need to roam. There's rewards that come from going through being with one person and breaking through to other levels with them.

ELEANOR: Yes, that's true that's very rewarding, because you do go through all of that and you have to be understanding. If you were completely totally in the know you'd be a woman, and I'd be a man, so viva la difference! You have to just understand it.

DBG: You think people want to be the opposite sex.

ELEANOR: Sometimes I think the guys have it pretty good. I never wanted to be a man - ever, ever! But I could understand that it's not so bad. But

*Duplex Planet is **a collection of conversations David Greenberger has with the residents of elderly facilities on Cape Cod and Martha's Vineyard.***

I just like the things that are very female. I like to have a home, I like to cook and sew and get partied up and dress and do all the female things.
But I envied the guys the lassitude of being able to walk away from everything if they wanted to, or to do things more than I could. I always marveled at a guy could pick up big things and carry them, you know, I could never do that. I'd say, "It's awesome! Look at the strength that guy has." But I could ever do that – and I wouldn't want to!

LAURA WILSON: You mean what health trouble?
DBG: No, more like shenanigans.
LAURA: Oh.
DBG: Mischief.
LAURA: We were always pretty goody-goody. We didn't do a lot of crazy things when I was growing up.
DBG: With twelve kids, you probably better not.
LAURA: Yeah. They would tell on each other, you know. I don't think I can think of anything. You mean like mischievous things?
DBG: Yeah.
LAURA: I think one night we came home too late and had to climb in the window.
DBG: That's not so bad.
LAURA: No, that's not so bad.
DBG: Doesn't involve the police.
LAURA: No, I never got into bad trouble.
DBG: I didn't think so.
LAURA: (laughs)
DBG: You don't strike me as somebody who would.

WHAT'S THE WORST TROUBLE YOU WERE EVER IN?

FRANCES BARLOW: When I was little I was always in trouble. Never anything serious, but I was a tomboy and a lot of the girls didn't like me. There was a little boy that used to pick on a girl, and this was way back when the outhouse was way out from the school, you know, wooden. And she had to go to the bathroom or she'd wet her pants. So he used to try to hold her, and I grabbed ahold of him and he started to punch me and I punched him back. And then I punched him a second time, hard, so he went down. I couldn't believe I'd done it, and I thought sure I'm in trouble. I was called in and the teacher and principal asked why I did it and I told them exactly why. It was a man teacher, Leo Frazier, and I told him why I did it, and he said, "You know something, I have to tell you young lady, I admire you for that. You were defending the helpless. She couldn't fight for herself so you helped her." He said, "You know what? They thought you were gonna get a demerit, instead of that I'll give you a plus!" I told my father and he was so proud that I stuck up for the kids. I've been doing that all my life. Anyone I see that's being treated unfairly, it makes me angry. My daughter could vouch for that, because I'll say, "You know, he's a miserable person, he doesn't even like himself!" She says, "Mother, you're never gonna change." I said, "It's too late to change me, honey." She says, "I know, I wouldn't change you anyway."

189

V. Law, editor
c/o Black Star Publishing
PO Box 20388
New York, NY 10009
cradlecap00@yahoo.com

Stephanie Walters #621650
Scott Correctional Facility
47500 Five Mile Road
Plymouth, MI 48170

### Let My Voice Be Heard

Let my voice be heard. I am a 27-year-old woman who is HIV positive. I am not ashamed that I have this disease. My name is Stephanie Walters and I am young, talented, caring, loving, kind, funny, married and someone's daughter. This does not sound like what you picture when you think of HIV. This disease has no face or nationality.

I am also a prisoner in a Michigan prison, sentenced to ten to thirty years. I am property of the state. Who am I? A person or just a number: 621650? This can't be real! Where did my life go?

I received news on December 4, 2006, that I was HIV positive. I could not believe it. There was no sympathy or warmth, just "Hey, you did know that you are HIV positive. So, can you sign this paper? You did know, right? Go ahead and undress so I can do your exam."

What? Me? Are you sure? I was in shock! The door was left wide open while I received the news. Prisoners walking by could hear the most devastating news of my life. This had to be a bad dream. I told the nurse I needed a few minutes.

It's not allowed.

I need a minute. I need to smoke! I'll be back!

As I walk out of the room, I see the faces of my peers staring at me. Trying so hard to hold myself together, tears begin to flow down my cheeks. As I hit the cold air outside, I feel myself almost collapse against the brick wall. I can't even light my Newport, my hands are shaking so badly.

A young lady comes out of health care and says to me it will be okay! "I heard! I am so sorry, truly." She is in her twenties and I realize how lucky she is. All I could do was put my head on her shoulders and cry. I remember saying, "What am I going to do about this? How? Why? I just can't believe it."

I have to pull myself together. She is saying, "You'll be alright."

"Hey! Hey! You two! What are you doing? Get moving! Get moving now!" Back to reality as the officer yells across the walkway.

I turn and face the health care building and say to myself, "This will be okay. They will treat me. I can live as long as Magic Johnson has. I will receive the same treatment."

As I walk into the building, I see everyone staring at me as I put my head down and walk through. I have never felt more ashamed as I did at that moment. I go back into the exam room as I sit on the table. I am numb. I have to sign the paper. It is yellow and it says HIV-positive in big bold black letters.

I undress for my exam. As I lay there, I feel nothing. There is a nurse and a physical assistant. As they talk, I lay there with tears streaming down my face. They continue to talk to each other and do my exam. As they finish, she says, "Do you have any questions?"

I don't say anything. What question could I ask? I still could not even talk.

The nurse says, "Get dressed. Someone will be out to talk to you about this in a few days."

As I leave the building, I realize, "Oh my god. My husband!"

I return to my unit and walk quietly to my cell. I sit on the bunk. I cry. I can't seem to stop. I have to use the bathroom so I go to leave my cell and I hear, halfway down the hall, "She is the one with AIDS. Don't use the stall after her. Oh god, she showers where we do." All I can do is turn back around with tears in my eyes and head to my cell.

What am I going to do? How do I deal with this? I will ask questions. I will study. I will learn all I can. I will gather all the literature I can about the virus. I will make it. I refuse to live like this! I refuse to die like this!

I lay in my bunk that night and stare out the window and I pray to god to help me. I don't want to die. They won't stop, all the tears. I think about suicide and a thousand ways to do it. My Bunkie says to me, "I'll show you how to hang yourself. It's easy! I'll leave the room so you can."

Days go by. I called my family. We cried. They all said the same thing: "You can live a long time with this. Don't worry Stephanie. They'll treat you. Don't worry baby. It will be okay. We will get through this."

Then came the letter to my husband. It was painful to write. How do I tell him that I am HIV positive? I love you but I have some real bad news. By the way, you are most likely positive too. And honey, I pray you forgive me because I most likely gave it to you. I can only imagine what it would feel like to hear those words from someone you love. I knew it would break his heart and I knew he would cry. That hurt more than finding out myself.

All our dreams were gone. Dreams of having children together. A life of growing old and living to a healthy old age. A life of living in comfort. All gone.

It has been four months since that day. I still remember it like it was yesterday. I felt as if I had lost everything. I was hopeless, fearful, angry.

What next? What do I do? I wait to see someone. I wait on answers. I was full of questions. I needed answers.

Then fear set in. I was afraid of everything. I was even afraid of myself. People started talking. Officers started making comments. I hated myself. This continued for a few

s. It will stop now. I will speak out. I will just put it out
⬚re. During an HIV awareness class, I'll step up and just
⬚ them all. I talked to the ladies who were doing the class
⬚ they said "You'll be the first in all the years I have been
⬚re that has spoken up about it. I have been here for twen-
⬚years."

⬚ the next class, I came out and joined them. When it got
⬚e for questions, I just simply said, "Do you know what
⬚ looks like? Well, I am positive. I don't care what you
⬚, but know that you are talking to a real person. See who
⬚m. See the pain I feel. Look at who you are hurting."

⬚egan to cry in front of all of them. There were about twen-
⬚ladies in that class.

⬚id, "Do you think I am scared at all? Do you think I
⬚oose this? I didn't!! I am all alone, five states away from
⬚ family, sentenced to a 10 to 30 year bit. And you know
⬚at? I most likely infected my husband. How do you think I
⬚l?"

⬚e class looks up and I see tears in most of their eyes. I
⬚ them it could be them, their daughters, their sons, their
⬚sbands. It only takes one bad decision to alter the rest of
⬚ir lives.

⬚ I let them know that when they feel like whispering about
⬚meone with this, remember, there is a face that goes with

⬚m that day on, I have embraced it. I started learning and
⬚king to everyone about teaching about the HIV virus.
⬚swering questions that people had. I studied all the info I
⬚. I wanted and decided that I was not going to live in
⬚ame.

⬚ear from my husband a few weeks later and it seems I
⬚s correct. My worst fear had come true. The letter read,
⬚by, I love you but I need to tell you something. I am HIV
⬚sitive." I can't even finish reading the letter. I have to
⬚se it and ask God to give me the strength to finish it.
⬚ase let him forgive me. I open it back up and he says,
⬚'t just play the blame game." I couldn't believe he was
⬚ng so forgiving.

⬚w I wait. I wait to see a doctor. I wait to ask questions. I
⬚t to see if they will treat me. I start a medical journal to
⬚ep records of my health. I begin to request health care
⬚arding my symptoms. I request mental health counseling.
⬚re is no response.

⬚sk when I will see a doctor.

⬚'t worry. You will see him soon.

⬚eks go by. No doctor. Finally, in February, I am taken to a
⬚cialist. But once I get there, I find out my appointment
⬚ been cancelled. I still have questions that can't get
⬚swered. The nurses tell me that they don't specialize in
⬚V. They tell me that my liver enzymes are elevated and
⬚t my T-Cell count is 501 and that my viral load is 7,586.
⬚at does that mean? I feel sick all the time and have no
⬚rgy. I simply don't feel well.

⬚ through periods where I have had bad diarrhea. I real-
⬚ that I will have to deal with these symptoms as they
⬚ur, but there should be an easier way to do so.

⬚ose to live a life of drugs, sex and money. These are the
⬚sequences of doing so. Since finding out the news, I
⬚ve decided to live a better quality of life. I stay positive in
⬚te of the circumstances. I don't sit still! I continue to write
⬚eople about HIV awareness. I write to advocates that
⬚ with problems relating to HIV and life in prison. I refuse
⬚sit quietly! I have a life to live and I know there is a lot left
⬚ me to do. This is the start of my journey and the healing I
⬚d to do to live.

Since writing this story, I was taken to the specialist on
March 21, 2007. I was told that at this point, he does not
see a need to start me on medications. He said that once
my t-cells are at 350, he will consider it. I have to try to live
as healthy as possible and pray that my immune system
keeps fighting. I was told by the doctor that he was prescrib-
ing me a multi-vitamin. Once I returned to the prison, I was
informed that I had to purchase them off the store.

This is the type of battle I must fight constantly. But I know
that I am not alone. Hopefully my story will inspire someone
else to continue to fight for their lives. Life is not over! You
are not alone.

Let's continue to fight for our lives and not give up!

PRISON ISSUES TALK 65:
# FOUR HOURS HOME VISIT

Another privilege at the half way house is a 4 hours
home visit. In order for you to obtain the first 4 hours home
visit permit you must:
1) Have worked at least 30 hours in a week;
2) You must have a sponsor. The sponsor can be your
husband/wife, a family member, a relative or a friend,
he/she must sign a contract agreement and be free of
criminal records;
3) the house must pass the half-way-house inspection
(free of firearms and a place for you to sleep in the future);
4) A new phone line must be install just for the half-
way-house to call, it has to be a plain line ;
5) You must answer the phone anytime they call;
6) You must agreed to be shake down, provide urine
analysis and alcohol test upon your return; etc.
When my first 4 hours home visit permit was approved,
I was so excited and full of ideas of things to do (I am a
dreamer) that it was impossible to do in 4 hours. However
there was one thing that I wanted to do it, no matter what. I
had decided that I was going to cook. I was yearning to
cook in a real kitchen, with real knife with my preferred
ingredients and my style.
Some of you may know that the father of my sons (my
husband) was kind enough to allowed me to stay in his
house with my sons; regardless of the status of our
relationship. So, my husband asked me: "what would you
like to eat, so I can order food and you just enjoy the time
with the boys?". I answered: "Oh no!, no I want to cook".
He replied: "well, what would you like to cook?"; I said: "I
will cook Arroz con Pollo( rice with chicken) in my style".
He answered: "the boys do not like Arroz con Pollo"; then I
said: "what about this?; what about that?". He answered:
"no, the boys do not like this, that, ....". I said: "well, you
decide what I will cook". he replied: "Ok". (My first
disappointment)
When I got home, my husband had the food already
seasoned sitting in top of the stove. I said to him: "why did
you do that, did not I tell you that I wanted to cook?". He
replied: "I know you said that, but the boys like the food in
a certain way that it is not your style," he paused and
added: "you must first learn how they eat". (My Second
disappointment).
At that point I could not handled a third
disappointment, so I gained my posture, I wanted to be
brave and I hided my frustrations from the reality that I did
not know anything about my sons. I said to my husband:
"you are right, but I can handle it from here". He left the
kitchen, but he was silently watching me from the distance.
Dear friends, I was completely lost in that kitchen, I did
not know where anything was, I opened and closed drawers
and cabinet doors back and forth; to then ask my husband:
"where it is this...., where it is that....?"
I managed to finished the meal and I was ready to serve
the table. While I was trying to do my best and be
efficient, all that I heard was: "mom, I do not sit there";
"mom I do not drink that", "mom I do not like tomatoes",
"mom I do not....", "mom. I do not ....".
I was so embarrassed in front of my sons that I was
close to explode in tears, but I was able to control myself;
however I could not eat. After we finished, I hardly had
time to do the dishes. It was time to go back to the half-
way-house.
On my way back, I was scared of my own thoughts. I
even thought to turn myself back to prison (the only
environment that I knew very well). I said to myself: "who
I am now?, a mother that does not know anything about her
sons"
This week I am starting a series of PIT related to the Re-
entry into my sons' life. It has been the hardest and most
painful experience after my release also most difficult to
write about it.

I am still struggling to get their (my sons) love,
confident, trust and respect. Our relationship is better now,
but I am in need of your prayers and/or positive energy.
When I am with them (my sons) I have to take one (1)
minute at a time and if I cry, then smile because I know
that tomorrow will always be a new day with a bright sun
that will lighten my life in my sons' eyes. I love you all.

Yraida L. Guanipa

After spending 10 years, 6 months and 18 days in prison,
Yraida L. Guanipa now lives at a halfway house in Florida.
In 2005, utilizing the BOP's new e-mail system for
inmates, she began "Prison Talk On-line" (PTO), e-
mailed descriptions of life in Federal Correctional Camp
Coleman. After her release in December 2006, she
changed the title to "Prison Issues Talk" and continues
to describe the effects of incarceration on not only her
but also her family and community.

She can be reached at: ylguanipa@yahoo.com

# Storage Scavenging for Dummies

STORAGE SCAVENGING FOR DUMMIES?
OR......

Building portable modular storage units with found materials.

Geoff Tanner
lewddite@hotmail.com

This is based on shelves I designed & built for the Anchor Archive Regional Zine Project/library in Halifax, N.S.. It's a very flexible system that can be designed around the things it will hold, the space it is to fit in, the materials at hand, etc. I'm sure the materials needed can be scavenged just about anywhere in the wasteful west. It's also a very portable system. Depending on what's in it, you should be able to move it with it's contents & set it up somewhere else in a matter of minutes.

The first step is to decide what you will be storing in it. In this instance it would be holding zines of all sizes which were to be stored in uniform, homemade cardboard boxes. We made the boxes first, then designed & built the units to fit both the boxes & the space available in the room.

The boxes were a direct copy of a file box on hand. I suck at drawing, but this is what they look like —

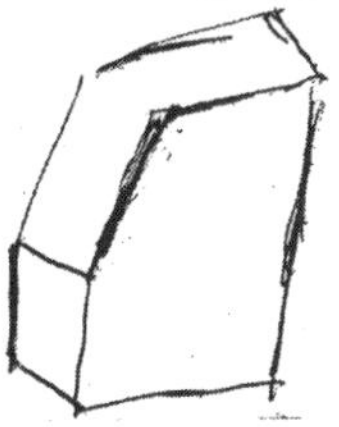

opened and spread out the existing box, like this — and traced it on a thin piece of masonite. To make them, I

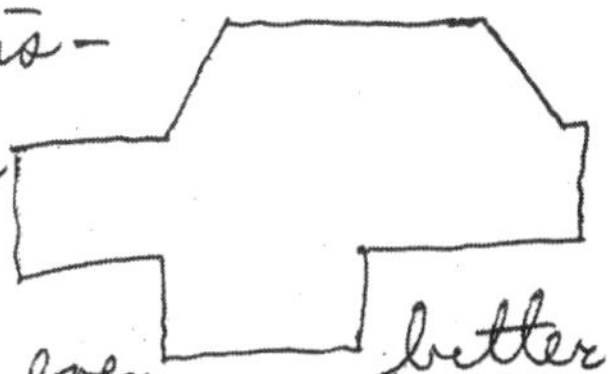

plexiglass would work even better if you had it, and a means to cut it. The next step is to find large pieces of corrugated cardboard. Lucky for us, there's a cardboard dumpster half a block away from the zine

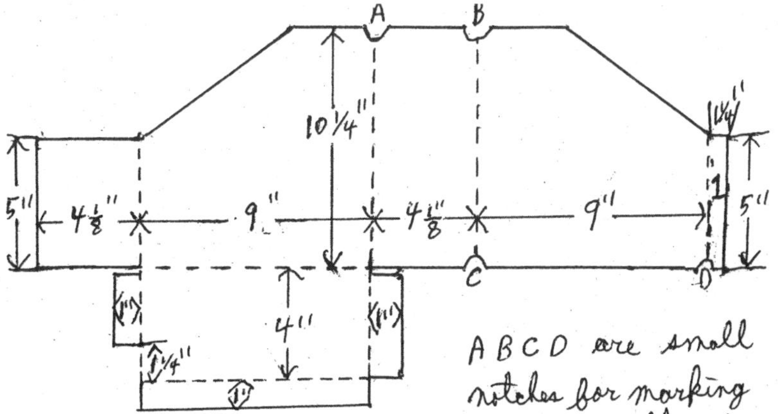

Suggested layout for file box

ABCD are small notches for marking ends of folding lines

193

# Your Mometer #7

**P.O. Box 66835**
**Portland, OR 97290**
**cfastwolf@hotmail.com**

## MOM'S RECORD CORNER...

Black Flag-Damaged 1981 SST Records. While certainly not as good as anything they put out before it (compiled as "the first four years"CD) it is ugly, loud, and mean. Humor and anger. Sarcasm. Why is this worth a mention you ask? Because 1980's copies came with a warning sticker "AS A PARENT I FOUND THIS TO BE AN ANTI PARENT RECORD". Plus it's a good example of new generational music that a previous generation will find confusing. My mom listened to protest music when she was younger. Dylan, Baez, Jefferson Airplane. But she can't get behind newer stuff. It is still about hating cops, but now it's faster and comes with a fist and a brick.

Velvet Underground-White light/ White heat 1968 Verve Records. I had this record on the stereo in our living room while Meklo and I were playing games on th ATARI 2600. Mom walked in. I though she might dig it cuz it's from her

1960's but she said "I've heard better"and left the house.

PIXIES-SURFER ROSA 1988 4AD Records. A different time,the same thing, "I'VE heard better".

PINK FLOYD-THE WALL 1979 columba Records. A friend of mine taped this dinosaur for me when we were in the 10th grade and it wasn't too bad for a rock opera. They even made a movie about it. I played the tape a few times around the house to cool out (you don't need to be agro all the time, dude). One day mom came into my room and sat down and says, "son, we've noticed that you've been having some problems lately. If you need to talk about it..." No wait, that's the wrong band. One day mom came into my room while I had this tape playing and she wanted to know who it was and what it was all about. I told her it was a story set to music about an overly controlling mother and how her son's life falls apart. She seemed satisfied with this but she didn't

speak much with me the rest of the week and we ate chilli that night. I don't think I've listened to the album since that week. I know I taped some BUZZCOCKS albums over it (thanks forever to Themos). Nowadays mom listens to a radio station that plays no new hits, just older ones. She likes "the radioheads",REM, and THE TALKING HEADS. But she most certainly **did not enjoy** THE BUTTHOLE SURFERS EP 1983 Alternatine tenticles Records. Seven damaged songs played over and over. "This is just plain stupid" "Trash". Mom also thought Madonna's music was "Trash". I should say something nice now, so I'll let you know a secret. Despite what she thinks about blacks, she did totally love SIR MIX-A-LOT's video for BABY GOT BACK. "BOYS! BOYS! COME IN HERE THIS MINUTE! THE BUTT VIDEO!"

# Spread Vol 3, #2

**Darby Hickey, author of article**
**Rachel Aimee, editor**
**PO Box 305, Cooper Station**
**New York, NY 10276**
**info@spreadmagazine.org**
**www.spreadmagazine.org**

"White men who use violence get to be porn stars and preachers (not to mention Presidents), while women of color and low-income women who use violence get shipped off to the cuckoo's nest."

"We don't need protection, we need a revolution."

"What were the gushing moviegoers who wept at Charlize Theron's on-screen demise busy doing on the morning of October 9th, 2002, when the "real" Wuornos was sent to her death by lethal injection?"

"In a country of criminalized prostitution, in which women in Richardson's line of work supposedly forfeit their entitlement to safety, she demands it anyway, with a switchblade."

## The Cutting Edge: On Sex Workers, Serial Killers, and Switchblades
By Sarah Stillman

I remember how Ronnie, my third-grade playground crush, used to whisper that illicit little ditty from the top of the jungle gym as if it might be the secret password to the gates of American manhood: "Lorena, Lorena, the nightmare wife…Sliced her husband's hot dog with a butcher knife!"

I remember, too, how it made me giggle hysterically—not just Ronnie's home-spun folksong, but the deluge of cartoons, media wisecracks, T-shirt slogans, and weenie-whacking tunes that flooded my nine-year-old head in the months after John Wayne Bobbitt lost his penis to the glimmering knife of his then-wife, Lorena.

No one in the national press bothered to mention that the infamous deed had occurred only after John Wayne, an ex-marine with a history of domestic violence, allegedly returned from a drinking binge, raped Lorena, and then fell fast asleep in their bed. Between chuckles, no one read me Lorena Bobbitt's courtroom testimony, in which the Ecuadorian immigrant described the "beating, kicking, punching, shoving, slapping, dragging, [and] choking" she suffered at her husband's hand in the preceding years of economic dependency. Instead, I heard mostly of limericks and advertising gimmicks, like the radio disc jockey who

offered free Slice soda and cocktail weenies with ketchup from a booth nearby the courthouse where Lorena was eventually acquitted of "malicious wounding" charges—not in the name of self-defense, but rather on a diagnosis of temporary insanity that required a stint in a mental hospital.

It was only a decade later, under the guidance of a wise feminist or two, that I discovered the bizarre story of John Wayne Bobbitt's rise—no pun intended—to stardom as an accused rapist-turned-pornstar. Following his debut in such hardcore hits as *Frankenpenis* and *John Wayne Bobbitt … Uncut*, Mr. Bobbitt eventually moved on to an equally illustrious career as an evangelical minister. By then, however, he'd already taught me a valuable lesson about gender, sex, and knives: white men who use violence get to be porn stars and preachers (not to mention Presidents), while women of color and low-income women who use violence get shipped off to the cuckoo's nest.

Recently, I've been thinking yet again about Lorena Bobbitt because I've been brooding even harder about a woman named Tonya Richardson. A self-described "working girl" with a Lara Croft air about her, Richardson walks the streets and jack-shacks of Daytona Beach, Florida, "specializing" in the notoriously bottle-strewn expanse of Ridgewood Avenue. She boasts a Southern twang that's just slightly more ass-kicker than sleep-walker—like a woman who's mastered Martin Luther King's famous art of righteous rage but who's starting to feel the wear and tear of it. She dresses in simple collared shirts. She warms to churchgoers. And, most relevant to the story at hand, she carries a sharpened switchblade with the intent to kill.

I first encountered Richardson on Florida's Local 6 nightly news, amidst reports back in March 2006 of a serial killer on the prowl. Three women, described in the press only as "addicts and prostitutes," had been murdered in the previous months near Richardson's Daytona Beach stomping grounds. As spring emerged, the silence enveloping their deaths thawed, largely due to fears that "innocent" spring break vacationers might now be at risk alongside their whoring counterparts. While Fox News dispensed footage of gyrating, bikini-clad college girls in reference to this possible threat—as if the killings only merited coverage now that attractive state school students were arriving in droves—Local 6 had a very different story to tell.

"Daytona Prostitutes Hunting Serial Killer" read the title on the monitor. "Rather than run from the man police labeled a serial killer," Local 6 reporter Tarik Minor began, "streetwalkers here in Daytona Beach along Ridgewood Avenue say they are seeking the serial killer out." As cameras panned the palm-lined street, Minor continued, "They believe the man responsible for murdering three women here is someone they have come in contact with."

Within no time, Tonya Richardson commanded the screen, framed in that familiar tight-angle crop of a politician or a spokeswoman for an international NGO. "We'll get him first," she declared of the serial killer. She nodded vigorously, "Yeah, we are going to get him first. When we find him, he is going to be sorry. It is as simple as that."

My jaw fell slack. It wasn't the extremity of Richardson's pledge that took me by surprise; her words fell miles away from "sugar and spice and everything nice," but her seriousness matched the gravity of the threat she faced. Nor was it the melodramatic buzz of the broadcast that struck me, although it was certainly the stuff of a Hollywood screenwriter's wet dream. Instead, the straightforward way the details were presented—right from Richardson's confident lips—brought me to a striking realization: never before on mainstream TV had I seen a story about sex workers' resistance told with this brand of matter-of-fact simplicity. Or even, come to think of it, told at all. This insight sparked my curiosity: how often have women like Richardson and her Daytona Beach cohorts taken up arms, and what kind of portrayals await them when they do? Where do sex workers and their allies turn in times of heightened violence—when a serial killer, for instance, is at large?

Since hearing about Tonya Richardson's case in the spring of 2006, I've set out to look for answers from those who know best: not news anchors or crime beat reporters, but self-identified street-walkers, call girls, strippers, dommes, and sex workers of various stripes. And what I've collected over the past year are strategies for self-protection that run the gamut from the mundane to the no-holds-barred, the indulgently commercial to the intensely practical. Not far from my home in England, for example, I discovered a group of sex workers and their allies who took to the streets of Ipswich after a serial killer murdered five sex workers there in December: resisting national broadcasters' entreaties that women stay inside their homes until the "Ipswich Ripper" could be apprehended, the protestors

stormed the area, chanting, "We don't need protection, we need a revolution." On the other side of the ocean, not far from a Canadian pig farm where more than two dozen indigenous sex workers were brutally murdered over a period of 25 years, I encountered a group of prostitutes in thigh-high boots who offered me a copy of their low-budget zine targeting johns, which, they explained, is meant to curb violence by communicating their standards for personal safety directly to the most relevant audience.

Street-savvy technologies and products seem to be the saving grace for many sex workers' these days: everything from cell phones to bras with secret linings for hiding the evening's earnings. True, some examples are rather pricey and elaborate; a stripper named Veronica at the Catwalk in New Haven told me about a new kind of platform shoe for urban sex workers that has a built-in alarm system, a GPS receiver, and emergency buttons that signal both law enforcement and local sex workers' rights groups. [*See Style page INSERT PAGE NUMBER – Ed.*] But other ideas cooked up by women and transgender folks are more accessible to those with minimal resources at their disposal—from cheap rape alarms purchased in bulk to entirely cost-free practices like buddy systems. Some sex workers train together at firing ranges while others study non-violent strategies of conflict de-escalation; some rely on end-of-the-night text messaging while there are others still who have perfected the 100% free strategy of license-plate memorization.

More interesting than the individual, consumption-based strategies tend to be the collective ones. Groups like the Sex Workers Alliance of Toronto (SWAT) publish an annual "bad date booklet," where sex workers can anonymously report assaults, rip offs, or harassment from clients (as well as from police, neighborhood groups, and stalkers) in order to help others avoid similar situations. Another Canadian initiative fights for "safe zones" in Vancouver—special areas of shops and buildings clearly marked with window stickers where sex workers of all gender identities can run if they're in danger, or if they simply want to use a phone or kick back with some coffee.

Then there are more broad-based co-ops like Nevada's Sex Workers Outreach Project or Seattle's Home Alive, whose mission is to fuel "a cultural and social movement that puts violence in a context of political, economic, and social oppression and frames safety as a human right." Founded in the wake of several brutal rapes and murders of women in the city, Home Alive organizes everything from self-defense classes and boundary-setting workshops to public chalking events and community conversations. In a single year, the non-profit offered more than 100 presentations to schools, workplaces, and low-income housing projects and shelters. Their analysis continues to help place the struggle against sexual violence in a larger political framework. "We believe that debunking stereotypes grounded in sexism and racism is one of the keys to ensuring sex workers' safety," says Home Alive director Becka Tilsen. "This is why we advocate a community response to violence that targets all forms of institutional oppression, but also gives people the tools they need to defend themselves."

Returning to Tonya Richardson's story, it's worth noting that this, too, was an example of community mobilization and not an individual crusade. Richardson always spoke to reporters in the plural—"We will get him," not "I will get him"—and one doubts this detail was accidental. Some of the sex workers' commentary on the killer may have sounded individualist, like a woman cited only as Shalonda who told the *Orlando Sentinel,* "I don't go nowhere without my knife…[because] if nobody ain't gonna protect me, I gotta protect me." Ultimately, however, most women along Ridgewood Avenue took up arms as part of an informal communal strategy to both protect themselves and watch each other's backs.

And if it takes a village to thwart a serial killer, then sex worker allies in Daytona Beach have also played an important role in that task. Extremely problematic as the history of religious interventions might be, it's worth noting that the Halifax Urban Ministry's volunteers rallied to sex workers' defense with a streetwalking program of their own—going out to talk with sex workers about potential threats, providing space for them to brainstorm modes of self-protection, lobbying for better lighting on dangerous avenues, and reminding the wider community that the saintly Mary Magdalene herself was none other than a prostitute.

In each of the individual and collective examples of creative resistance I've cited so far, catching word of silenced stories is only half the battle. Next comes the challenge of representation. How do sex workers get their voices back into the public sphere, while also addressing difficult internal debates about, for instance, violent versus non-violent means of seeking change? On the one hand, sex workers' resistance is often ignored within or actively erased from our public records. On the other hand, it's sometimes scrawled in bright red ink on billboards and tabloids all across America: sexualized, sensationalized, glamorized, and re-packaged for the highest bidder.

Nowhere is this truer than in Hollywood, where few things sell better or titillate more than the cocktail of sex, women, and weaponry. Directors often want to have their stories both ways: cashing in on the tear-jerking image of the helpless female victim, while also harnessing the energy of the hysterical whore. A clear case in point is that of Aileen Wuornos, a sex worker in Florida who earned infamy as "the first female serial killer" after murdering seven johns whom she accused of rape or attempted rape. In a searing documentary called "Aileen Wuornos: The Selling of a Serial Killer," Nick Broomfield shows how Wuornos's own lawyer showed more interest in auctioning off the film rights to his client's life than in saving her from death row. A decade later, when Charlize Theron's portrayal of Wuornos in the Hollywood film *Monster* won her an Academy Award for Best Actress, more dicey questions about Wuornos's commodification arose. It was hard not to wonder what most gushing moviegoers who wept at Theron's on-screen demise and rallied to her character's imaginary defense were busy doing on the morning of October 9th, 2002, when the "real" Wuornos was sent to her death by lethal injection.

On the rare occasions when women who employ extreme means of self-defense aren't depicted as stark-raving loonies, they still tend to be punished in the end—think *Thelma and Louise* or *Madame Butterfly*. Frankly, Pedro Almodóvar's recent box office hit, *Volver*, is the first movie I've seen in which a young woman's retaliation against sexual violence doesn't ultimately boomerang around to destroy her, too. But this plot anomaly is possible only because the doe-eyed teenage daughter with the kitchen knife in hand is not, in fact, a sex worker. To the contrary, she is still young and virginal enough to be considered an "innocent" victim—one who has not yet compromised her right to be surprised by male violence due to the clothes she wears, the streets she walks, or the hours she walks them.

Not true of Tonya Richardson. In a country of criminalized prostitution, in which women in Richardson's line of work supposedly forfeit their entitlement to safety, she demands it anyway, with a switchblade. And that's why I return to her story again and again, filled with a deep and contradictory swirl of emotions: My admiration for a woman and her colleagues who have stood up for themselves against a serial killer who left three women with their pants down in a ditch. My surprise that a mainstream media source dared to cover their collective action so straightforwardly. My anger and heartbreak that a group of women—or, for that matter, *people*—would ever be placed in a circumstance where wielding a switchblade felt "necessary." Or, perhaps more inexcusable, where the burden of finding and restraining a person who wants to mutilate their bodies would be thrust on an already disenfranchised group instead of being considered a collective, societal priority. And of course, my awareness that as a privileged white woman, I owe Richardson and her colleagues far more by way of solidarity than I've offered—pulling my weight in pursuit of a world where safety is considered a sex worker's basic human right.

shortandqueer #8

I am not unreasonable

# shortandqueer #8

**Kelly Shortandqueer**
**PO Box 13559**
**Denver, CO 80201**
**shortandqueer@yahoo.com**
**www. shortandqueer.com**

An excerpt from "A Response":

**Hey Kelly,**

**oopsie, sorry about the gender pronoun mixup, but i must warn you, i make those mistakes ALL the time with my husband/wife :) its just cause i kinda think about gender as changeable, not black and white, so i constantly mix the pronouns up in my speech because Dan/Laura\* changes back and forth all the time and i just think of everyone being like that to some degree, including myself :) (i sometimes refer to myself as a "guy" or guys as "ladies", hee hee) anyhow, i will try to be more careful in the future but no guarantees :)**

**I cant wait to see the next issues of Trans(in)formation and Short and Queer!**
**Kate\***
**hope your summer is going well so far, talk soon :)**

(*Names have been changed)

Woah.

This was not what I was looking for.

I was overcome with emotion but was having a hard time figuring out exactly what was going on for me. Was I overreacting? Was I justified in my anger? Was I taking away other people's fluidity? Was mine being taken away? With all of this going on in my head, I knew I couldn't respond immediately. I remember lying in bed, writing e-mails in my head until I fell asleep (which took a while because I felt really wound up).

My first draft went something like this:
Dear Kate,
I think it's really awesome that you're able to embrace gender fluidity and switch back and forth with pronouns. It's definitely something that is a challenge for a lot of people. I identify as genderqueer and...

Then I'd get stuck.

I identify as genderqueer and I think it's important to be able to switch pronouns whenever is appropriate, whether that is what makes someone the most comfortable or is a survival choice. I didn't get into this in the e-mail in my head but

wanted to make sure to mention it here. I work for the Colorado Anti-Violence Program and have found myself in situations where service providers are trying to deny services to transwomen who are making survival choices about gender. She may be coming from an all-male facility where it would be physically dangerous for her to express the femininity that feels more comfortable. She may present as a man in order to find a job because transphobia is so prevalent in employment discrimination and "gender identity and expression" is not in a lot of non-discrimination policies, even when "sexual orientation" is included. She may need to present in a more masculine way in order to get through her day without harassment, to have access to bathrooms, to have access to health services, shelter, food, resources, etc. It is about survival, not a confusion or flakiness around identity. At the same time, there are people who feel more comfortable moving back and forth between ideas around masculinity and femininity, concepts of man and woman. These descriptors might both be applicable or maybe neither of them are but they're used alternately to bring attention to how they're not an adequate description of themselves. This is not confusion or flakiness around identity either. People who feel this way are often very confident in their identity and often run into language barriers because there aren't appropriate words to describe them.

I identity as genderqueer and I think it's awesome that you can support your partner (or husband/wife as you called him/her before), and go with the flow. I identify as genderqueer and...

I identify as genderqueer and... No. It's not ok that you're messing up my pronouns.

Every time, I'd end up in the same place. And every time, I'd get nervous. Maybe I'm not really genderqueer. Maybe I used to be and am becoming a gender essentialist. Pronouns are non-negotiable with me. I must have unintentionally handed in my "genderqueer card" and shifted to a binary when I was wasn't paying attention. And here I am co-opting an identity that's not even mine anymore! I am being so fucked up!

But wait... I don't believe in the binary. I embrace fluidity. I use gender-neutral pronouns for friends. I still think it's amazing when people consciously live in that in-between space; when people pick and choose what they like from various gender roles. So, do I only appreciate this in other people? Has being on testosterone moved me to a new place or myself? Now that I pass as male most of the time, I no longer have to navigate that in-between space unless I intentionally put myself there. Am I still putting myself there? Or am I allowing my new-found male privilege to let me coast through life in a way I had never experienced before? Oh my goodness! What's happened to me?

I was going in circles in my head about all of the ways that I was being inappropriate: using an identity that didn't fit anymore, taking advantage of my privilege. Gross! I've become exactly what I was trying to avoid. This is NOT why I wanted to transition.

I had to have several conversations with friends to get some of this worked out. I was struggling and was glad that as soon as I opened my mouth, I received the validation I so desperately needed.

I DO identify as genderqueer.

Yes, pronouns are non-negotiable for me. You cannot call me "she" or refer to me as "her". It's not a request. I will not be flexible. I am not being inappropriate for demanding this. It has been a struggle to get to this place. I lived in Denver for a year before I went to Chicago and came out as trans. I wondered why it happened in Chicago where I didn't have the social network that existed for me in Denver. After about a year away, I came back to Denver. And it was hard. People couldn't get my pronouns right. Some people just didn't know and I felt helpless and lonely and scared and was unable to tell them. And the people who knew and kept messing up... I felt completely alienated from a community from whom I used to draw strength. I was miserable. And then I realized that was exactly the reason I had to leave in order to come out. I didn't feel like I had the support I needed. There were too many people with assumptions about who I was and I didn't see much flexibility in changing their minds, especially when I felt so nervous and unsafe expressing myself. Even when I had strong moments, they never stuck with me as long as the times that I didn't stand up for myself, couldn't stand up for myself.

A supervisor at work told me that I wasn't trying hard enough, that I wasn't doing that much different, and so he couldn't think of me as a boy. I wanted to scream at him, but instead, I let a coworker come to my rescue, but then be fucked up in a different way, sacrificing someone else's identity to defend mine. That didn't feel good either.

While I enjoyed parts of my life in-between gender, being androgynous, dealing with others' confusion around my gender, I didn't feel like I had much power there. I wasn't able to decide to step out of that when it felt more comfortable or safe to do so.

Instead, I had to learn how to defend myself, act tougher than I felt, take criticism, inappropriate comments, etc. I developed coping mechanisms that made people in my life think that everything was ok when I was falling apart inside. It sucked. A lot. Now that I have facial hair and my voice has dropped, most people read me as male. When I begin contact with someone through e-mail, I often wonder if they assume that the Kelly they are writing to is a woman. There are often times that the first phone or in-person interaction begins with an awkward readjustment of gender expectations. I love that. It's amazing to see people confront their assumptions in ways that don't feel as dangerous to me or leaves me feeling vulnerable in those same ways.

I do still enjoy being able to live parts of my life between genders. Through mannerisms: the way I sit, the way I cross my legs, the way I gesticulate, the way I dance. Through clothing: I love dressing in drag, showing up to parties all dolled up in a wig, a super-cute dress and wearing a petticoat. I love that I can do these things and not have my gender challenged. My friends do NOT get confused, mess up pronouns, or wonder how this fits into my identity.

I AM genderqueer. And pronouns are NOT negotiable. Whew. I'm glad that's settled.

Ok, so starting again: I identify as genderqueer and I know how important it is to have identity respected, recognized and celebrated. I think it's amazing that you can support people in your life in that way. I think it's awesome that you can apply that to yourself as well. I love when people play with gender, with language, with pronouns. At the same time, I am very clear in my identity and I need you to show me that same respect and support. Refusing to respect someone's pronoun choice is transphobic. In this case, I understand that the intention is different. You're trying to widen language instead of restricting it. You're trying to give room for other identities, other people. In the process, however, the message is that my identity isn't valid. It isn't worth the extra effort to get it right. "I will try to be more careful in the future but no guarantees" says to me that this is my problem, not yours. But, after my initial reaction to take that on, I have to say, no, it isn't my problem. And if you can't guarantee that you'll get it right in the future, I don't have the time, energy or emotion to try again. I'm sick of doubting myself, of allowing other people to make me doubt my choices, my intentions, my identity. I like who I am and the person I'm in the process of becoming. If you're willing to meet me here, I'll be waiting.

# Kerbloom #68

*Ker-bloom!
Artnoose
5532 Baywood St.
Pittsburgh, PA 15206
artnoose@yahoo.com
http://craftycards.net/projects

Ker-Bloom! sixty-eight

...and Why I'm
Leaving.

I'm not the first to love the Bay Area, nor the first to leave it. I have to admit that in the past, when people I knew moved away, I felt a little resentful, especially if they said they were moving away because the Bay Area was too expensive. I felt betrayed in a way, both personally because they were choosing economics over proximity to me, but also a general disappointment that they were in my eyes giving up the struggle.

Yes, living in the Bay Area is a financial struggle. It's no secret. It's a great place with some great people, but you pay for all that greatness. You pay with high housing costs, and you pay by periodically losing your friends to less costly cities. However, I always had felt that the struggle made us tougher.

Oakland is a tough place. It's gritty, and I'm proud to be from here, even if I wasn't born here. I don't live in Portland. I don't live in Santa Cruz. I live in Oakland, and I was living here before it was cool, before the hipsterization of LoBot, when the packs of stray dogs still roamed Dog Town. I remember an era of punk houses and warehouse spaces that no longer exist. And yet, my own personal time here is miniscule compared to the long and rich history of this big city.

I talk about Oakland the way a lover can. I didn't just come here to check it out, putz around for a while and then move on to the next big thing. When I arrived in 1993, I intended to stay. I entrenched my life deeply into the city and after a while I couldn't see how I could ever leave. I built a life here, formed relationships, and acquired heavy machinery. I even bought a pair of "Oakland Booty" underpants.

Themed underclothing notwithstanding, I know that a city is only as cool as the people who live in it. My favorite people in the world live in the Bay Area. Why on earth would I leave the best people ever? I must be crazy.

Moxie and I have known each other for years, but when we started having more intense conversations last fall, one thing that came up repeatedly was the idea of limitations. Moxie asked me what I wanted to do with my life. As far as I was concerned, I was already doing it. I had friends, projects, a place to live, and my own business. I could see doing just that for the rest of my life. But when Moxie asked me why I wasn't doing everything I wanted to do, it usually came down to not having enough time, space or money. These are all related. Rent on living and commercial space is high here, so I work a lot and still seem to be usually pretty broke and can't afford to occupy a larger work space for more equipment. The more I thought about it, the more limited my current life seemed. Sure, I could probably do this my whole life, but just this and not much more. It almost seemed like as full as my life was, it was a shell of what it could be.

Moxie's suggestion was simple enough: move to where a house could be bought, thus eliminating the need to pay rent for me or my printshop. And not just anywhere but some place we like, some place we'll want to stay for a while, a place with cool folks, since it would be silly to choose houses and printing presses over human beings. I know the difference between people and things.

I'm not taking this move lightly. I'm not doing this just for a change. (I could cut my hair or paint my room if that's all I wanted.) In fact, I don't think people should really move that much. There's a depth of relationship that comes with being some place for a long time.

I also won't pretend that Moxie has nothing to do with this. Although I have occasionally fantasized about getting land in Oregon or something, Moxie was the instigator for this current idea to move. It was his interrogation that prodded me to expand my vision of what my life could entail. And I'll admit that I also want him to be happy some place, partially because I care about his happiness but also because I want to be where he's happy, too. I feel like if he's happy then he's more likely to stick around for longer, although I realize that this is ridiculous. He's a person; people leave. I mean, look at me--- I'm leaving. And someone of Moxie's caliber will have no shortage of opportunity. In fact, I would wager that he will have a lifetime of opportunities to leave.

And so I have to go somewhere that I can build my life independently, where I can conceivably nurse a broken heart. I have to be prepared to step out of the moving truck in Pittsburgh with Moxie never wanting to speak to me again. Simultaneity isn't the same as togetherness.

It has been said that you should learn to sail a boat solo, because that way you can take anyone out sailing, with the full confidence that if that person should become incapacitated due to anxiety, sickness, or incompetence, you can operate the boat alone. Similarly, if you go on a bike trip down the coast, you should know that your biking companion might get dreadfully sick and have to be put on a bus to go home, and you'll need to finish the tour yourself. You can't take companionship for granted, because things so often don't go in the direction you plan.

And suddenly while writing this I had a realization that I've been mistaken for a long time. Not in a trivial way but in an *I've-based-the-past-ten-years-of-my-life-on-an-assumption-that-I-just-now-discovered-was-wrong* kind of way. You see, I have wanted to have a kid for a long time, and I failed because I was always looking for a good person to have one with. I never did find such a person. I didn't want to be a single parent, so I refused to make the journey altogether. It just occurred to me that this was pure folly--- it might not matter who you have a kid with, because chances are that they'll leave anyway. Most single parents didn't plan to be single parents. Think about how many people decide they don't

actually want kids AFTER they've had them and then leave, either geographically or emotionally. Think about how many people plan to co-parent, only to be suddenly widowed with very young children at home. Circumstances can change drastically, and plans yellow and crumble like old newspapers.

People's desires change all the time, and in ways even they can't predict. No one can really be trusted to stay, no matter how much they promise or pledge. There's nothing anyone can say to ensure that their priorities won't change next week or next year.

Maybe you'll say that people do stay, or that you've been lucky, or that I've just been terribly unlucky. Or maybe I was the lucky one, because I've learned there are no guarantees.

Now I'm moving, tired of the rat race of Bay Area living but used to the phenomenon of people leaving when their passions change with the wind.

Sorry to bum you out.

It's time to go now.

# UK Zine Yearbook

**Circuit Bending**
182a Archway Road
London, UK  N6 5BB
projectserendipity@yahoo.co.uk
http://www.myspace.com/bentsurprises
www.myspace.com/projectserendipity

**Sweet Shop Syndicate**
**Art School comic**
56 Reigate Road
Brighton, East Sussex, UK  BN1 5AH
sweetshopsyndicate@gmail.com
www.sweetshopsyndicate.tk

**Toby Chelms, editor**
Ground Floor 42 Buckingham Road
Brighton, East Sussex, England BN1 3RP
myspace.com/thenewwaveofcutandpaste

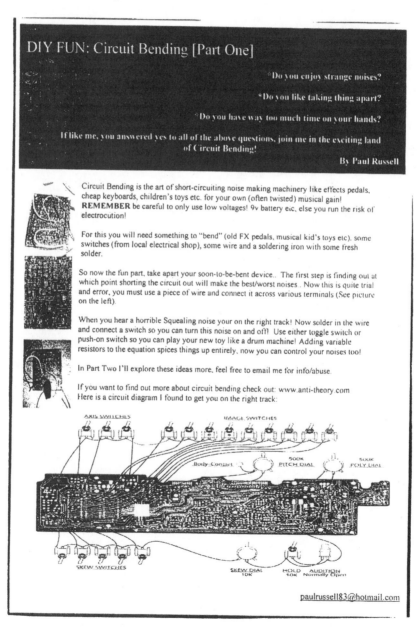

# ART SCHOOL

see what i did here was to make a pulp from some cardboard boxes and with that pulp make a far inferior cardboard box. Also the pulp was very smelly.

brilliant

I've spent the last 7 days exclusivley drinking gin. I recorded some conversations I had, mostly incoherent babbling and also wrote down some stuff which you can't read because I spilt gin on the paper.

amazing

we have to do work? I was under the assumption I was here to wear ironically bad clothes + god awful haircuts and have a general air of superiority because 'they' don't realise how cool I really am.

superb.

I painted this portrait.

out. now.

# Resistance of Dreams

**Geoff Slagheap**
**7 Beelen Street**
**Pittsburgh, PA 15213**
**geoff@okcancel.org**

## GROWING UP I DIDN'T LEARN SHIT ABOUT LIFE

I had never been to Chicago much. Even though I only lived half an hour from the city, it was a world away. The suburbs are antiseptic, the city is dangerous. Yeah, that's why all the white people ran away, isn't it? All their fear was inside me, that legacy. The first time I drove to (the legendary) Fireside Bowl to see a punk show, I didn't even know how to get to the city. I was scared of the highways, and in my naivete I was going to just drive straight down Roosevelt Road all the way into downtown, then just take a left on Fullerton . . . 100 stoplights and two hours later, we'd be there. Luckily, my friend Ryan actually knew the way.

The trip itself epitomizes the transition from suburban to urban. 'Player Dog Rest In Peace' tagged on an overpass is the golden arch that signals your transgression into the city limits. When we got off the highway, I felt the difference. Immediately on Western Avenue are a line of projects, usually someone begging for change at the first stoplight off the highway ramp. We locked our doors, hoping the click wasn't audible from the outside. Maybe that was somehow humanizing... we'd let them starve to death, but we didn't want to offend them. Or maybe it was just fear, us suburban kids feeling naked and vulnerable, not wanting these urban monsters to smell our fear.

Ryan used to tell of the time he was listening to Black Flag's "White Minority" with the windows open during the summer on the way to a show in the city. When they pulled off the turnpike, fast hands reached to turn down the stereo and roll up the windows...and then we all joked about getting shot. The exact same thing would happen to me later, and it was one of the first times I felt uncomfortable with the politics of the culture that was my life. But not the last.

The city is beautiful for that, the inescapable realism that forces one to continually re-evaluate. Would I ever listen to that song, or Minor Threat's "Guilty of Being White" in the city? In front of actual black people, now part of the experience instead of just a subject of it . . . How uncomfortable would I feel? Or would I just keep locking the doors, rolling up the windows, retreat to the 31st floor or the $1000/month loft or maybe even all the way back to the suburbs. The beautiful thing about the city is that it forces one to see the ugly contradictions in escape? Why is it so hard to create a counterculture that actually is supportive of individuals' exploration of their self and that doesn't have some kind of hierarchy of members?

After helping them move their shit, I was just hanging around. This was a city show with mostly city punks who I didn't know and who didn't seem too interested in knowing me. Walking down the street outside the club, a figure suddenly jumped out of a darkened doorway, jumped right at me. I was startled, adrenaline pumping in fight or flight response, and began to back away when the figure reached a hand from an overcoat pocket and asked "Hey man, can you help me out?"

I wasn't thinking, just running on instinct, and I jammed a hand into my jeans pocket to pull out the first bill I touched, handed it to the figure, that I now vaguely identified to be a withered old black man. I held my hand with the bill in it out really straight, keeping me a good distance from the street man. After all, I though, he could have a knife or a gun or something. He reached for the money. I was worried he'd grab my arm as he took it, drag me into the doorway and rob me. He was old and boney, worn-out sunken eyes. I was afraid of being attacked by a frail old man. I noticed the bill I'd given him wasn't a dollar, but five. In spite of my fear, the feelings of loss and disappointment began to rise up inside of me. I then looked at his eyes, and saw they were old but still alive, and I began to attribute human qualities to this creature. The hand and the bill disappeared back into the old man's overcoat pocket. Mentally, I was chastising myself for what I had lost. I could have bought a seven inch or maybe even a CD with that money, especially at punk rock prices. The old man smiled and I began to turn away, but he motioned me back and I stopped. He motioned me closer and I inched forward, just a bit.

He spoke. "I've got $6.25 in my pocket here, and I'm going to play a little song." Maybe he said it to me, or to the world in general, or maybe just to himself and I happened to overhear it. But then he pulled out a little silver harmonica from the great big coat that shielded his body, and I witnessed the soul of a tired old black man blow itself through the reeds of a silver harmonica cupped between two wrinkled hands in the cold. And there was so much life hiding in those old bones, concealed behind the overcoat, I caught a glimpse of it for thirty seconds, before the hands slid back down into their pockets, the back hunched once more, the eyes sunk back down in their sockets.

The silence afterwards was a funeral. I tried to give my respects but soon turned and left. We really had nothing to say to each other and it was pointless to even offer a goodbye, for what kind of connection could I really offer to someone from so obviously a different world than myself? Suddenly, everything in my life seemed starkly, painfully meaningless. Suddenly I wanted to stop talking. I wanted everyone and everything I knew from my life to stop making so much fucking noise and just listen. I felt sick. I hated my friends and myself even more. We were all pretending we know so goddamned much, when really we didn't know shit about life.

This is the first thing I remember that forced me to write. I needed to try to put this down on paper, sort it out somehow or try to make some kind of sense of it in my head. I guess I thought staring at a pale shadow of experience on paper would help. I guess it has. Within a few days I had an attempt. It was "finished" in a few weeks, until now. I used to end this recounting with the line "It was the best five dollars I had ever spent." I thought it was a really good closing statement, and so did my high school English teacher. She gave me an A+ and wrote "I love this last line" underneath the typed manuscript in red ink.

It is a terrible last line, representing a terrible kind of logic. In my head, the act of giving people money was still somehow synonymous with buying a product....I was still buying something. But what was I buying but their silence, spending away my guilt? Buying their silence because each open hand is an inescapable reminder of the wealth that I have, my privilege not to beg on the street. In amerika, where we expect so little of life, even that has become a privilege. And in spending money on panhandlers, I maintain that privilege. I maintain my power, and I expect some kind of value for my money. Their poverty, their suffering, it becomes a commodity like any other and I offer a token for the privilege to ignore it. I buy them out of existence with my parents' money. I drive away and sleep in a soft bed in a warm home. I sleep deeply.

But what can we do instead? The world is too fucked up, there are two many problems, that they combine to overwhelm our abilities. So we learn to respond in completely token ways, with no hope or intent of actually changing the situation in a meaningful way. But is that better than doing nothing? Probably it is, but if we are always working in half-hearted attempts that we do not believe will succeed, how can we ever challenge our own inaction? How do we responsibly react to all the oppressions of the world, and what can we realistically expect of each other? It's a question to which I do not know the answer. I think the least we can do is acknowledge the shared humanity of the person on the street and ourselves, and with that acknowledge the basic selfishness that we allow them to stay there while we have a home. But also i know that there is a relativism to it all - for how many of us would be as callous as those in power now, who would rather people sleep on the streets than to give them abandoned buildings and jeopardize the sanctity of private property? I know that most of us would act less selfishly than that, and that is better. So there is a lot of space

between our best and our worst...do we call that hope? And now, years later, I wonder why the man played? Was it because he wanted to? Or out of some sense that he owed me something for giving him money? The shadow of capitalism corrupted even this ghost of a moment of beauty.

# Scrabble Freaks

Lisa Dempster
info@lisadempster.com.au
www.lisadempster.com.au

## Lexicon vs corpus

The internet is fertile ground for Scrabble-enthusiasts. Heidi Harley, Associate Professor of Linguistics at the University of Arizona, used her blog as a forum to muse on the letter distribution of Scrabble's one hundred tiles.
(insert graphic #1

She had been surprised to discover that the letter distributions (i.e. that there is one Z, two F's etc) were based on an informal corpus count by the creator of the game, not a lexicon count. that means that, as 12% of the letters in Scrabble are E (12 out of 100), that's pretty much exactly the percentage of letters that are E in the corpus of written English.

Why is that surprising, exactly? Heidi wrote, "In a corpus there will be many repetitions of function words, which probably inflates the percentages of certain letters, e.g. T (the, to, it), E (the, he, she), etc., when compared to their percentage appearance in the lexicon, which contains only one token of each functional word."

It struck Heidi that it would be much more appropriate to use a letter distribution system based on the percentage of each letter occurring in a list of dictionary head words; after all, she noted, "Scrabble is all about producing nice individual words, not producing a corpus-like set of words." In fact, someone who repeatedly uses words like TO, IT and THE would not get very far in a game of Scrabble. Was the initial development of the letter distributions making the game tougher for players than it needed to be? She began to wonder how different the lexicon-based letter distribution in English is to the corpus-based letter distribution.

A reader of her blog, Lance, rose to the challenge and created a series of graphics showing the respective letter-distribution counts…
(insert graphic #2)

The leftmost bar represents Lance's lexicon letter counts, the centre represents corpus letter counts and the rightmost bar represents Scrabble's tile distribution list.

Lance and Heidi found that the graphs showed some notable differences between the lexicon and corpus counts. For example, H and T occur in the corpus more frequently than in the lexicon, and, curiously, the S is underrepresented in the corpus compared to the lexicon. Letters whose frequency is less than 1%, such as Q, are necessarily over-represented in Scrabble, as you can't have a letter with less than one tile.

"What's interesting," Heidi wrote, "Is that the Scrabble tile distribution matches lexicon frequency in some cases of discrepancy, corpus frequency in other cases, and neither in a couple of cases." Which is an odd result, considering that Alfred Butts supposedly based the tile distribution on a corpus count of the *New York Times* front pages. Heidi thinks that Butts adjusted some of the frequencies based on is intuition about what would make the game flow better.

The letter S, for example, is less frequent in Scrabble than in either the lexicon or corpus; obviously, S makes high-scoring hooks easy, increasing its value as a letter. Heidi supposes that Alfred foresaw this and made the letter scarcer. Similarly, there are fewer Cs than there should be; two rather than three, but, as Heidi said, "That's kind of nice since there's no legal two letter words with C." Not so nice is twice as many Vs as there ought to be, and there are no two words with Vs in them. Heidi says, "I find it hard to imagine that Alfred was thinking about the availability of two-letter words," Heidi said, conceding, "but maybe he was."

It will probably always remain a mystery why Butts chose the final ninety-eight letters that he did. My impression is that he did a pretty good job, seeing as the game has been played and used as he intended for the best part of a century… and in ways he didn't intend either.

## Tile bank

Another person who works in Scrabble, though in a very different way to Allan, is Meg Henderson. Meg became interested in Scrabble and got involved in the Scrabble club scene in about 1980. Roughly ten years later, she had an ingenious idea.

"I became aware people were losing tiles," she said, "and it's very expensive buy a full set." So she set up a Scrabble tile bank using a few old, incomplete Scrabble sets her club had. When people heard what she was doing, they contributed boards as well.

The tile bank idea is simple and effective: people send in a sample of their tile and an SSAE, tell Meg what letter they need, and she sends out a replacement. It saves them buying a set (which can cost up to $20.00) and surely buys Meg a whole lotta good-deed karma.

Meg estimates that she has averaged about two requests a week since the tile bank has been in operations – that's over a thousand tiles distributed. In that time, she has become something of an expert in Scrabble tiles.

Apparently there are many different styles of Scrabble tiles in Australia, over 20 or more. When someone organizes to distribute Scrabble, they get the board from the manufacturer but you have to source tiles locally, hence the difference in styles. Meg had seen the quality of tile improve over the years also. They were formerly wooden. Instead of printing the letters, they are now engraved. And there is even a new style of tile called Protiles – the letters are embedded in, which is good because the tiles can't wear out.

Meg has a wide variety of tiles at her home, though she doesn't catalogue them, but simply pops them into a plastic bag with similar-looking tiles. It sounds like she must have the most extensive Scrabble-tile collection in Australia; only once or twice a year Meg gets a request she can't match.

Meg says she plays Scrabble for recreation and enjoys the problem-solving aspect of it. Well, she solved the problem of missing tiles for Australia's Scrabble players! She said, "It's a simple thing to do to help, because you can't play a proper game without a tile and they are so easy to lose!"

# Fuzzy Lunch Box #11

**Laura and Deborah Nadel**
**309 Cedar st. #34**
**Santa Cruz, CA 95060**
**lauranadel@aol.com**
**www.myspace.com/fuzzylunchbox**

## FAVORITES FROM the PORTLAND ZINE Symposium Trip

- Getting a whole table
- Not doing one trade that resulted in a poetry zine
- The zines we received in trades were Really good!
- Sitting next to the 24-Hour CHURCH OF ELVIS.
- Seeing Elvis.
- Eating really good hummus from a Lebanese restaurant
- Meeting our "friends" from myspace. They're real people!
- Getting gifts of C.D.'s & movies from zinesters
- It wasn't 1000 degrees this year
- Sneaking bikes into the Hilton (take that Paris!)
- Getting your water filled promptly & often by the bartender.
- Making people fill out extraneous pointless surveys.
- Seeing a weird mobile political campaign of some hick town recall election. Drama!
- Witnessing an awesome zine related tattoo. (you know who you are, Mark-ah)
- Going to the Hawthorne area.
- Being surrounded by D.I.Y. enthusiasm & FRENZY
- Making someones day by giving him a broken pen.
- Being in a bar with live music & still being able to hear each other

"I'm clown bait."

# THINGS THAT SUCKED FROM THE PORTLAND ZINE SYMPOSIUM TRIP

- Getting a whole table because people thought we were lepers and wouldn't sit next to us.
- Getting stuck in bumper-to-bumper traffic at least twice on our ride home.
    - especially the second one of us says "I have to pee!" or "I'm hungry"!!
- Because it was colder than usual, Laura actually had to wear sneakers on her day off!
- Inhaling 200 cigarettes in 2 minutes in the basement of the "Shanghai Tunnel"
- Meeting a twin who gleefully perpetuated stereotypes of twins.
- People who tried to be a "hard sell" for your zine & made you work for it.
- When people said "no" to receiving a free fortune from our cheesy paper junior high fortune teller.
- That no one got the 16 Candles reference
- When you ask people in a survey to choose "one" & they wuss out & won't-writing "either", "neither" or making up their own answer. Damn non-conformists!
- Have mustaches become (gasp!) hip again?
- Excessive presence of shreiking bachelorette parties.
- Waiting until we are beyond starving to feed ourselves
- Being too uncoordinated to participate in a spontaneous double dutch jump rope session (although trying to attempt anyway)
- No one wanted our free stickers :(
- Fear that the scenes from MAXIMUM OVERDRIVE might come true when driving on I-5

# Grit & Glitter

Hazel Pine
Cursive Bomb
PO Box 12596
Seattle, WA 98111
hazel.pine@gmail.com

Neely bat Chestnut
221 s. 43rd
Tacoma, WA 98418
tea_heart@hellokitty.com

## HOW DO YOU DEFINE

### Neely

For me, femme my femme identity is something that i hold dear and something that hankers back to a false idea of my own chldhood. Playing dress-up and going on teddy bear picnics. I dress like I have no one to tell me what to do, and that includes ending up wearing clothes intended for girls 20 years younger. I have a deep love of peter pan collars and lace. Knee socks, fake pearls and every color of the rainbow. Doll houses and something else I cannot quite place. It doesn't always work right because I don't do a lot of the things that society tells us is "right" for a woman of my age, make-up, shaved skin and being nice. But really i am nice, just not in the "right ways". Most of the time I feel as thought I am this stranger outsider in the world of women. It's

as though I never "grew into a woman" when i started to bleed or decided i wanted to have children. I don't really fit. As a punk, it works. But when I go to the Anna Sui counter to buy eyeshadow, i always feel a little disconnected. No, I will not feel like i need a sexual partner to feel like a valid adult. i call myself femme because it fits the best. I do like "girl" things, but maybe not womanly things. Most of my habits would make my grandmother proud. Sewing, baking and art. I love to cook large meals for people, I love to take tea with honey and lay around in my handmade clothes and day dream about braids and ribbons and names for my child. I love to curl my eyelashes and to paint my nails and god how i wish i could have been a ballerina. I call myself femme not because these things make me weak, but because they make me strong. For me femme is about taking all of my gender learning, thinking about it long and hard and taking the bits back that work for me. The things that feel right and forgetting the rest.

 ribbons
 cake
 necklace
 crown

# FEMME

*Hazel*

The heart of femme-ness, for me,
is the frivolousness.  It is the
conscious, over the top expression of
femininity. It is blushing at doors
held open because it is so obvious,
- so obvious it is something I can do
myself, But someone doing it for me i

is a little gift, a stab at courtesy.
I know where it is based (white
gloves and lack of upper arm

strength) and that is why, when
it gets past the frivolous,  I am so
eager to prove myself. I may let
someone open a door, but I will not

.et them take something that could
actually be too much for me - a bag
too heavy, a lid too tight,

because

t challanges me as
woman. Not as a femme,
ecause femme to me is
lso someone strong
daring (outspoken, loud
nd brash)

211

# There Is A Danger

Shaun
PO Box 1282
Fullerton, CA 92832

The hills are filled with rust and gold.

It's funny how one has a tendency to become the other, in a roundabout way.

Not so long ago passage across this Great Basin was a risk that claimed many. A landscape that is both enigma and canvas, intangible and predatory. Using stillness as barrier – anything that intrudes upon its terrain must be willing to endure time. Summers its heat can turn glass to liquid, winters that can fall like a blanket, perfect and absolute.

To walk in this desert is to feel suspended within a held breath, a landscape mercurial – solid and definite until one tries to grasp it.

Distance bound us on every side, and beyond that distance the mountains towering to the clarity of the late-afternoon heavens. In silence. In layers. The sheer immensity that reflects vulnerability. The exposed layers in the stone hold time on display in jagged bands.

A story is as a landscape, made up of turbulent and often contrasting forces. It's the visible lines, the apparent details, that get told, that are charted and recorded in the histories and biographies. But it is the unseen, the tides and currents beneath the surface, that govern the narrative.

History – memory rewritten and enforced. Though, as is unstated in all texts but always true, its validity is only as authoritative as one's acceptance of it.

Dig beneath the layers and you will find the veins, the stories.

Nevada. The name encompasses risk and masquerade. Lawlessness and a human coexistence with the desert as fragile as the sullen feminine vibrato voice of an old blues record, crackling, ethereal, unable to leave the haunting fringes of a tragic serenity.

Frequently I wonder to what degree an environment is shaped by those who inhabit it and to what degree the opposite is true.

Some people can't be bound by conventional notions of work, of security, of love. What is it about the desert that draws the gamblers?

We situate ourselves beside the highway, somewhere between the violet skies and the silver veins, in the safe path carved out by other trespassers, autumn air crisp as disintegration, facing the vastness…

Nevada, tell us a story.

'Y'all are welcome to a beer' he said, motioning to the case of Budweiser sitting on the seat between he and us as he opened one himself and drank.

Speed limits in Nevada are 75 mph, meaning a driver on a crowded highway could hit about 85 and not worry about police. A driver on this desolate open stretch – such as a beer-swilling miner by way of Texas – could hit the upper 90's without thinking about it.

'What brought you to Nevada?' we asked.

'Racing' he answered briskly. 'My dad built engines for racecars. Traveled all over the country and ended up here. Live in Winnemucca. But you're looking at the largest gold deposits in North America up in these hills. So I got into mining.'

Maps like memories can tell of the towns that this desert has consumed. If one was to compare the maps of this landscape over time, one-time towns would be absent from future editions. This landscape can swallow them up, make them disappear, leaving rusting machinery as the only landmarks of these settlements, steel and cement skeletons of the boomtown gone bust. Airstreams and mattress coils framing the sagebrush that grows from within its decomposing ribs. All along this highway are settlements spanning the phases of collapse, the ghosts of the map.

I wonder if time itself has a memory. That intuits when to bring the freezing nights and inclement storms. If the unseasonable weather is merely an experiment carried out by the heavens with the ease and curiosity with which one may add a new spice to a familiar meal.

People defend the theories of civilization the same way that at one time they would laughably dismiss challenges to the idea of the flat earth.

That the earth is flat is recorded in the texts. Another landmark rusting off the map. A notion collapsed except for the ink that remains, authoritative, when the only consistency throughout time has been that no rule has gone unbroken.

'Open pit mines. I drive the machines. We got machines that'll level the earth down to two inches. From there we load it into trucks and ship it off. Got no old lady or kids. Been here five years now. I'm going to get my check right now and it goes straight to the bank. I'm set to retire in three or four years.'

He couldn't have been past his early forties.

'What are you planning to do once you retire?'

'Don't know. Maybe get some land away from everyone. Maybe I'll just work more. There's one old guy that's there, been there 57 years. Still working. He puts me to shame. I wish I had his talents.'

He had a crazy grizzled miner's laugh. And he'd burst into quick laughter without provocation.

Solitude has a way of uncovering your weaknesses.

Maybe this is why this landscape carries with it an air of tragedy, a way of creating mythologies of vice where others have their heroes. Those who are canonized out here are the self-made individualists. The courtesan given the key to the city. Those who squatted the land abandoned by Mormons fleeing back to Utah Territory, turning an opportune river crossing into a metropolis. The criminal money that turned a railroad stopover into a billion dollar tourist destination.

The desert's mythologies evoke highwaymen and lushes with the same celebration that other places praise physical strength or virtue.

Disaster-struck, it wears its scars of pit mines and nuclear test detonations. Though what is disaster but an event that shakes people from the direction they've become comfortable in.

The gold is there, in the veins beneath the surface. Therein lies the hope that brings the gamblers. Riches have been found and lost in these mountains.

Rust and gold.

There are those who have dug for gold and struck madness, those who hit rust, or those who hit nothing at all.

There are those who invested their time and money, striking a vein of rust, another cast-off layer in a desert full of valueless expanse. They gave up and moved on. They challenged time and were defeated. It wasn't until later when the rest was examined that it was realized that what they had abandoned
was the largest silver strike in history.

These mountains can hide veins of precious metals, or sometimes nothing save for the remains of steel spade and weathered bone. Towns that were built to withstand time lie like bodies fallen. Time has moved on. The maps have followed. Their stories have dispersed, or disappeared altogether. The phases of collapse.

Other towns remain standing, where glitter and neon dance for non-existent cars. They would have died too were it not for the tendency of cars to break down on the highway or that habit of hunger to beckon at regular intervals.

'These are the biggest deposits in the country right now. Last year these hills produced 800,000 ounces of gold. Now 800,000 ounces at three to four hundred dollars an ounce, up to five hundred during the wartime, for some reason war increases the price of gold, and that's just one of the companies. I work for a smaller company based out of Canada contracted out to these larger companies. It's better than working for the big companies.'

I asked if there were any small mining operations or if it was primarily larger corporations.

'A lot of it is for the government. It's mostly big corporations, along the lines of the government, and practically as stupid. One company has a nineteen-year contract, and that's just to process what's already been turned up. The money's here. You see those mountains? Just behind them are some open pits. They're all over these hills.'

The desert is a landscape that keeps no secrets, but whose terrain itself is barrier. Carrying vastness and patience the way one makes visible their talons or incisors, this distance has been able to hold at bay the civilization that has asphyxiated so much of the rest of the country. Calm and violent, as the tides of the sea. Standing like a dare to those who wish to conquer land – the prospectors, the mapmakers, those who sought to turn the wild into a garden. This landscape has seen the creation of what were amongst the most modern and decadent cities in the nation, and also seen them fall into dusty stopovers.

A stranger's truck barreling through the desert.

Layers like time. They each have a tendency for movement, re-formation. The land changes, shifts, collapses – as absolute as disaster. The maps follow, the surface layers of the past.

It's a mistake to imply that the story has an ending, that any history is definitive. For it's only the surface of memory, while the hidden tides of rust and gold, of stories and landscape, of disaster and tragedy deep as the desert remain unwritten.

It's no secret that stone is more malleable than a photograph.

'The government gets the gold. I don't know what they do with it. You know those Wells Fargo armored cars? Out here they have big rigs like that. And they say for every one they send out full of gold, they send out three that are empty.'

What is it about the desert that draws the gamblers. For whom disaster is contained in their veins as surely as the gold lies beneath the surface. For if survival were enough you wouldn't challenge death.

'Have there been any successful robberies?'

Desert mythologies.

'Well the one I heard about, there was this man who worked in the melting area. And when they pour it, some splashes out and dries on the ground, and they're supposed to scrape it up and melt it again. Well he was taking that and hiding it in his thermos. Just somewhere in there. So when he went through the metal detector, it was a metal thermos, no one looked at it. Seems he was able to do this for a while.'

He pulled over, an offramp marked by a lone road sign and the road immediately turned to gravel.

'Ain't no traffic out here but you got fifteen minutes down the road and a beer.'

Mountains bound us on every side. Desert and sage in shades of frontier and isolation, the sky a boundlessness you can taste and the air a scent of being forgotten, and being satisfied with that.

[postscript]

Crossing northern Nevada by way of small towns and strangers' cars. Through highwayside waits and 2 am casino diners, we passed our time with stories and memories.

Gamblers have always occupied a fascination of mine. Those who wagered despite risk despite precedent, despite convention. For the history that you find in the texts is often the self-congratulatory banter of the victor. I've always been drawn to the tragedy and desperation, the acts that fringe on – and oftentimes are fully indulgent in – lawlessness and utter abandon. A gut reaction to the rationalized constraints of civilization. My heroes have always been the ones who defied those who wield the authority. Those who set aflame the machinery, those who have taken knives to the slaveowners' throats.

Rust and gold.

Here's the rest of the story…

'Seems he was able to do this for a while. And no one would've known except for his wife and he got divorced and she went and told them. Now gold's all regulated by the federal government, fell under federal jurisdiction.'

It's funny how one has a tendency to become the other.

And then falls the night. Showing stars that were never gone, only hidden for a time. The hum of day is replaced by the lonely and debaucherous language of the insects. We awake at night – on desert floors and theatre rooftops. The desert concealed by darkness and our world what lies in each others' arms, and the night gives cover to those scavengers who move invisibly throughout the tides beneath the surface.

# Xerography Debt #21

**Davida Gypsy Breier**
**PO Box 11064**
**Baltimore, MD 21212**
**davida@leekinginc.com**

## RIP Tower

I was the last major zine buyer in America, and you have no idea how strange it is to see those words in black and white. True, there are still some places buying lots of zines- Joe still does wonderful work at Microcosm, Ubiquity is still alive, kicking, and by all accounts generally taking care of business, and there are lots of regional distro types- but there's no outfit anywhere that operates with the kind of freedom that I did. I could bring in as much (or as little) as I wanted of whatever I wanted from wherever I wanted. I ordered punk zines from Hong Kong. I paid tens of thousands of dollars to a series of graffiti artists in Europe, Canada, Australia, New Zealand, and South America. If I wanted several hundred copies of a fantasy art zine from Down Under, I got several hundred copies, and no one ever asked me a question about it. Heck, I even *printed* zines in the Tower Print Shop when the zinesters couldn't afford to print them themselves, or because I liked them, or because I thought they were important. I sent these zines to Tower Records stores all over the country and, for a while, all over the world. And I'll tell you how I did it, too: Tower Records was committed to supporting zines and indy press publications, and no matter how much the company changed over the years, that never did. It also helped that an erratic genius named Doug Biggert laid an incredible foundation back in the 80s, creating a model within which the Mag Division operated on its own to an unprecedented extent, starting the zine distribution warehouse in the back of the first Tower Bookstore and eventually moving it into a real warehouse space, and shipping more than $10 million worth of zines and magazines every year.

## Imagine that.

And now Tower Records is gone, twice bankrupt and ultimately liquidated. What happened? Well, back in the early part of 1998 I was sitting in my office in San Diego (where I was still a regional manager) talking to one of my colleagues when the new issue of Billboard Magazine came in. On the

cover, a headline announced that Tower had just secured hundreds of millions of dollars to expand by opening a line of credit and selling bonds to private investors. My friend and I looked at each other in horror. After all, by 1998 it was clear that the music industry was set on selling fewer and fewer records, and we had no idea where the money to repay these loans was going to come from. We could have turned out to be wrong (Tower's upper management could have spent the money wisely, expanding the company carefully and thoughtfully) but we weren't (amazing amounts of money were lost in bad real estate choices, and in overseas markets like Argentina and England, among others). Now fast-forward to 2004. The loans are coming due, music sales are flat or declining, DVD sales are flattening out as the marketplace finally saturates, and the only product lines showing growth are books and magazines... which only account for somewhere in the neighborhood of 5% of Tower's revenue, so the fact that they were doing well wasn't going to be of much help. Tower enters bankruptcy the first.

The company reorganizes, people are laid off, departments shrink. The stores are forced to cut payroll, meaning already poorly-paid employees (including managers) are being asked to do much, much more work than ever before. As you might imagine, some of them become surly. An excruciating game of musical CEOs commences, apparently to coincide with the ongoing game of musical CMOs. The advertising department continues its policy of being mainly interested in its own ideas, many of which seem to have been beamed directly into their brains from outer space. The newest CEO engineers a terrifically fast bankruptcy, from which Tower emerges in less than 30 days; all you have to do is look at a newspaper to see that this is many times faster than most companies, and employees become cautiously optimistic. Unfortunately the bondholders now own 85% of the company, and whatever profit comes in now goes directly to them; they could have foreclosed and shuttered the company's doors, after all, so they should be reimbursed... and in the absence of raises or any kind of investment in the stores, the next two years are: tense. The new CEO dedicates himself to fostering an atmosphere of paranoia, in-fighting, and pocket-lining. I stay though the Autumn of 2004 and then step down for reasons unrelated to the bankruptcy- but keep the zine buying duties to myself because I'm liked well enough that I can design my own part-time job. I decide to make a change to our zine distribution system that turns out to be good for everyone: we start buying zines outright, without returns, which means people get paid for everything in about 6 weeks with nothing held back against sales. And the system works, too. Tower is still breaking even on zines (and contrary to what some might believe, Tower never did much more than break even on zines, what with all the shipping and handling and paying employees and so on), zine people are getting paid faster, and everything goes well until the summer of 2006.

I'm in Pittsburgh for the summer, far from where the milk finally curdled, when I get the call: no more zines are to be ordered. And not just zines, either; nothing is to be ordered by anyone unless it's new release CDs or DVDs. I tell the Mag Division's crack staff (which means that I told Diana, the office manager) to start calling zines and telling them to hold their shipments back, and to start refusing shipments at the warehouse whenever possible. I figure that this way it's possible that folks'll be out their shipping money, but not out the zines themselves. We even send back some of the zines that were still waiting to be shipped, although the finance people put a stop to that pretty quickly. Diana begins emailing and calling as many people as we have contact info for, letting them know that they shouldn't ship us anything unless we call and say it's cool. This call will never take place. Tower enters bankruptcy the second in the early part of August. Two months later the company is auctioned off and purchased by a liquidation company.

The good news is that because we were buying zines on a non-returnable basis, and because we turned so many shipments away and caught many zinesters in time, relatively few people got ripped off. The bad news is that shipments that managed to somehow get through between the middle of June and August's bankruptcy declaration have become "unsecured creditors", most of whom have not been paid as of this date. They get to file claims- the deadline was in January and they might eventually get paid, although I don't know how that process is going to work. This sucks, but I take some small comfort in the fact that when Tower finally went down, it didn't do to the zine community what Fine Print did, or what Desert Moon did, or even what Big Top did (just ask Dan Sinker at Punk Planet what Big Top did The damage was in the range of hundreds of dollars, and not thousands, or tens of thousands. And if they someho do get paid, then even that damage will be undone.

I'm not holding my breath. I'm holding on to that whole "small comfort" thing.

I recently found out that there's one more piece of bad news. Somehow, the accounting people at Tower have decided that some zines actually owe Tower money, and have sent out collection letters. (This is what happens when corporate people finally have at the zine accounts without someone like me or Diana around.) So even though Tower sent me my final paycheck back in Octobe I found myself in their offices just a couple of weeks ago arguing about some of these letters. So far it hasn't done any good... but I don't think any more have been sent ou

I was the last major zine buyer in America. It occurs to m that I was probably the last major zine buyer in the world which is a decidedly strange thing to consider. (It is also sad and depressing, and so are its implications: these are probably subjects for another column somewhere down th line.) When I started writing this, I thought I'd tell the story in as detailed a fashion as I could, but it turned out t be much too long. That's right- this is the short version. With that in mind, I'm going to shut up now, and open the floor to questions. You can send them to me at johnsclj A yahoo DOT com. If I get a bunch, maybe Davida will publish them in the next issue of XD.

# Glossolalia #9

Portland, OR
www.sarahmccarry.com

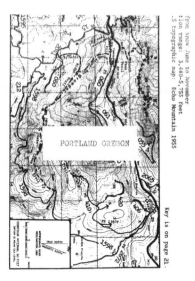

In Portland summer is golden, better than summer in any other town in the world, the days are long and balmy and it's bike rides, bike rides, swimming, bike rides, sunburned shoulders and ice cream. Landon made up this drink with Old Crow and coconut soda and pickled ginger, the Hollywood, all summer long it's your afternoon cocktail. Every night barbecues and staying up too late with all the people you love.

Portland is a porch and summer kind of town and everyone has jobs they don't care about, maybe you will call in sick to ride bikes to the river, swimming and lounging on the sand and talking about the day you are going to get all your favorite people together, inner tubes, float down the river with coolers full of beer.

Portland, it's so lovely there, all the flowered trees are blooming, everyone is happy, the streets are full of bicycles and pretty girls, you live in a big old gorgeous house with your best friends and there is always someone who will stay up with you on the porch steps, when the nights are finally warm enough to be outside late without a coat and your arms are tan in the warm glow of the streetlights and all night long people ride past your house ringing their bike bells when they see you, the solidarity of good living.

Even on the hottest days the horizon is full of green things and the air smells like flowers, the neighbors' kids running shrieking through sprinklers, your backyard full of berries and jungly plants the cat likes to bound through pretending it is prowling the savannahs of its forebears. The yard has become hopelessly overgrown and you are always promising yourself you will plant lovely things and tame the wilderness and then running off to drink beer in the park instead.

Every weekend you drive to the ocean and run up and down the hot sand, fling yourself into the waves until everything tastes like salt and afterward there are fish-and-chips and the long drive home. This summer, the last summer for pretending you can live like this forever, a peter pan kind of summer where no one will ever grow up or go away, it's never true but no matter, not right this moment. Swimming in waterfalls, swimming in the river, cotton sundresses and ridiculously huge five-dollar sunglasses and cowboy boots, no cares and nowhere to be, no future, only this one lazy afternoon in the bright yellow sun, only the perfectness of now.

glossolalia number nine was letterpress printed with handset type on a grumpy old challenge proof press in my garage in portland oregon at the end of the summer of 2007 with a heart full of love for someone far away. the soundtrack of my summer vacation was andrew bird and the mysterious production of eggs, and bruce springsteen, and that hot chip song that is really catchy and overplayed and is probably in a car commercial by now. i read a whole lot of raymond chandler, too. this one is for bryan reedy and emiko, the people who make new york and portland places i want to be. you can write me a letter or you can get back issues through paper trail distro, www.papertraildistro.com

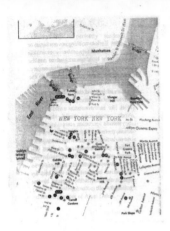

In New York everything is very large, or else it is very tiny, there is no middle ground, the buildings are gigantic and the horizon is a sparkling wall of immensity, everything goes on forever, all the streets. The subways are like cavernous circles of hell and the crowds of people stretch across vast expanses, this is what it is like in the outside world of New York, enormous things. In your boyfriend's apartment everything is very small, there is a tiny kitchen with a tiny stove, a tiny percolator for making tiny coffees, the bathroom is so cramped you knock your knees on the wall when you pee and your boyfriend's bedroom is so diminutive he has to put the bed up against the wall in the morning or else you can't walk to the door.

Everything is perfectly rendered in miniature except for the cat which is enormous and howls incessantly at the door to be let out, until it is outside, when it howls incessantly to be let in. You have never seen such an enormous cat, it has come all the way from Japan with your boyfriend's roommate who is tiny and as furtive as a cockroach. Your boyfriend's apartment has a deeply soporific effect upon your person, plunging you into a terrible and incapacitating lethargy, all you can manage to do with your days while he is at work is lay about drinking beer and watching Jean-Pierre Melville movies, wishing you still smoked and were being filmed in a Parisian garret so that you could lie on your back and blow smoke at the ceiling with the magnificent doomed glamour of Alain Delon.

New York is the most important city in the world and everyone who lives there know this, the pedestrians of New York

are alive with the importance of their city, with a great animating purpose that drives them in packs from one end of New York to the other on uncountable errands of great urgency, their faces are fixed in determination and they will push you aside if you are less certain of your destination, and apt to stop in the middle of the sidewalk to gape at the dogwalkers walking sixteen dogs of variegated sizes, or the man on twenty-eighth who wears the homemade Superman suit and cowboy boots and likes to shout in the middle of the street, or if you are easily distracted by all the pretty ladies in their small wispy garments.

Summer in New York, that most terrible and impossible of cities, everything smells like garbage and rot and shit and the air is so thick your skin gets slick with it, sweat and dirt and something else, the awful stickiness of New York, the dank putrid subways and the filthy streets. Sometimes you think it is the most awful of all imaginable cities, how can anyone live in this wretched sinkhole of so many unlivable blocks, no trees anywhere or anything beautiful, New York, it's disgusting.

But sometimes you are walking home alone and Purple Rain is playing free at McCarren Pool, loud enough that all the streets are alive with its music and the moon is full and there is a breeze, cool enough so that the air smells of flowers and not garbage, and you are walking in the perfect summer twilight past a stoop full of funny old Polish ladies drinking beer and playing cards and they all crack the hugest grins at you like you have a secret together, and you remember what it was like to have the future coiled up in your heart unwritten, when you were young enough to think you could move somewhere new and start over, leave all your history behind, and you think maybe here.

Maybe here. Maybe the possible is still possible, here, New York, like magic. New York your name in lights, New York where you will make it big, so big the whole world will remember your name and you will say this is where it all started, this little studio, this tiny room, this place where you came when the future was only a world of unwritten stories, New York.

# Southern Fried #9

Jerry Smith
3344 Horner Dr.
Morristown, Tn 37814
skybot99@yahoo.com

# Functionally Ill

functionally ill:
adventures with mental health

## intake at the mental health clinic

**Laura-Marie**
robotmad@gmail.com
dangerouscompassions.blogspot.com

My first appointment was lost. I called to verify the time and was told that there was no record of my appointment in the computer. The worker I'd talked to before was apologetic, but there was nothing they could do. "Are you doing okay?" she asked. I wasn't, but when I'm not well, I can't articulate that. The holidays were coming soon, and the earliest she could get me in was a month away.

So when I went to my appointment, I knew it was only an intake appointment, which meant two more hours of forms. The clinic is nearby, and I drove myself. Erik was working, and I didn't think I needed my friend P.

I found the place, forced myself to walk in, went up to the window, and handed the worker my letter. I didn't say a word. She looked at the letter and handed it back to me, called someone on the phone to say their two o'clock was waiting, and told me to take a seat.

The waiting room was full of crazy people—poor crazy people, mostly white, and they looked at me. I was obviously new. Many of them seemed dirty and were wearing too many jackets. I was dressed conservatively and felt very clean. Someone said hi to me, and I couldn't manage to respond.

I seated myself right by the coffee machine and took a zine out of my bag, but it was hard to read. A man who didn't look too good was chattering to himself and rocking. Art projects on the wall looked like they were made by kids, but I understood that they were made by grownups. I read encouraging phrases on colorful bulletin boards, and I read announcements that were taped to the wall: a tai chi class was bring offered on Tuesdays. Would I be able to take that tai chi class, and would I want to?

A woman opened the door and called my name. I got up and went to her. I followed her down halls, past rooms of people to an area of cubicles. She directed me to hers. I sat—she sat at her desk and didn't talk to me. I held my bag on my lap and looked around.

Her cubicle was undecorated. There was a metal bookshelf with piles of forms—the bookshelf had some old dinosaur stickers stuck on it. There was her desk with her computer. She had a stack of papers that she was putting into an envelope for me. She was folding them into thirds.

On her desk was a clear plastic cup with pens in it, and a few packets of salt and pepper. "These are for you," she said.

"You can look at them at home." I took the papers and put them in my bag.

She seemed about my age, around 30. She was fair and had pale hair, and her accent was strongly Eastern European. Her handwriting was as well: ornate and beautiful.

My mind was full of questions: how long she had been in this country, what was her job title, and why didn't she decorate? I wanted her to talk to me as a person and see me as I am. But I was too nervous. I had to pretend everything was a dream in order to get by. When I'm afraid, I often go silent like this, but my mind races with thoughts.

She read my file for a long time, and I watched her. There was a note that my first appointment had been lost. There was a summary of my symptoms that I caught a glimpse of. I mostly couldn't see what she was reading.

"Are you on Medi-cal?" she asked, but she pronounced it like "medical."

"No," I said.

"How much money do you make?"

"Just me?" I asked.

"Yes," she said, and I told her.

"But my husband makes more," I said. She wrote down numbers and frowned. She looked at a chart and saw that my monthly payment would be almost three hundred dollars a month.

"This isn't good," she said. "You should be on Medi-cal. Are you and your husband legally married?"

"Yes," I said.

"I'll speak to my supervisor," she said. "We need to do something about this—this is too much." She was staring at the three hundred dollars a month figure and seemed extremely troubled.

"Maybe I overestimated how much my husband makes," I said. Erik's employment has been sporadic over the past few months. I had been giving her numbers based on our taxes from the year before.

She got a new form, and we negotiated. The new monthly payment was something reasonable.

Looking at the information in my file, she filled out more paperwork, and I was patient as her beautiful handwriting filled the blanks.

Meanwhile, I could hear a man and woman rush down the hall and enter the cubicle next door. Every word they said was clear. The woman explained in animated language how her psychiatrist wouldn't give her her prescription and how she was violating probation by self-medicating. The man seemed competent and compassionate, and his energy matched his client's. They talked about court dates and personality conflicts. They spoke quickly, and something in me longed to be like them.

When they left, it was abrupt. The man was going to help his client—she would be assigned to a new psychiatrist. They continued to talk as they walked away quickly down the hall. The silence after they left was deafening.

"There's no privacy!" I said.

"What was that?" my caseworker asked, pausing in her writing to look at me.

"There's no privacy!" I said, gesturing in the direction where the voices had been.

She gave me a sheepish look. "I'm sorry," she said, and she went back to the form. Periodically she would separate some papers and give me a pink or yellow copy to put with my other papers.

Then it was time for more evaluation. She asked me questions much like the ones I had already answered with the discouraging worker who I had hated on the phone: detailed, terrible. Questions where to say the answers, I had to admit things I had never told anyone before except maybe Erik. It was almost physically painful to answer them, and the most difficult part was when she asked me to specify how often certain problems bothered me. "A little, or a lot?" she asked. I constantly battled my desire to understate.

I didn't see why I had to answer these questions over again, and I was afraid that since I was unprepared, I wasn't doing a good job this time. I kept telling myself to breathe and be honest, calling myself back from elsewhere, taking myself off auto-pilot because my auto-pilot can't be trusted. I needed to make a conscious effort to be super-honest.

But how could I really answer these questions? So many of them, I considered myself a poor judge. When she asked whether I have unrealistic expectations of people, I started to giggle because it all seemed absurd. Of course I have

unrealistic expectations of people, but her question was really about degree. How unrealistic was she thinking? But she wasn't thinking at all—she was reading off a list.

My perspective kept switching—I would think of an answer that was honest and true according to my use of terms, then think of how an imagined regular person would use the terms—how I look from the outside, how someone else would answer this question for me, or what Erik would say, if he was there. I would also consider the spirit of the question, what the question was getting at, and imagine how I should answer it.

The situation was complicated, and my caseworker seemed tired. I didn't trust her to write down accurately what I was saying anyway, or even to hear me correctly.

"Do you feel isolated?" she asked.

"Yes."

"A little, or a lot?"

"Mmm...a lot."

"Do you participate in leisure activities?"

"Mmm...."

I've spent my entire life trying to convince every person I meet that I'm okay. Trying to portray my secret inner reality to a stranger who asks a series of confusing questions—every second, I had to override a lifetime of habit—habit born of self-preservation. It felt dangerous, though rationally I knew that the overworked Eastern European woman wasn't going to hurt me.

"I go to church?" I offered. "I sing in the choir." She wrote something down.

"Do you exhibit any bizarre behaviors?"

I was in no position to decide whether my own behaviors are bizarre. I have some odd habits, but would they qualify? Bizarre sounds terrible. "I don't think so," I said.

"Do you have any visual or auditory hallucinations?"

I tried not to let my voice crack. I tried very hard not to sound like I was crying.

"A little, or a lot."

She took me back to the waiting room so someone could make me an appointment with a psychiatrist. She was behind the window with the man who peered into his monitor. "I have February 22nd with Dr X, and February 26th with Dr Y. Which one of those would work for you?"

"I'll take February 22nd."

He printed out a piece of paper and showed me the date and time of the appointment.

"Nice to meet you," the Eastern European woman said. But I didn't feel that we had met. I didn't even know her name.

Thank you for reading *functionally ill*, my first mental health zine. Thanks to Erik and my closest friends and relatives for their ongoing support.

robotmad@gmail.com
www.dangerouscompassions.blogspot.com

# Zinester's Guide to US Mail

**Zine World**
**PO Box 330156**
**Murfreesboro, TN 37133**
**www.undergroundpress.org**

# The Zinester's Guide to U.S. Mail

The new shape-based U.S. postal rate scheme is certainly more confusing and cumbersome than the old system... but with little more than a ruler and a scale, you can still Do It Yourself. In this guide, we'll break down the various options zine publishers can use for mailing within the U.S.

All information in this guide was obtained from the Domestic Mail Manual (DMM), accessed at pe.usps.gov/text/dmm300/dmm300_landing.htm in July 2007. Throughout the text we have included citations to specific sections of the DMM, which you can refer to for more information (or use if you're challenged by postal clerks).

Because of space constraints, we haven't included the postal rate chart in this guide; however, you can find a postal rate chart (containing U.S. First Class and International rates) on the back page of **Zine World** #25 or at www.undergroundpress.org/pdf/postalrates5-07.pdf.

By the way, if the Post Office in your town doesn't have the stamps you need, consider buying your stamps online. At shop.usps.com, you can buy any stamp denomination currently available, and they'll mail them to you (via Priority Mail) for just $1.

## First Class Mail

Rates for First Class Mail are now based not only on an envelope's weight but also its size, as detailed below.

## Letters: Size Requirements

Letters must be between 5 and 11.5 inches long and between 3.5 and 6-1/8 inches high and no more than .25 inches thick. Letters can weigh no more than 3.5 oz. Envelopes must be rectangular.

This means any envelope within this size range can be mailed at Letter Rate (unless it has nonmachinable characteristics; see below). Half-size or digest zines (weighing less than 3.5 oz.) can be mailed in a 6 x 9 envelope at this rate, but a 6.5 x 9.5 envelope would

have to be mailed at the more expensive Large Envelope rate.

## Nonmachinable Criteria for Letters

If a Letter is deemed nonmachinable, you have to pay a 17¢ surcharge in addition to the postage rate. Any one of these characteristics could make your envelope

nonmachinable:

☒ If the aspect ratio (length divided by height) is less than 1.3 or more than 2.5. (For example, an envelope that is square or is very long and very short.)
☒ If it is enclosed in plastic material.
☒ If it contains items (such as loose coins or buttons) that cause the thickness to be uneven. (Such items should be taped or wrapped in paper, to prevent them from shifting and to help make the envelope evenly thick.)
☒ If it is too rigid. (It should be bendable to about 1 inch.)
☒ If the delivery address is parallel to the shorter side of the envelope. See DMM 101.1.2 for other characteristics.

## Large Envelopes (aka Flats): Size Requirements

Flats are more than 11.5 inches long, or more than 6-1/8 inches high, or more than 1/4 inch thick. Flats cannot be more than 15 inches long, or more than 12 inches high, or more than 3/4 inch thick. In other words, an envelope smaller than 11.5 inches long is still considered a Flat if it is more than 6-1/8 inches high or more than 1/4 inch thick (such as a heavy Letter-size envelope or a 6.5 x 9.5 envelope). Generally, envelopes that are too big for Letter rate by any dimension fall into the Large Envelope category. Flats that are rigid, nonrectangular, not uniformly thick, or exceeding the above maximum dimensions must be mailed at Parcel (aka Package) rate, which is much more expensive.

*Note: Any mail weighing more than 13 oz. and using stamps must be handed to a clerk at a Post Office retail counter. (This new rule does not apply to mail with metered or PC-printed postage.)*

## Rigidity and Thickness

To test the flexibility of your Flat, USPS offers these guidelines:

1. Place the envelope on a flat surface, with the longer side parallel to the edge, so that it is only resting halfway on the surface.

2. Press down on the envelope at a point 1 inch from the outer edge, in the center of the length. (See illustration.)

3. The piece must bend at least 1 inch vertically without being damaged to be considered flexible.

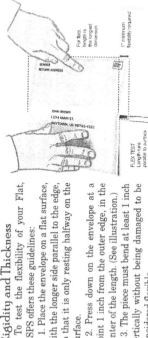

4. If the envelope contains a rigid insert, you must also test the flexibility along the shorter side, in the same manner as described above. Flats less than 10 inches long must bend at least 1 inch in this direction, too. For Flats 10 inches or longer, the shorter side must bend at least 2 inches.

A variance of more than 1/4 inch in thickness will make your Flat considered nonuniform. If your zine has a spiral binding or the envelope has any bumps, protrusions, or other irregularities, you should try to wrap the item in paper or bubble wrap to make it uniform. Nonpaper contents (think buttons) must be secured to prevent shifting within the envelope. (DMM 101.2.4)

## Other Mailing Options

For envelopes weighing above 10 oz., Priority Mail is not your only option. It is more economical to mail them using Media Mail or Bound Printed Matter. The delivery may not be quite as speedy – average delivery is 2-9 days – but it will be cheaper, especially as the package gets heavier.

If using one of these options, be sure to write MEDIA MAIL or BOUND PRINTED MATTER in the postage area, either below or to the left of the stamps.

## Media Mail

In the past few years, many zine publishers have turned to Media Mail for heavier envelopes – in part because we've been led to believe that Bound Printed Matter no longer exists or is not available for us to use. That's not true, but we'll get to that momentarily.

The USPS says only these items may be mailed using Media Mail:

☒ Books of at least 8 printed pages. Cannot contain advertising (display or classified ads).
☒ Films
☒ Printed music
☒ Test materials
☒ Sound or video recordings
☒ Playscripts and manuscripts
☒ Printed educational reference charts for training
☒ Loose-leaf pages containing medical information for doctors, hospitals, or students
☒ Computer-readable media

As you can see, it's debatable whether zines fall into this category – especially if they contain advertising. Media Mail is subject to postal inspection, and the Post Office has gotten stricter about its use. However, if it looks like a book and feels like a book... Let's just say we've rarely heard of a zinester who has had problems using it.

Media Mail cannot be personal correspondence, but it can include an invoice or a "personal message or greeting" (DMM 173.4.4 & 4.5). *Any method of postage can be used, and Media Mail postage can be purchased at a USPS retail counter*, making it easy to use. Media Mail rates are based on the weight of the package, regardless of destination. Don't forget the new 13 oz. rule (see Note on previous page). For more information (including a rate chart), read the Media Mail section of the DMM at pe.usps.gov/text/dmm300/173.htm.

## Bound Printed Matter

Bound Printed Matter should be the secret weapon of any dedicated zinester. It is designed for discount, bulk mailing, which requires a permit, special sorting, and other hoops to jump through. However, it can also be used for nonpresorted, single pieces. *For BPM mailings, you have to figure out the postage yourself and apply the postage yourself; USPS retail clerks will not calculate and apply postage for you.* And BPM rates are based not only on weight but also on the destination, which means you have to figure out which zone applies based on your zip code.

Bound Printed Matter is for items:

☒ Consisting of advertising, promotional, directory, or editorial material (in any combination).
☒ Securely bound by permanent fastenings such as staples, spiral binding, glue, or stitching.
☒ Consisting of sheets of which at least 90% are imprinted by a process other than handwriting or typewriting (think photocopy or offset printing) with letters, characters, figures, or images (or any combination).
☒ Not having the nature of personal correspondence or stationary.

Like Media Mail, BPM is subject to inspection. You can include an invoice or a "personal message or greeting" in the envelope (DMM 363.3.3). You'll be using the nonpresorted BPM rate, which applies to mailings of fewer than 300 pieces and not sorted.

For postage, you can use regular adhesive stamps or postage from a meter or printed from your PC (DMM 364.1.1.1). You can take nonpresorted BPM mailings to any post office or station, or give them to any Postal Service carrier (DMM 366.2.2d), but don't forget about the new 13 oz. rule (see Note under Large Envelope section). Use the criteria stated in the Large Envelope section of this guide to determine if your package qualifies as a BPM Flat or if it must be considered a Parcel.

The tough part, really, is figuring out the zones. Zones are based on proximity to your zip code; for example, the zip codes closest to yours will be Zone 1 or 2. Go to: postcalc.usps.gov/Zonecharts/ and you can get a printable list of zones based on your zip code. Once you have the zones (and your package's weight), you can use the BPM postal rate chart to figure out the postage.

You can also use the USPS online Domestic Business Rate Calculator to determine the postage (dbcalc.usps.gov). In the Flat (or Parcel) category, select Bound Printed Matter. Then, scroll down to the Nonpresorted section and enter your package's weight. It will calculate the postage per item for each zone.

Yes, it is a lot of work, but if you're doing a lot of heavier-envelope mailing, it may be worth the trouble, as BPM is usually cheaper than Media Mail and definitely cheaper than First Class.

Postal clerks don't regularly handle BPM, so don't expect them to answer your questions, and they may challenge your right to use it. You may be able to get more info from 800-275-8777, but you should specify you're asking about "nonsorted bound printed matter," or you'll just be referred to the bulk mail division of your local post office. For more information, including a rate chart, read the BPM section of the DMM at pe.usps.gov/text/dmm300/363.htm (Flats) or pe.usps.gov/text/dmm300/463.htm (Parcels).

This guide was created by *Zine World: A Reader's Guide to the Underground Press*, PO Box 330156, Murfreesboro TN 37133, www.undergroundpress.org. Permission is given for anyone to copy and redistribute this document as long as: you do not charge for it and this notice remains intact. The information in this guide was obtained from the USPS Domestic Mail Manual but has not been approved or confirmed by any USPS employees.

# Honorable Mentions

**Mute As Bottles**
Po Box 4.
Enmore, 2042, Australia
Lostcity99@yahoo.com

**Elephant Mess #19** (Nice Mess)
Dan Murphy
Po Box 3154
Moscow, ID 83843
messyelephant@hotmail.com

**Trying...**
Dominic Armao
dominic@bust.com

**These Here Are Crazy Times #1**
Sarah May
83361 Rodgers Rd.
Creswell, Or, 97426
teerexteeth@gmail.com

**Anarchism and Litigation**
Eric D. Smith
DOC # 112675
WCU P.O Box 473
Westville, Indiana

**Living Proof #5: Rapprochement**
Andrew
P.O. Box 14211
Chicago, Il 60614
livingproof@atm4.net

**End of a Perfect Day #10**
The Captain Joyce Leslie
joycealeslie@yahoo.com

**Love Like Pop #5**
Rachael Kuan
6a Tully Rd.
East Perth WA 6004
Australia
rachaelk@gmail.com

**Sojourner: Critical Reflections on Travel**
Suze B.
52 Hamilton Pl.
Oakland, CA 94612
suzeb@riseup.net

**Confrontations: Selected Journalism**
Kristian Williams
Tarantula Publishing
818 SW 3rd Ave. PMB 1237
Portland, OR 97204

**Overtime**
Corey Mesler
P.O. Box 250382
Plano, TX 75025-0382

**Quitter #4**
Trace
trace@wilmingtonblues.com

**Lower East Side Librarian Winter Solstice Shout Out, 2007**
Jenna Freedman
521 E. 5th St. Apt 1D
New York, NY 10009
leslzines@gmail.com

**Art Bureau #13 and #14**
Bert Benson
Po Box 1823
PDX, OR 97207
Artbureau.org

**La Frontera: the border**
Melissa
girleveryday@gmail.com

**Barfing 7's: The Chronicles of Bat and Moon #1**
36 Bedford Ter. #18
Northampton, MA 01060
Radishonparade@myway.com

**I Still Believe**
Jessica Rae
8990 Haggerty
Plymouth, MI 48170

**Coordinates**
Jon Allen
934 Illinois St. #C
Lawrence, KS 66044
noexpectations@hotmail.com

**Late Night Thinking #0:Circumspice**
Thomas Kula
Po box 7417
Ann Arbor, MI 48107
kula@tproa.net

**Smarmageddon #1**
Michael Gerkovich
mgerkovich@gmail.com

**19 C.**
Jamie
jdanehey@gmail.com

**Yoga Moves For Dudes**
J.G. Sookecheff
6-205 4th St. W
Cornwall ON
K65 2K9
Canada

**Grrrl Noire #7**
Kim Riot
Po box 33654
San Diego, CA 92116
hexestarr@yahoo.com

**Biblio Funk #1 and #2**
4904 28th Ave S. #4
Minneapolis, MN 55417
bluevalentinepress@hotmail.com

**Thirty Hour Sloth #2**
Sarah Wayward
Po box 31224
Halifax, NS
B3k 5yl

**A Love Letter to Pennsylvania City: The Unauthorized Biography of John Street**
Billy Fatzinger
billyfff@gmail.com

**Absolutely Zippo #25**
Robert Eggplant
Po box 4985
Belk, CA 94704

**Erinsborough Exploits ep. 16**
Gpo box 4201
Melbourne
Victoria 3001
Australia

**Cracks in the Concrete #5 and #7**
Luke Romano
Radical Rabbit Distro
234 Jamestown Blvd.
Hammonton, NJ 08037

**Lion in a Teacup**
Tabby Kaye
Po box 471343
Chicago, IL 60647
editor@lioninateacup.com

**Smile, Hon You're in Baltimore #9**
Po box 11064
Baltimore, MD 21212
wpt@eightstonepress.com

**Nothing is Real: Weird Comics for Your Brain**
c/o Daniel Brandt
722 Warsaw Ave.
Winnipeg, MB Canada
R3M 1C9

**220 Days of Movies with an Enormous Ball: Stupid Journey #6**
Jonathan Culp
Satan MacNuggit Popular Art
3584 John Street
Vineland Station, Ontario
L0R 2E0

**Miranda #17**
3510 SE Alder St.
Portland, OR 97214
oceanreader@gmail.com

**The Rise and Fall of the Harbor Area #10**
Craig Ibarra
info@theriseandthefall.com

**I Carried a Watermelon**
Cheryl Sonstein
3728 SE Kelly St.
Portland, OR 97202

Cheryl_superc@yahoo.com

**Baltimore County Public Library Zine Collection**
9833 Greenside Drive
Cockeysville, MD 21030
bcplzines@gmail.com

**Body Language**
Jessica "Max" Stein
caprice@riseup.net

**Tangential Fervor**
tangentialfervorzine@yahoo.com

**Bitter Pie**
Tena
2419 Mission St.
SF, CA 94110
bitterpie@hotmail.com

**Ditty Bag Devotional**
J. Brown
thedittybag@gmail.com

**Crescent City Stories**
nicki!
po box 743
Olympia, WA 98507

**Tempo Giusto**
maeo@bust.com

**Syndicate Product#12 Year of the (Pack)rat**
A.j. Michel
Po box 877
Lansdowne, PA 19050
synprod@gmail.com

**Somnambulist #9**
Martha Grover
Po box 14871
Portland, OR 97293
marthagrover@hotmail.com

**Rattletrap #2**
skybot99@yahoo.com

**Ad Astra Per Aspera**
Sarah Kate
1820 Grove #207

Oshkosh, WI 54901

**F-Word #2**
Melody Berger
howlingharpies@gmail.com

**Sidewalk Bump #2**
Dan Moynihan
danmoynihan@verizon.net

**Out of the Closets**
thebangarang@riseup.net

**Better Looking Than a Blog**
Shawn Granton
TFR industries
Po box 14185
Portland OR 97293-0185
Tfrindustries@scribble.com

**How to Make a Super 8 Film: Super 8, Super Zine**
anchorarchive@gmail.com

**When It's Time to Go**
wileymohawk@gmail.com

**Anti-Immigrant Hypocrisy**
Sallydarity
Sallydarity@yahoo.com

**Wave Project/Signals #5**
singinggrove@conknet.com

**The Crusades**
Simple History Series #2
J. Gerlach
1827 NE. Fifth St.
Minneapolis, MN 55418
jgrubby14@hotmail.com

**Post is the Most #1 and #2**
The Obvious Child Press
c/o Ryan Finnerty
4210 12th Ave. NE Apt. C
Seattle, WA 98105

**Prepubescent**
asummerj@hotmail.com

**The Lavender Hoe #1**
Shannon Perez-Darby & Amelia
Crewe
Po box 48131
Denver, CO 80204
Shannon- perez-darby@hotmail.com
Amelia- pandoras.law@gmail.com

**Phases of the Moon #2**
Ms. Skeleton Key
185 Mathews Ave.
Athens, GA 30606
cicada@selenographie.net

**Toothworm #2**
toofworm@gmail.com

**Puddnhead #4**
wilk0214@umn.edu

**And Then One Day #6**
Ryan Claytor
Elephant Eater Comics
Po box 15552
San Diego, CA 92175
ryan@elephanteater.com

**Superman Stories #2:**
**The Second Coming**
Mark Russell
The Penny Dreadful
3148 SE Salmon Ste #C
Portland, OR 97214

**Cursive Bomb #5**
Hazel Pine
Po box 12596
Seattle, WA 98111
Hazel.pine@gmail.com

**Mixtapers Do It Better #2**
Karen H.
49 Winterhalder Dr.
Zeeland, MI 49464
Recycled_youth_@hotmail.com

**School Daze Year 1:**
**Middle School**
Michel Valdes
schooldazezine@yahoo.com

**Turn the Page:**

**The Complete First Season**
Jayson
librarycartoons@gmail.com

**Farmer's Daughter #2**
mujeralbored@hotmail.com

# ZINE LIBRARIES INDEX: 2007

By Jenna Freedman (zine librarian) and Julie Turley (zine intern), Barnard College Library

**Zine libraries solicited for this article:** 74

**Zine library updates received:** 40
Academic libraries 11
Online libraries 2
Public libraries 14
School libraries 1
Volunteer libraries 12

**Newspaper quotes that made us laugh:** 1
"There is no preexisting librarians' code pertaining to how one should handle a document that includes a free prophylactic." Hsu, Hua. "File under other." *Boston Globe. May 6, 2007. p. E3.*

**Proposals for zine collections accepted:** 2
Ela Area Public Library (Illinois)
University of Pittsburgh, Information Science Library

**Zine collections launched:** 7
Cuyahoga County Public Library, Independence Branch, Ohio
Linebaugh Public Library (first zine collection in Tennessee)...
....followed by the first academic library zine collection in Tennessee (Watkins College of Art and Design)
Multnomah County Public Library, Portland, Oregon (They had a party—with donuts!)
Plymouth Regional High School, New Hampshire
Samuel H. Wentworth Library (in Sandwich, New Hampshire, population 1200 or so)
Seattle Public Library, Washington
University Library at Portsmouth, UK
Wellington City Libraries, New Zealand

**Approximate number of zines at Toronto Zine Library:** 1850

**New materials added at existing zine libraries:** 6
ABC No Rio (NYC) added zines and periodicals from the now-defunct Wetlands Preserve
Barnard College (NYC) received donations from two individual donors in particular that enhanced its collection of trans zines and zines by women of color
Bingham Center Women's Zine Collections at Duke University (North Carolina) acquired a full set of *ROCKRGRL* magazines
Bowling Green State University (Ohio) received a large gift of zines
The Labadie Collection at the University of Michigan acquired Bob Black's collection of zines and other serials.
The Punk Zine Archive completed their set of *Maximumrocknroll* and added a number of *Flipsides*.

**Old school fanzine collections:** 3
Bowling Green: Dipzines (Diplomacy zines—Diplomacy is a game)
Bowling Green: Kirk/Spock slash fanzines
University of California at Riverside: Bruce Pelz Fanzine Collection (including the Rick Sneary Collection)—67,500+ science fiction fanzines now held

**Libraries with approximately 4,000 zines:** 2
Bingham Center Women's Zine Collections at Duke University
San Francisco Public Library (California)

**Soliciting donations:** 7
Barnard College collects personal and political zines by urban woman-identified people, especially women of color, particularly on the topics of third-wave feminism and riot grrrl. Will pay shipping when it's time for you to clear your old zines out of your parents' attic or basement and send 'em to Barnard for preservation, use by future scholars, and leisure reading.
The Bingham Center collects zines by women, girls, and woman-identified people. Their particular interests include riot grrrl and feminism, gender and sexuality, and Southern women. Will pay for shipping materials, and your zines will actively be used in classroom instruction and scholarly research.
Colorado College (particularly zines from Arizona, Colorado, Nevada, New Mexico, Texas, and Wyoming)
Cuyahoga welcomes all zines, but specifically collects zines by, for, and of interest to teens.
Omaha Zine Library (Nebraska)
Papercut Zine Library (Cambridge, Mass.) They want zines and money—they were robbed this year! They'll also take more zine librarians.
San Francisco Public Library collects zines produced in the San Francisco Bay Area, and is always happy to consider donations. Anything that doesn't fit is traded to zine libraries around the country, ensuring long and useful lives for lots of zines.

**Changes in facilities:** 5
Nova Scotia's Anchor Archive Zine Library expanded to include the Ink Storm Screenprinting Collective studio
Same location, but Papercut Zine Library's status went from "uncertain" to "stable."
Papercut added new shelving to accommodate an "insane amount of zine donations."
Papercut started alphabetizing their zines.
Same location, but the Salt Lake City Public Library Zine Collection (the one that started it all)* has been renamed the Alternative Press Collection

**Changes of location:** 4
The Bat Annex Free School Library at the Belfry Center, Minneapolis
Bibliograph/e, Montreal
Chicago Underground Library (due to a "bizarre hostile takeover of the coffee shop in which we'd set up")
Omaha Zine Library's website moved to http://www.freewebs.com/omahazines

**Nonprofit status granted:** 1
Denver Zine Library (Colorado)

**Card carrying members of the Papercut Zine Library:** nearly 1,000

**Libraries that began circulating their zines:** 7
Barnard College
Carnegie Library of Pittsburgh
Linebaugh Public Library
Multnomah County Public Library
Plymouth Regional High School
Seattle Public Library
Toronto Zine Library

**Average number of times each zine circulated at Baltimore County Public Library in 2007:** 4

**Web projects:** 15
Baltimore County Public Library uploaded two videos to YouTube
The Bat Annex wiki
http://belfrycenter.wetpaint.com/page/library.
LibraryThing catalogs
Bat Annex: belfrycenter
Carnegie Library of Pittsburgh: clpteenszines
Plymouth Regional High School: PRHSZineLibrary
Seattle Public Library: spl_zines
Zine Libraries Flickr group
Barnard College
.m.e.c. (library student)
Multnomah County Public Library
Plymouth Regional High School
Warren Disgrace (not sure!)
Watkins College of Art & Design
Entry added to ZineWiki for San Francisco Public Library
Blogs launched
Anchor Archive Zine Library started a blog about cataloging their collection:  http://blog.anchorarchive.ath.cx
Barnard College LiveJournal: BarnardZines
Punk Zine Archive http://punkzinearchive.blogspot.com
ZineLibraries.info, a communal project administered by Stephanie Iser, KCPL

**Online catalog debuts:** 3
Bingham Center Women's Zine Collections at Duke University:
http://library.duke.edu/specialcollections/bingham/zines
        (Site also includes a guide to the collection, an
        essay by Sarah Dyer, and a "Brief History of Zines"
        timeline.)
Cleveland Public Library (Ohio)
Multnomah County Public Library

**Online catalog improvements:** 1
San Francisco Public Library updated their online finding aid and added a collection level record

**Zines available online via pdf at the Queer Zine Archive Project (QZAP):** over 200

**Granted the Punk Zine Archive permission for online publication of out-of-print issues:** 3
*10 Things Jesus Wants You to Know*
*Ink Disease*
*Profane Existence*

**Inventories and Archival Rehousing Projects completed:** 1
San Francisco Public Library Little Maga/Zine Collection

**Onsite events:** 10
ABC No Rio Zine Library fundraiser, open house, and reading (three discrete events)
Anchor Archive Zine Library hosted a 24 hour zine making marathon
Baltimore County Public Library had an Indie Comics A-Go-Go program that generated a lot of press
Baltimore County Public Library (Maryland) hosted field trips from the Zines and Mini-Comics classes taught at the Maryland Institute College of Art
The Bat Annex hosted a benefit for the super fancy zine *Profane Existence* and various crafts workshops
The Sallie Bingham Center for Women's History and Culture at Duke University gave information sessions to undergraduate classes in feminism and literature
The Carnegie Library of Pittsburgh did various workshops with teens, teachers, and librarians
Oregon third annual Zinesters Talking series (w/teen poetry slam) at the Multnomah County Public Library
Abby Bass and Hazel Pine led a zine making workshop at an all day zine symposium to celebrate Seattle Public Library's zine collection launch. There were also a panel discussion and open-mic zine reading.
The Western New York Zine Archive (poetry zines, SUNY Buffalo) hosted college art classes

**Libraries that offered zine workshops:** 11
Anchor Archive Zine Library
Barnard College
Bingham Center Women's Zine Collections at Duke University
Carnegie Library of Pittsburgh
Cuyahoga County Public Library
Independent Publishing Resource Center (IPRC) in Portland, Oregon
Linebaugh Public Library
Multnomah County Public Library
Queer Zine Archive Project (QZAP)
Samuel H. Wentworth Library, given by Margarat Nee of Grrrl Zines A-Go-Go
Seattle Public Library

**Offsite events:** 24
American Library Association conference event, "Zine-a-Palooza 2007!" a Zines in Public Libraries panel featuring Miriam DesHarnais and Julie Harrison from Baltimore County Public Library, Jennifer May and Emily-Jane Dawson from

Multnomah County Public Library, and Julie Bartel (formerly) and Brooke Young from Salt Lake City Public Library

Bako Zines (Bakersfield, CA) had an "anniversary thingie" with workshops, discussion groups, zine trading, with food from Food Not Bombs

Mid-Atlantic Radical Book Fair table (Baltimore County Public Library, Barnard College)

Small Press Expo table (Baltimore County)

Barnard College curated a zine reading at a coffee shop

Society for the History of Authorship, Reading and Publishing (SHARP) conference panel presentations by Jenna Freedman of Barnard College and Kelly Wooten of the Bingham Center Women's Zine Collections

Twin Cities Zine Fest, zine libraries discussion led by Jenna Freedman of Barnard College and Lacey Prpic Hedtke of the Bat Annex Free School Library (at the Belfry Center for Social and Cultural Activities)

Twin Cities Zine Fest table, Bat Annex

Lacey Prpic Hedtke of the Bat Annex presented a poster session at the BOBCATSSS conference in Prague

College of St. Catherine zine panel, by the Bat Annex

Bibliograph/e presented at the Humanities and Social Sciences conference in Saskatoon

McGill University zine librarianship talk by Bibliograph/e

The Bingham Center developed "Portable Zine Talk" for classroom presentations

The Bingham Center gave a Zines/Feminism talk and workshop for girls aged 12-16 at the North Carolina Girls Rock Camp

The Bingham Center's Kelly Wooten presented at the Society of American Archivists conference

Chicago Underground Library launched a "multi-media series creative reinterpretations of items in our collection," presented at the Hyde Park Art Center

Boston Zine Fair—organized by Papercut Zine Library with Black Ocean Publications

Queeruption: workshop by Queer Zine Archive Project (QZAP)

Institute of Museum and Library Services/Urban Libraries Council presentation by Andrea Grimes of the San Francisco Public Library

Tennessee Library Association presentation by Jerianne Thompson of the Linebaugh Public Library (and *Zine World*)

The University of Minnesota illustration classes, by the Bat Annex

Librarians from the University of Washington Bothell delivered a poster session at a University Teaching and Learning Symposium

## Zine exhibits: 6

ABC No Rio (The Art in Zines) *See article elsewhere in the Zine Yearbook.*

Barnard College (The Zine Scene and College Knowledge)

Bingham Center ("Hidden and Forbidden: Literary Secrets and Transgressions")

Bingham Center ("Stretching the Canvas: Women Explore the Arts.")

California International Book Fair (San Francisco) by SFPL

University of Pittsburgh, Information Science Library (zines by library workers)

## Zine library spawned groups: 2

The Bat Annex, with Arise! Resource Center launched a Radical Book Club

The zine collection led to the formation of a local literacy group at the Linebaugh Public Library

## Artist/writer/zinemakers-in-residence hosted at the Anchor Archive Zine Library: 7

## Zine event that got busted by the cops: 1

A Chicago Underground Library co-hosted literary event

## Things that doubled:

Baltimore County Public Library's zine circulation

Number of zines in the Bat Annex's collection

## Zine Librarians list members in good standing (email isn't bouncing): 225

http://groups.yahoo.com/group/zinelibrarians

## Zine Librarians list posts in 2007: 276

## Zine library staff who produced zines: 7

ABC No Rio: Vikki Law (*Tenacious* and others)

Barnard College: Jenna Freedman (*Lower East Side Librarian* and others)

Barnard College: Jennie Halperin (*So, you're a freshman? Or how I learned to stop worrying and love college or top ten things I wish someone had told me about my first year*)

Colorado College: Jessy Randall (*The Huge Underpants of Gloom*)

IPRC: Greig Means (*Best Zine Ever* and others)

Pratt Institute: Alycia Sellie (*Unanswerable Questions* Vol. 1 No. 2: *Coping*)

University at Portsmouth: Jackie Batey (*Future Fantasteek*)

## Staff Changes: 4

Greg Means left the IPRC after 8 years of service and was succeeded by Marc Parker.

James Danky retired after more than 30 years of collecting underground publications at the Wisconsin Historical Society (but WHS is still collecting all zines made in Wisconsin or with political subject matter).

Alycia Sellie also left the Society and is now working on reviving Pratt Institute in Brooklyn's zine collection

Hazel Pine resigned as director of Richard Hugo House's Zine Archive & Publishing Project

## Pen pal relationship formed: 1

The Bat Annex and the IPRC

## Publications by or about zine libraries: 8

Baltimore County Public Library zine

http://www.bcpl.info/centers/library/Zine.pdf

*Baltimore Sun* article. Schaefer, Andrew. "Cartoonists find fans at Cockeysville library." April 12, 2007 Thursday: p. 4B.
*Boston Globe* article: Hsu, Hua. "File under other." May 6, 2007. p. E3.
http://www.boston.com/news/globe/ideas/articles/2007/05/06/file_under_other
*Christian Science Monitor* article: Dreilinger, Danielle. "Wanted: pen, plain old paper, imagination." Dec 14, 2007. pg. 12
http://www.csmonitor.com/2007/1214/p12s02-algn.html
*Philadelphia Inquirer* article: Haegele, Katie. "Visit to LibraryThing can bring together readers and collectors." December 2, 2007.
http://www.philly.com/inquirer/currents/20071202_Visit_to_LibraryThing_can_bring_together_readers_and_collectors.htm

*Phonebook* essay on community archiving: Nell Taylor of the Chicago Underground Library, published by Threewalls and The Green Lantern Press http://phonebook.squarespace.com
*Tennessee Libraries* article: Thompson, Jerianne. "Zine: it rhymes with teen, how a zine collection can help you connect with young adults." Volume 57 Number 1, 2007
http://tnla.org/displaycommon.cfm?an=1&subarticlenbr=138

**Awards: 2**
Best branch library in Baltimore County: Cockeysville, because of the zine collection
Association of College and Research Libraries "Significant Achievement in Women's Studies Librarianship" award for panel that included a presentation on zines in libraries by Jenna Freedman, Barnard College

**Radio shows: 2**
Anchor Archive Zine Library started a bi-weekly zine themed show at a local community station
The Bat Annex librarians were featured on a show promoting the Twin Cities Zine Fest

**Disasters: 4**
Floods
Chicago Underground Library
Richard Hugo House's Zine Archive & Publishing Project (ZAPP), Seattle
Robbery: Papercut Zine Library
Website hacked: Queer Zine Archive Project (QZAP)

**No activity, missing in action, in flux, or on hiatus: 5**
Kansas City Public Library (no new activity)
New York Public Library (no new activity—maybe next year)
Pratt Institute (Brooklyn, NY. No new activity, but zine enthusiast Alycia Sellie joined their staff in 2007, so expect some news in the 2008 Yearbook)
ZAPP—zines in boxes, post flood
Urbana Champaign Independent Media Center (UCIMC) Zine Library

**Newspaper quotes that filled our hearts with joy: 1**
What makes Cockeysville the best, however, is its zine collection, organized by librarian Miriam DesHarnais. From it you can borrow tiny little periodicals about everything from eyeglasses and bike repair to summer vacations and cats' personalities—and minicomics, too." In a *Baltimore City Paper* article naming them the best public library in the county. http://www.citypaper.com/bob/story.asp?id=14143

*The Information above is courtesy of reports solicited from the ZineLibrarians Yahoo! Group*
*http://groups.yahoo.com/group/zinelibrarians, libraries from our list of zine collections*
*http://www.barnard.edu/library/zines/links.htm#libraries, the Underground Press/Zine World list of zine libraries and Infoshops*
*http://www.undergroundpress.org/infoshops.html, and ZineWiki's list http://zinewiki.com/index.php?title=Category:Zine_Library.*

* Note that other public and research libraries had begun collecting zines years before Salt Lake City Public Library launched its collection in 1996, but that SLCPL was as far as we know the first to develop and promote a standalone zine collection, and one that was created by library workers who were themselves part of the zine community.

# COLUMNS

 Dave Fried Taco Puppy

Kisha and I arrived in Portland, Oregon late one night. We caught a ride from a cab driver named Reno. He was an award-winning barbecue champion, and had a beard I wanted to run my fingers through. He gave us a ride from Seattle to Portland - late one night, dropped us off near downtown. It was up to us to find our way to the house we had been promised a place to sleep. It was a little after midnight, and all I had was a foreign looking address on a sheet of loose leaf paper. I didn't know where it was or how to get there. Kisha and I lugged our bags around, going to several bars, showing it to people. Four out of six had no idea where it was, and three out of the six weren't even from the area. A bouncer at a very loud Irish themed pub finally sent us on our way to the right street, to the right bus, in the right direction. We were so tired we were hallucinating.

When we finally got to where we needed to be, it was everything we didn't want in the world at that moment. We had spent the past ten and a half hours traveling. The last thing I ate was an $18 tuna sandwich at the airport; I was gassy as could be. Kisha was constipated. We were nauseous, tired and thirsty. There was an all night show going on at the punk house that would be our crash pad before the Zine Symposium. We groaned. It was all we could manage to do.

After finding one and a half people we knew, we made our way to the living room, and tried to find a place to sleep - someplace where nobody would step on our heads or vomit on us. A tall order for this house, indeed! Kisha and I looked at each other and laughed, feeling like we had come to some full circle, or were some sort of culture vulture upon this house. The living room was a busy intersection of people and noise. People excited about the next band or just happy to be drunk on a Friday night. Having more than a decade between us, of living in and out of punk houses, squats, and other flavors of squalor - this house was nothing new or shocking. Loud music in the basement, flyers for anything and everything on tables, pyramids of beer cans – it's all you can see. Looking the part of the weary traveler, some drunk guy told us about Food Not Bombs, informing us of the free vegan meal at the park. We thanked him for the locale of the free chow right before he convulsed, put his hand up to his mouth, and sprayed red spaghetti vomit all over the wall and blacked out. I think we were curling our toes over the edge of insanity at this point.

We poked around and found a closet on the upper floor. It was full of old blankets and VHS tapes. It was so small, you'd have to go outside to change your mind. It was dark and far away from the noise of the spur of the moment dance party that blossomed after the last band ended. We pushed everything aside and tried to sleep. We were folded in half, on a cold hardwood floor, with Kisha sneezing every nine seconds. In rigid upright positions we nervously tried to sleep.

After the sixteenth or seventeenth time I woke up, I saw light coming from the crack on the door. We had made it through the night. So what that it was seven fifteen in the morning? We survived. Kisha sneezed herself awake and groaned, rubbing every sore spot on her body. My back hurt like hell, my nose was clogged, I was just as tired as when I went to sleep, but it was morning — and the Portland Zine Symposium was starting in a few hours.

On the way to the Symposium, I still managed to convince myself that this was better than going to work. In a few hours, I'd get to rub elbows, and have my elbows rubbed by dozens of zinesters from across the lands. People who I only know by way of this unique context, I'd catch up with - the people I only see once a year. Sitting at my table, I realize that I'm a part of this, and I'm involved in this, and I'm happy to be here. I write a goddamn zine. I'd hear things like "Issue six! I haven't got issue six!" or "Have you seen the new oh seven long arm staplers?" It was nice to have a level playing field of unbridled excitement. These were my people, like it or not!

This is why I continue to do zines. Enthusiasm. Nothing less than genuine enthusiasm for what we're writing about. It sure as hell beats not

doing a zine. I could just as well be playing the harmonica for sport or eating mayonnaise out of the jar. In case anyone was wondering, I just want to go ahead and say it: I think the best zine in the whole stupid world is *You Don't Get There From Here* by Carrie McNinch. There, I said it.

 With Some Hope and Some Despair
Joe Biel

I first encountered Lance Hahn on a record in a record store. It was 1993 and I had been combing the record reviews in Maximum Rock n Roll obsessively at that time, looking for new bands that would be cooler than the ones I was familiar with, or at least ones my friends hadn't already checked out. J Church seemed to have at least a few new records every single month and Lance Hahn was a regular contributor to the zine itself.

After reading reviews of multiple J Church records month after month, I decided to pick up the "This song is for Kathi" seven inch. I loved it and played it religiously. It was funny, clever, socially relevant, and smart in a way that I hadn't yet encountered in punk.

A few years later J Church came on tour to Cleveland and played at our local DIY showspace. They were refreshingly earnest and available to talk about all manner of things in a way that I hadn't yet come to expect from a band that I respected. I did not know it at the time, but that night my peers Jake and Steph interviewed Lance for their zine "Summer". I did manage to make it home with a copy of Lance's zine "Some Hope and Some Despair".

It wasn't until the following year that the issue of "Summer" was published with the interview but by coincidence, I picked it up at the next J Church show, which was coincidentally at the same place. I loved them even more with every passing encounter.

I started writing back and forth with Lance over the next year and ordering their records directly from him. His mailorder was very slow but that somehow convinced me further about how "real" they were and how Lance had a real life outside of playing in this rock band and writing this zine.

By 1997 I had setup my own interview with them for my own zine. Strange things had happened in the last year – they had signed to Honest Don's Hardly Used Recordings, a subsidiary of Fat Wreck Chords, and were playing at a big rock club in the drinking part of town on St. Patrick's Day instead of the DIY self-managed club. I had a lot of probing questions for them indeed.

In retrospect, I was probably an annoying kid who thought he knew more about the financial realities of their band than anyone involved and that obviously signing to Fat Wreck was worse than selling out, it was ruining their production values (their first full length is about 40 minutes and credited as being recorded in one hour).

Instead of being annoyed with me, they gave me one of the best interviews of my life. They leveled with me. They explained how their record label worked. They told me how complicated it is to have dozens of records out on dozens of friends' bedroom labels that are constantly in and out of print. Lance and Gardner were two of the most likeable, transparent, and forthcoming people I had ever met. That interview was printed in pieces in about four or five different zines. I felt like a journalist who had cracked the questions everyone was curious about.

They were sharing a drummer with Pee, who they were on tour with, and he would play songs with them, on request, that he had never heard before. It was great.

That night he also gave me a zine that detailed being the touring guitarist for Beck and what that tour was like throughout Europe. I was floored that Lance had somehow worked his way into that position.

I somehow finagled my way into doing some recordings of them. I still honestly didn't know them very well but I sent them the finished tapes of the recordings and they released it as an album. The idea of them being so prolific and off the cuff that seemingly anyone could record them on tour and it turns into a record a few years later is what really struck me as "on the level" and magical about this band.

The following years were sad ones. Gardner quit the band after being unable to write songs and was tiring of touring so much. Lance got sick with kidney and heart problems. He got new band members and carried on, recording new albums. He moved to Austin a few years later and started the band over again there with a new lineup.

We kept in touch pretty well and he sent me every new zine that he did. He sent me postcards every few months and I used J Church's music in a documentary that I made about zines in 2003. That was also the same year that I saw Lance for the last time.

I was living in Portland, OR and they were coming through on tour. I setup a show for them at my friend Heather's house and it turned out really well. The old punks came out and sang along and hefted beers and the new lineup was pretty together. I got them about $150 for the show, which seemed pretty reasonable for a living room.

The following year I got only one postcard from Lance and a videotape of live performance that he was compiling. I ran into his bandmate Ben Snakepit who told me that Lance's heart had stopped at one point on tour after he had run out of medicine on the road. Ben was unsure if they'd ever tour again and what Lance's future would be like.

Lance was always in good spirits despite whatever was going on in the world or in his life. He seemed to laugh about everything and have insightful comments. His apartment caught on fire and he sent out a newsletter with a list of things that needed replacing; not a plea for help or complaining or frustration. People put together numerous funds to help raise money for his seemingly infinite medical bills and earlier in 2007, a tribute album was put together to help pay his medical bills.

He seemed to be friends with everyone in the known universe. He associated with the old anarcho scene, the riot grrrl scene, the alternative scene, the zine scene, the DIY punk scene, and simultaneously seemed to have personal relationships with members of every local and touring band.

He was working on a book about anarcho-punk history for the better part of ten years, if not longer. It's contents have been printed one article at a time in the pages of Maximum Rock n Roll, as it seems uncertain if the finished book will ever see publication.

I was in Halifax for Canzine in 2007 when I got the news that Lance had died that day, on Oct 21. It had been a turbulent life. It wasn't a tremendous surprise but at the same time it was crushing my spirit to know that someone who I would always picture smiling, shrugging it off, and changing the subject couldn't just ignore his health problems forever and be the eternal fighter that he deserved to be.

Taylor Ball
Parcel Press

In the very beginning of 2007, I moved Parcell Press back into its home state of Virginia after six quick months away. Starting the year in Richmond was realigning to this very personal project to which I've devoted myself for four years. The year started strong with a reprinting of Niku Arbabi's wildly popular *Ms. Films DIY Guide to Film & Video,* which was Parcell Press's first official book release. The second run was beautifully printed by the folks at 1984 Printing and continues to get great book trade distribution support from their neighbors and prominent worker-owned publisher AK Press.

In April of 2007, Parcell Press participated in the Richmond Zine Fest here in its new hometown. The Richmond Zine Fest was incredibly well-attended and well-received by both Richmond and Virginia residents as well as independent writers and artists from further down the Southeast coast than most of the regularly-held Northeastern zine fests are able to cater to. I was lucky enough to be able to help out with coordinating and organizing the fest at the tail end of the planning stages, though I admit that Sarah, Liz, and Nicole had done most of the necessary work to ensure that the fest was the best in recent collective memory and they were gracious enough to give me little more than a figurehead role in the capacity of planning. At the fest, I was fortunate enough to sit on a panel discussion with Alex Wrekk of *Brainscan* and *Stolen Sharpie Revolution*, as well as Jerianne Thompson of the legendary *Zine World: A Reader's Guide to the Underground Press* review publication. It was a real honor to share the panel with such influential and important members of the zine community.
After the natural high of the Zine Fest began to subside, I moved Parcell Press operations out of my apartment (finally!) and into a shared workspace in the beautiful Fan District of Richmond. At last, I was going to have space to expand the Parcell Press catalog and inventory without sacrificing any more of my living space. I've now shared the space for nearly a year with artist, zinester, and friend Travis Robertson, whose screen printing abilities are matched by few, and whose company is consistently motivating, inspiring, and most importantly, enthusiastic. Travis and I spent a long, hot summer together in our two-car garage warehouse/office/studio space sniffing around our new, intimidating, and confusing procurement of an offset printing press and enough supporting equipment to make any zinester swoon: automatic folder, automatic paper cutter capable of effortlessly slicing through a phone book-sized stack, foot-powered stapler, and other automatic this-things and electric that-things, all tinted in that evocative and nostalgic 1970s "office-industrial green," or, in some cases "warehouse brown," and exceptionally, blue. After a few months of arranging the half- or whole-ton machines into a configuration that appeared to be the most user-friendly and practical — not to mention space-saving, since 400 square feet tended to disappear under the weight of our combined projects — we flipped the press on a few times to witness its steady rhythm of factory ca-chink, ca-chink, ca-chink before collapsing into an oblivion of ignorance. Not only were we confused about how to run the machine, we weren't clear on how the machine ran itself, so it appeared impossible for us to even articulate the correct questions to ask anyone in order to better understand.

It took at least four or five months of persistent curiosity and determination to acquire even the most elementary of the skills and knowledge necessary to successfully run a print shop. There were too many nights of pure devastation to count on a set of hands, but there were also miraculous moments of beautiful breakthrough: the satisfying success of unexpectedly consistent and flawless prints produced by one slight manipulation of the press itself, the empowered sense of accomplishment upon identifying and remedying a tiny, unsuspecting machine part by repair or replacement, and the awareness that, in exchange for a set of finely-printed business cards, we were actually capable of finding people in town who were willing to pay us to essentially teach ourselves what the hell we were doing in this windowless garage with these pretty machines.

By autumn, things were rolling. We printed *Adrift*, a beautiful comic book for my friend JP Coovert of One Percent Press, and we've done a lot of other fun jobs as well. At this point, I spend about half my working time coordinating print projects and running the press, and the other time focusing on the redevelopment of Parcell Press's website (the design of which has been generously generated by my brother, Mike Ball), and planning for future publishing projects. I have a small book of my own which I'm continuing to write and re-write before printing it. It will be titled *The Big Shrink*. In the meantime I will be creating small books and zines out of single stories, printing broadsides, and more. Parcell Press is also working with a group of folks to compile and publish an updated *Radical South* journal, and an anthology of independent art and writing related to mental health, *Mental Skillness*.

2007 was a year of rearrangement and expansion for Parcell Press, and I hope in 2008 to be able to showcase the fruits of these new skills, resources, and labors. The future holds, for Parcell Press, a continued devotion to independent media and art — writing, printmaking, bookmaking, illustrating, theorizing, expressing, and challenging — and a sincere effort to bring the means of production and resources for expression closer to the hands of those whose voices should be amplified and whose minds deserve and crave empowerment. If you happen to be walking through the alleyway between Hanover and Grove Avenues in Richmond, stop by the unsuspecting carriage house/garage building that emits an odor of soy inks and a steady sound of ca-chink, ca-chink, ca-chink, because I'm in there, probably printing *The Big Shrink*, and I'd love a visitor. (Taylor Ball, taylor@parcellpress.com, Parcell Press, P.O. Box 14647, Richmond, VA 23221)

## Samantha
## Civic Media Center

When I was three days old, my mother wanted to escape the summer heat of Queens, which was hellish when you lived in an old apartment with no air conditioning. Since then I have always been a traveler.

I've eaten in tiny hole-in-the-wall diners, which probably haven't changed their menu since they opened back in 1950-something. I've broken down in the middle of nowhere, in the age before cell phones. I've developed an accent that is a blend of the places that I've come to refer to as "my future home." Basically, I've made myself a child of the road.

While I've had both good and bad experiences, I've always been able to find comfort in the fact that I am not alone in my travels. Since the 7th grade, after discovering Quimby's bookstore on a trip to Chicago, I have been collecting other zinesters' stories about travel (mis)adventures, and sharing experiences in some sense. I have felt sympathy for travelers who have found themselves stuck with no money, excited for those headed out on their first big road trip, and envious of those who were already where I was headed to in the car.

When I first got into zines, I remember being jealous, because everyone seemed to be in a place where everyone seemed to be doing something cool and wishing that my hometown was more like the one that I had read about, instead of the tourist trap that I was constantly trying to leave.

Before a trip, I would order zines on the internet from distros, carefully reading the descriptions, hoping to find a zine about one of my destinations, so I would already be familiar, in some sense, with the town. I would arrive to a city like New York or Portland, and already know where I could find something interesting to do that would allow me to see the city in less of a touristy way, and through a more local perspective. When I would visit a place, I felt like I already knew it from reading about it.

When I moved to Gainesville, I immediately found a community that was filled with creative minds and progressive thinkers. I had read about the Civic Media Center an alternative, non-profit library that frequently hosts community events, and as soon as I was unpacked, walked in and two months later was hired as co-coordinator.

In my position at the Civic Media Center, I, along with several other volunteers, have made it our mission to not only promote the library as a whole, but specifically our extensive zine collection, which tends to be the most ignored part of the library. I feel that zines are an important part of community, allowing the communication and expression that is necessary for any counter-culture to survive.

The reason I originally became interested in zines is because I wanted to find cool places to explore in my travels, and Seventeen magazine and Frommer's travel guide weren't satisfying me. I felt like zines were written by someone like me, curious about the world and hoping to satisfy that curiosity through exploration.

In the age of Myspace, Blogspot, Facebook, etc. it can be easy to forget the importance of independent and self published, printed materials. Mainstream media is becoming more and more controlled by a select few who are rich enough to buy all the TV stations, newspapers, websites, etc. When I first got politically involved, I began to view zines as more than a way to ensure a good vacation. I realized that they were an act of resistance against a world in which Corporate America is boss. Zines gave me a much needed political outlet. In a time where my government was invading a country under false pretenses and taking innocent lives, I read zines (as well as independent newspapers and magazines) that talked frankly about the war, ways to try and stop it, what our soldiers were doing/having done to them, and just allowed people to speak about how horrible it was to go in to war under false pretenses.

Although I had been fiercely anti-war for as long as I could remember, I always felt that I was one of the few who felt the way I did. I credit this partly to the town I grew up in, which had a large Redneck population, but also to the state of the mainstream media, where the voices of the people are suppressed in order to keep the corporations supplying the advertising dollars.

While zines still have a thriving world community, there has been a recent shift from print to online zines. It seems that zinesters are slowly becoming bloggers, which creates a moral conflict of sorts for some. The internet allows many to get their zines out for a fraction of the cost of printed zines, as well as potential reach a much wider audience, but it allows corporate involvement into a community which tends to believe in the opposite.

I believe in remaining independent and have dedicated nearly the past year of my life in the fight against corporate media. While many people I talk with read blogs and get information from the internet (I know I am guilty), zines allow for a much more personal experience. I never would have made the life for myself that I have if I hadn't read zines, the information is on the web, but I would not have stumbled upon it, but instead probably passed by the Civic Media Center everyday on the way to some other job.

Growing up in a small town, if I wasn't on the road, I had two ways to get zines, wait for either Punk Planet or Maximum Rock N Roll to arrive in the mail, or go online and order them from distros. I appreciate what the internet allows for zinesters; we

can share copy machine tricks, promote ourselves, find new zines, etc.What I am fearful of is the extinction of the printed zine. Many zinesters are now going at it online, for a variety of reasons, leaving behind the days in which I would read their words in the car to somewhere new.

 More than just a zine:
Grrrl Zines A-Go-Go
by Kim Riot

Coming into a room of blank-stare faces to share the wonderful knowledge of zine-making isn't as easy as it sounds. One of the biggest challenges Grrrl Zines A-Go-Go always faces is how do you connect with your audience and participants not just on a zine education level, but as a non-authoritative and respectful community network advocate. When standing up in front of a classroom, community center, or even out in the park, one can't assume that your curious observers will either A) even know what is a zine and B) will even relate to zine culture in the first place. Having taken many strides in respect to these issues, over the last year we've jumped over many hurdles to make zines a fun, easy, and relevant force in the community.

In 2005, we penned "Let's DIY: Tips and Tricks on Organizing Zine Workshops." We felt we needed to take this idea further, so in conjunction with the 2006 Portland Zine Symposium workshop

presentation, we expanded upon the notion of getting the zinesters out of the bedroom comfort zone to use your zine as a collaborative community project idea. This last year at Portland, we stressed the importance of zines providing avenues for social change and how to further identify your focus group, and published "Let's DIY #2: Taking Zine Making to the Community" based on that presentation. Add to that really getting to the point of taking your skills and experiences as zine educators to improve community bonds and relationships. There were participants that really wanted to get out of their rooms, so to speak, and challenge themselves by building strong culture!

We continued our workshop presentations that we really honed in our busy 2006 season (we got a grant that year that brought us extra attention). Our most satisfying work of the year has been our workshops and mentoring with the Hillcrest Youth Center of San Diego, which serves LGBTQ youth and their allies. We began our work with them in January 2007, when their Women's Group asked us to come and do a workshop. From this workshop they were inspired to begin producing their own zine, *Rainbowlution Now*, in partnership with The Storefront, a shelter for homeless youth. They gather under the guidance of Nikyta Palmisani, an artist working at The Storefront, with additional mentoring from GZAGG. During the production of the first issue we met with them several times, sitting in on their weekly meetings to provide tips on zine production. That proved quite a task given a room full of flirty teens!!!! Now working on their third issue, the kids continue to take on more and more responsibility, and a curriculum is developing to carry this model of zine teaching into other youth settings. We drop in from time to time to check in on what they're working on and to provide encouragement. We've also begun purchasing queer zines for the Youth Center to develop a zine library. There is such a need for more queer youth zines, so we're glad that these kids are adding to the scene. This collaboration reinforced the whole idea of building continuity from within, using creative means, that is on its way to being self-sustaining.

Think we branched out in 2007? You betcha! We did our first out-of-state workshop in New Hampshire, in the small town of Sandwich (pop. 1300+). Not only was our workshop a first for them, we donated a starter collection of zines for their library. This small town library is hoppin'! All ages congregate here, and books are flying out the door. Our goal, shared with the library staff, was to engage the youth in valuing the printed word outside of the classroom, where reading is always assigned. While there is some teen reading going on at the library, most of their energy is focused on the wi-fi web access available there, a more participatory and shared experience that they control. Our workshop was mainly youth aged 9 to 15 (plus 2 moms), some home-schooled, some public schooled, and some who attend a local independent Community school. The kids got seriously involved once they understood that they controlled the "assignment" of producing a page, and once the copies were made the main room was littered with silent youngsters reading their zine (which itself was added to the library's collection). We hope to continue our collaborations here, bridging the gaps in literacy definitions with additions to their collection and future workshops.

As far as numbers go (And honorarium payments, woohoo!), our biggest and busiest workshop of the year was at Chaffey College in Rancho Cucamonga, CA. Part of their *Girly Show* museum exhibition, we went on after a professorial presentation on zines that we were itchin' to add our comments too. We introduced our own personal history in zines, personalizing the history that had been only glanced at in the lecture. When we asked who had been in the (righteously cool) zine reading room set up in the museum a few steps away, only a few hands went up in the college crowd. We told them that if they really wanted to see what zines were about, they needed to spend some time in there perusing the wealth of real zines by women rather then relying on a teacher's distant perspective. The collaborative zine produced that day was filled with personal commentary and reflection, on feminism and more. Turned out one of the museum interns had done a zine, and talking to her about it made us feel like we'd made a connection with at least one person who wanted to continue what we started that day.

We spread our limbs out this year even more and did three Zine Picnics to encourage people interested in zines to get together in a pleasant "afternoon at the park" free vegan cupcakes kinda way. Here in San Diego there isn't a visible zine community, and almost no places to read and buy zines, so we wanted to offer a space in which zine-makers and the zine-curious could get together. While they were small affairs we did succeed in these goals. We would have street travelers, dog walkers, veteran zinesters, and activists hang out in our modest tent. We even had some young folks take the time (and go through the hassle!) to cross the border from Tijuana to share their zine with us. The zine picnics are a good option for groups without a budget, as they are very low cost. Since our grant from The Foundation for Change wasn't renewed that was an important consideration when we were brainstorming ways to get out in the community. It's really this idea of accessibility much like a library, but we are in some ways bringing the library to the people.

So why not? Take the knowledge and make it as limitless as possible. The majority of people are marginalized into thinking that knowledge is privilege. Even the most community-centric of places like libraries are intimidating for many. The zine workshops, picnics, and collaborations are springboards for how we can better de-institutionalize print media. Our goals for 2008 involve mobile "zine reading rooms" and more visibility for zines. The time is now to be seen and heard!

Grrrl Zines A-Go-Go
www.gzagg.org

 The Art in Zines at ABC No Rio
by Victoria Law

"Somebody doesn't know what a zine is?!?" my six-year-old daughter screeched. "That's crazy!"

Her amazed comment came at the end of a small zine reading. Everyone there knew what a zine was and laughed.

My daughter has grown up around zines. She not only has a mama who makes zines, but has spent numerous hours in ABC No Rio's zine library since she was one-month-old.

The zine library is only a few years older than her. Started in the mid-nineties as a project of Blackout Books, an anarchist bookstore on the Lower East Side, the collection lived in the South Bronx, more than an hour subway ride away. In 1998, it was moved to ABC No Rio, a DIY community arts center a few blocks from the bookstore. Volunteer zine librarians began cataloging the zines and keeping open hours for the public to do research and browse the materials. (Zines are non-circulating) Individuals donated their personal collections and zinesters began to regularly send new issues to add to the library. Within less than a decade, the collection more than tripled in size. Subjects span music, culture, politics, personal experience, travel and, given No Rio's location and ties to the local squats, recent Lower East Side squatting and anarchist history.

The zine library attracts different types of people: Students, activists and writers have used the zine library to research neighborhood history and events, like the 1989 Tompkins Square Park riots and squat evictions. During the summer months, travelers recovering from too much partying the night before spend quiet afternoons reading queergrrrl and punk zines.

In 2006, after two decades of struggling first against eviction and then to raise money to renovate its dilapidated four-story tenement, ABC No Rio bought its building from the City for $1.

The money to begin construction hasn't been fully raised yet. In the meantime, the plans have changed: Instead of renovating the existing structure, the building will be torn down and rebuilt from the ground (or the foundation) up.[1] This will allow us to build each facility according to its needs: The design for the new zine library allows for nearly three times the amount of shelf space, enabling the collection to comfortably triple in size.

While No Rio volunteers continue to try to raise the two million dollars necessary for rebuilding, the zine librarians are working to make the facility more user-friendly: The library's on-line database will be revamped and updated. The librarians will also be creating a guide to the collection and organizing displays of their favorite zines. There are also plans for a springtime benefit to raise money for much-needed preservation materials for the older and more fragile zines.

This past fall, Steven Englander, ABC No Rio's director, proposed mounting an exhibition showcasing the art found in the library's over 10,000 zines. Two zine librarians expressed interest in helping select the works to be shown; a third, who is also a graphic design student, offered to design the publicity and informational materials for the exhibition, utilizing the facilities at his school.

For the next several weeks, we spent many hours in the zine library pulling box after box of zines off the shelves to find examples of cover art, illustration, comics, collage, graphics, design and layout. We each had our own preferences: Aliqae selected zines that obviously relied on cut-and-paste techniques, such as "Cybervision," "Speed Demon" and "Giant Kielbasa." I preferred those with hand touches, such as the silkscreened paper bags that "El Diablito" had arrived in or the hand-stamped silhouette of a woman against green and gold metallic ink illustrating a poem inside "Caryatid Rises." I also set aside zines with stories behind them, like the waterbuckled cover of "I Hate This Part of Texas" that had been submerged during Hurricane Katrina and later salvaged for the fifth issue. Jack found examples of ways in which certain styles and techniques crossed national boundaries (the French zine "Demarchie," for example, employs a cut-and-paste/ransom note aesthetic). Wanting to ensure that the exhibit included historical representation, Steven pulled earlier and later versions of well-known zines like "Factsheet Five" and "The Match." My daughter's favorites were easy-to-read pieces that deconstructed gender stereotypes ("Mama, this zine is all about how it doesn't matter if you're a boy or a girl; you can still wear sparkly shoes," she said after reading "Viva La Toddler," the coloring book insert in the mamazine "Fertile Ground.") She also chose art that appropriated Disney characters and images of large-eyed aliens.

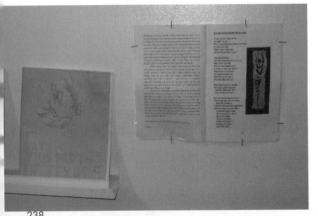

From those 10,000+ zines, we came up with 146 examples. In true zinester fashion, we spent hours at Kinko's xeroxing our selections. (Not in true zinester fashion, we actually paid for our copies.) We divided them into categories and mounted most onto four 8-foot pieces of black foamcore. Sometimes the juxtaposition emphasized the wide array of content found in zines: An early cover of the punk parenting zine "The Future Generation," which the creator colored with her daughter's crayons, sat beside the cover of "Rabble Rouser" with its black-and-white cartoon of a masked anarchist about to throw a bomb. At other times, the exhibit highlighted the changes that occurred during a zine's lifespan. The black-and-white xeroxed cover of a 1985 issue of "Factsheet Five," with its hand-drawn cartoon-like figures, was mounted beside a duo-tone, off-set printed cover that came out only two years later.

Zines with tactile touches that could not be conveyed through xeroxes were displayed on rows of thin wooden shelves. Art zines, which Aliqae characterized as having "no name, no year, no identifying information," as well as the actual zines whose art we had culled, were also set out for viewers to handle and read.

The Art in Zines wasn't just for those already in the know. We provided a Zine About Zines with essays by both zinesters and those who study them. While we couldn't guarantee that my six-year-old wouldn't laugh at their ignorance, those new to the medium could walk away with a zine that explained not only the differences between zines and blogs, but also explored zines as aesthetic forms, social networks, and resistance to both mass market culture and gender stereotyping.

There have been numerous discussions and debates about whether blogs, myspace and other Internet modes of communication have rendered zines obsolete.[2] Interest in the Art in Zines showed that they have not. The two accompanying events (an evening of zine readings and another evening of slideshows by artists and zinesters Cristy Road and Fly) packed the gallery space. A former zine reviewer from "Punk Planet" donated boxes of punk and hardcore zines from the 1980s. Another zinester arrived with a backpack full of zines to give to the library. During the open exhibition hours, viewers stayed to examine the zines, often looking and reading for half an hour to forty-five minutes.

"I've been wanting to start a zine for a while," said one visitor, who rushed in shortly before the close of the gallery one evening. After establishing that my daughter and I were in no rush to leave, she spent more than half an hour looking at the examples on the walls and browsing the zines on the shelves and ledge. "Thanks," she said when she was finished. "Hopefully this will motivate me to finish my zine."
I reminded her about the Zine Library one floor above. She promised to return and donate a copy of her zine.
The Art in Zines was curated by Jack Z. Bratich, Steven Englander, Aliqae Geraci and Victoria Law, with much input by Siu Loong Law Englander.

The Zine about Zines and other exhibition-related materials were designed by Suckzoo Han.

[1] The cost of tearing down and rebuilding is, relatively speaking, only slightly more than the cost of supporting the existing structure and safely and correctly renovating it. For more information, go to www.abcnorio.org

[2] Since this piece is about the Art in Zines exhibition, I am not going to rehash any of that debate here. If you are interested, check out Jenna Freedman's Zines are Not Blogs at: http://www.barnard.edu/library/zines/zinesnotblogs.htm (a shorter version was published in the Zine about Zines). *Bitch Magazine* ran a short piece that also compared zines and blogs, entitled "In Praise of Zines: Pushing Paper in the Digital Age." (*Bitch Magazine* #31, 2006. Not available on-line.)

We are unsure yet if we are going to attempt this project again next year. Should we? Is this an important medium for zines to be read? If we aren't going to do it, is someone else? In the meantime, feel free to send your zines over, if nothing else, for us to read and enjoy! Thanks! -Microcosm